THE *Create-Your-Plate* DIABETES COOKBOOK

A PLATE METHOD APPROACH TO SIMPLE, COMPLETE MEALS

Toby Amidor, MS, RD, CDN, FAND

American Diabetes Association

Associate Publisher, Books, Abe Ogden; *Director, Book Operations*, Victor Van Beuren; *Managing Editor, Books*, John Clark; *Associate Director, Book Marketing*, Annette Reape; *Acquisitions Editor*, Jaclyn Konich; *Senior Manager, Book Editing*, Lauren Wilson; *Composition and Cover Design*, pixiedesign llc; *Photographer*, Mittera; *Stock Photography*, Shutterstock; *Printer*, Imago.

Printed in Malaysia
1 3 5 7 9 10 8 6 4 2

The suggestions and information contained in this publication are generally consistent with the Standards of Medical Care in Diabetes and other policies of the American Diabetes Association, but they do not represent the policy or position of the Association or any of its boards or committees. Reasonable steps have been taken to ensure the accuracy of the information presented. However, the American Diabetes Association cannot ensure the safety or efficacy of any product or service described in this publication. Individuals are advised to consult a physician or other appropriate health care professional before undertaking any diet or exercise program or taking any medication referred to in this publication. Professionals must use and apply their own professional judgment, experience, and training and should not rely solely on the information contained in this publication before prescribing any diet, exercise, or medication. The American Diabetes Association—its officers, directors, employees, volunteers, and members—assumes no responsibility or liability for personal or other injury, loss, or damage that may result from the suggestions or information in this publication.

Madelyn Wheeler and Sacha Uelmen conducted the internal review of this book to ensure that it meets American Diabetes Association guidelines.

∞ The paper in this publication meets the requirements of the ANSI Standard Z39.48-1992 (permanence of paper).

ADA titles may be purchased for business or promotional use or for special sales. To purchase more than 50 copies of this book at a discount, or for custom editions of this book with your logo, contact the American Diabetes Association at the address below or at booksales@diabetes.org.

American Diabetes Association
2451 Crystal Drive, Suite 900
Arlington, VA 22202

DOI: 10.2337/9781580407045

Library of Congress Cataloging-in-Publication Data

Names: Amidor, Toby, author.

Title: The create-your-plate diabetes cookbook : a plate method approach to simple, complete meals / Toby Amidor, , MS, RD, CDN, FAND.

Description: Arlington : American Diabetes Association, 2020. | Includes index.

Identifiers: LCCN 2019048180 (print) | LCCN 2019048181 (ebook) | ISBN 9781580407045 (paperback) | ISBN 9781580407311 (ebook)

Subjects: LCSH: Diabetes--Diet therapy--Recipes. | LCGFT: Cookbooks.

Classification: LCC RC662 .A47 2020 (print) | LCC RC662 (ebook) | DDC 641.5/6314--dc23

LC record available at https://lccn.loc.gov/2019048180

LC ebook record available at https://lccn.loc.gov/2019048181

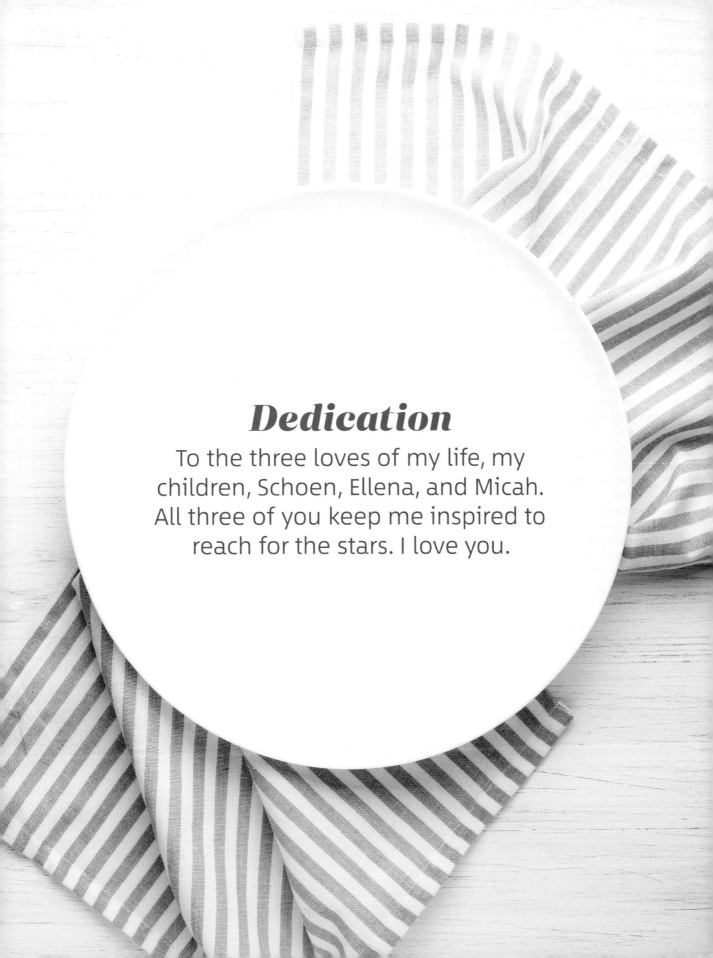

Dedication

To the three loves of my life, my children, Schoen, Ellena, and Micah. All three of you keep me inspired to reach for the stars. I love you.

Contents

Acknowledgments

To write a cookbook takes a team effort. There are many people I want to thank for making this very special cookbook possible. First and foremost, I want to thank my three children, Schoen, Ellena, and Micah, for supporting my long nights and weekends cooking. I know my schedule has been hectic, but all three of you always hang in there and provide encouraging words. You are the forces that drive everything I do. I love you. Schoen and Ellena, thank you for being my very truthful taste testers, and Micah, thank you for being my assistant when testing recipes. You are the best kitchen assistant a mom could ask for and hopefully you have learned some cooking and recipe writing skills along the way. Thanks to my boyfriend, Tom Wexler, for being a fabulous taste tester and always supporting me. I love you.

A huge thank you to Gail Watson, MS, for your assistance on this project and to Christine Camargo for helping me with anything and everything that needed to get done.

A big thank you to my literary agent, Sally Ekus, from The Lisa Ekus Group, who has always believed in me. Thank you Jaimee Constantine and Sara Pokorny from The Lisa Ekus Group for your support and kindness throughout this process. Many thanks to the wonderful and kind team at the American Diabetes Association, especially Jaclyn Konich and Lauren Wilson, who have been a pleasure to work with.

Introduction

At 24 years of age I began my dietetic internship at New York Methodist Hospital in Brooklyn, New York, to ultimately become a registered dietitian. I remembered learning about diabetes in my classes at New York University, but of course no one can prepare you for working one-on-one with someone with diabetes—adults, kids, and those newly diagnosed. Once I started counseling folks with diabetes it became clear how challenging following a diabetes-friendly diet could be. I remember thinking, "Why can't there be a more simplistic way of eating to help those with diabetes?"

When I was approached to do this cookbook, all those thoughts came rushing back. Plus, I thought of my own family who has a history of diabetes. I was so glad I could be a part of making eating easier for the many people who live with diabetes. The Diabetes Plate Method created by the American Diabetes Association is a simplistic, realistic, and delicious way of eating. This cookbook brings the Diabetes Plate Method to life and can help those with diabetes select healthy and tasty foods at every meal. There are various tools included throughout the book to help make meal planning for those with diabetes easier including tags to indicate recipe type, nutrition information, and tips on how to tweak recipes to your liking. Ultimately, this cookbook was created to help those with diabetes take charge of their food and lead a healthier life one bite at a time.

Chapter 1
Create Your Plate

What you eat makes a difference for your blood glucose levels, cholesterol, blood pressure, and weight. Eating healthful foods does not have to be difficult. Using the Create Your Plate approach to meal planning (also known as the Diabetes Plate Method), which includes five easy steps to balance your meals, helps simplify your food choices.

This cookbook will give you step-by-step instruction on how to create a balanced plate to help manage your blood glucose and other health conditions. You will also find 125 recipes to help you create delicious, healthy meals to fill your plate. Finally, you will find 1 full week of sample plates for each meal and snacks as well as additional breakfast, lunch, and dinner sample plates all featuring recipes in this cookbook. The ultimate goal is to have you create your own personalized plates using the recipes in this cookbook so you can enjoy delicious and varied meals that help keep your blood glucose in your target range.

The Diabetes Plate Method is a simple and effective meal planning method to help you manage your blood glucose levels and lose weight. Instead of counting carbohydrates and measuring portions, you can use your plate as a visual guide to create balanced, diabetes-friendly meals. With this method, you fill your plate with more nonstarchy vegetables and smaller portions of starchy, carbohydrate foods and protein foods. There are no special tools or counting required.

Five Simple Steps to Create Your Plate

The Diabetes Plate Method lets you still choose the foods you want, but changes the portion sizes so you are getting larger

HOW TO CREATE YOUR PLATE

Start with a dinner plate that is roughly 9 inches in diameter. (If you are someone who needs more calories than average, you can use a larger plate, such as an 11- or 12-inch dinner plate, while some people with lower calorie needs may decide to use a slightly smaller plate, such as an 8-inch dinner plate.)

Imagine your plate is divided into three parts with one half and two quarters.

 STEP 1. Fill half of your plate with nonstarchy vegetables, such as cauliflower, broccoli, spinach, kale, or others (see page 2 for a list of nonstarchy vegetable options).

 STEP 2. Fill one of the small sections (one-quarter) of your plate with lean protein foods, such as lean meat, fish, eggs, or plant-based protein.

 **STEP 3.** Fill the other small section (one-quarter) of your plate with carbohydrate foods, such as grains, starchy vegetables, fruit, milk, or yogurt.

 **STEP 4.** To complete your meal, add water or another zero-calorie beverage.

STEP 5. Choose healthy fats in small amounts.

portions of nonstarchy vegetables and a smaller portion of carbohydrate foods, such as grains, starchy vegetables, fruit, or milk or yogurt. When you are ready, you can try incorporating new or different foods within each food category into your meals. Below are the five simple steps to follow in order to create your plate.

Step 1
Fill half your plate with nonstarchy vegetables

Vegetables are full of vitamins, minerals, fiber, and phytochemicals (natural plant compounds that help fight and prevent disease)–and with so few calories and grams of carbohydrate, you can enjoy more nonstarchy vegetables! There are two main types of vegetables–starchy and nonstarchy. Nonstarchy vegetables are very nutrient dense, meaning they are high in healthy nutrients like vitamins, minerals, and fiber, but low in calories, fat, and carbohydrate. See box below for examples of nonstarchy vegetables. Nonstarchy vegetables provide many health benefits for people with diabetes, and do not have a big effect on blood glucose levels; that is why they should

---

NONSTARCHY VEGETABLE OPTIONS

The following is a list of common nonstarchy vegetables:

- Amaranth greens or Chinese spinach
- Artichoke
- Artichoke hearts
- Asparagus
- Baby corn
- Bamboo shoots
- Beans (green, wax, Italian)
- Bean sprouts
- Beets
- Brussels sprouts
- Broccoli
- Cabbage (green, bok choy, Chinese)
- Carrots
- Cauliflower
- Celery

- Chayote
- Coleslaw (packaged, no dressing)
- Cucumber
- Daikon
- Eggplant
- Greens (collard, kale, mustard, turnip)
- Hearts of palm
- Jicama
- Kohlrabi
- Leeks
- Mushrooms
- Okra
- Onions
- Pea pods
- Peppers

- Radishes
- Rutabaga
- Salad greens (chicory, endive, escarole, lettuce, romaine, spinach, arugula, radicchio, watercress)
- Sprouts
- Squash (cushaw, summer, crookneck, spaghetti, zucchini)
- Sugar snap peas
- Swiss chard
- Tomatoes
- Turnips
- Water chestnuts
- Yard-long beans

take up the largest portion of your plate. An easy way to fill half your plate with vegetables is to double the serving size of your favorite nonstarchy vegetable side dishes. Starchy vegetables are vegetables that are higher in carbohydrate and can cause a significant rise in blood glucose. They fall into the category of "carbohydrate foods," which are discussed in step 3.

Step 2
Fill one of the small sections (one-quarter) of your plate with lean protein

Foods high in protein, such as fish, chicken, meats, soy products, and cheese, are all called "protein foods." You may also hear them referred to as "meats or meat substitutes." Protein is one of the three main nutrients in food (the other two are carbohydrate and fat). Proteins are used in the body for cell structure, to produce hormones like insulin, and for other functions. The biggest difference among foods in this group is how much fat they contain and, for the plant-based proteins, whether or not they have carbohydrate. Here is a list of the various types of proteins you can include on your plate.

PLANT-BASED PROTEINS

Plant-based protein foods provide quality protein, healthy fats, and fiber. They vary in how much fat and carbohydrate they contain, so make sure to read labels.

FISH AND SEAFOOD

Fish or seafood is recommended at least two times per week (but limit fried seafood because it is high in fat and calories).

PLANT-BASED PROTEIN OPTIONS

Here are some common examples of plant-based proteins, arranged in order—from highest to lowest—of the carbohydrate content in one serving of the food. Please note that the serving size varies for these foods (for example, a serving of beans is about 1/2–1 cup, but a serving of peanut butter is 2 tablespoons):

▲ HIGHEST

- Bean products (for example, baked beans and refried beans)

- Beans (such as black, kidney, and pinto)
- Lentils (such as brown, green, or yellow)
- Peas (such as black-eyed or split peas)

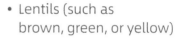

- Edamame
- Hummus and falafel
- Soy nuts
- Nuts and nut spreads (such as almonds, almond butter, peanuts, peanut butter, cashews, cashew butter, walnuts, or pistachios)

- Products like meatless "chicken" nuggets, "beef" crumbles, "burgers," "bacon," "sausage," and "hot dogs"
- Tempeh, tofu

▼ LOWEST

HOW TO INCORPORATE HIGH-CARB PROTEIN FOODS INTO YOUR PLATE

Plant-based proteins are higher in carbohydrate compared to animal-based proteins, such as chicken, fish, or meat. If you're following a vegetarian or plant-based diet, you may find yourself filling your plate with higher-carbohydrate sources of plant-based proteins, like beans or lentils, and a carbohydrate side dish too, like brown rice or quinoa. If you choose to follow a plant-based or vegetarian diet, your plate will likely be slightly higher in carbohydrate than the plate of someone who eats animal proteins. However, you can make some simple swaps from higher- to lower-carbohydrate starches or plant-based proteins. Here are a few guidelines:

- If you choose a higher-carb protein like beans, lentils, or another similar food, then try to choose a lower-carb vegetable (see the list of nonstarchy vegetables on page 2) to add to the quarter of your plate reserved for carbohydrate foods. For example, if you choose black beans for one-quarter of your plate (as your protein serving), pair it with zucchini noodles.

- Opt for nuts or nut butters as a protein choice as nuts are a lower-carb protein. For example, try whole-grain pasta with a peanut sauce (and/or topped with chopped peanuts) and vegetables.

- Remember that higher-carb plant-based proteins do provide more carbohydrates than animal proteins, but they are also generally very high in fiber, which is beneficial for blood glucose management.

FISH AND SEAFOOD OPTIONS

Types of fish to incorporate into your eating plan include:

- Fish high in omega-3 fatty acids (for example, albacore tuna, herring, mackerel, rainbow trout, sardines, and salmon)

- Other fish including catfish, cod, flounder, haddock, halibut, orange roughy, and tilapia

- Shellfish including clams, crab, imitation shellfish, lobster, scallops, shrimp, oysters

POULTRY

Poultry includes chicken, turkey, Cornish hen, and duck. Choose poultry without the skin for less saturated fat and cholesterol. Also, choose healthy cooking methods to cook poultry like grilling, sautéing, baking, and stir-frying, and avoid cooking methods high in fat like deep frying.

EGGS AND CHEESE

Eggs and cheese also provide protein. Select eggs that are large. As a general rule, recipes use large eggs (as opposed to jumbo or extra-large). When selecting cheese, low-fat and nonfat varieties have less saturated fat and cholesterol, but may contain more sodium. Examples include:

- Reduced-fat cheese or regular cheese in small amounts

- Cottage cheese

- Whole eggs

RED MEAT

Red meat and game are also protein foods. Red meat includes beef, pork, veal, and lamb. Game includes venison (deer), ostrich, and buffalo. When selecting red meat there are many lean and very lean options to choose from. The United States Department of Agriculture (USDA) and the Food and Drug Administration (FDA) define lean as less than 10% fat by weight, or less than 10 grams of fat per 100 grams. Limit high-fat red meat, which is often higher in saturated fat. Processed red meats like ham, bacon, and hot dogs are often higher in saturated fat and sodium.

RED MEAT OPTIONS

The leanest red meat options include:

- Beef: Select or Choice grades trimmed of fat, including chuck, rib, rump roast, round, sirloin, cubed, flank, porterhouse, T-bone steak, tenderloin

- Game: Buffalo, ostrich, rabbit, venison, dove, duck, goose, or pheasant (no skin)

- Lamb: chop, leg, or roast

- Pork: Canadian bacon, center loin chop, ham, tenderloin

- Veal: loin chop or roast

Step 3
Fill the other small section (one-quarter) of your plate with carbohydrate foods

Carbohydrate foods include grains, starchy vegetables, fruits, and milk and yogurt. When it comes to grains, there is no end in sight to the debate as to whether they help you lose weight or possibly promote weight gain; or, even more importantly, whether they help or hinder blood glucose management. But one thing is for sure. If you are going to eat grain foods, pick the options that are the most nutritious: whole grains. They are rich in vitamins, minerals, phytochemicals, and fiber.

WHAT ARE WHOLE GRAINS?

A whole grain is the entire grain, which includes the bran, germ, and endosperm (starchy part). The most popular grain in the U.S. is wheat, so let's use that as an example. To make 100%-whole-wheat flour, the entire wheat grain is ground up. "Refined" flours like white and enriched wheat flour include only part of the grain– the starchy part–and are not whole grain. They are missing many of the nutrients found in whole-wheat flour. Flours and breads that do not use the whole grain tend to be enriched, meaning the nutrients lost are added back in. Examples of whole-grain and whole-wheat products include whole-wheat bread, pasta, tortillas, and crackers that contain 100% whole wheat or 100% whole grains. The list is

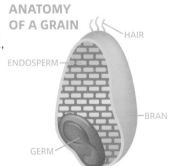

ANATOMY OF A GRAIN

HAIR

ENDOSPERM

BRAN

GERM

very long, and the good news is that there are many whole grains and whole-grain products to choose from.

Finding whole-grain foods can sometimes be a challenge, but it gets easier once you know what you are looking for. The problem is that some foods only contain a small amount of whole grain even if the front of the package says it contains whole grain. For all cereals and grains, read the ingredient list and look for the following sources of whole grains as the first ingredient:

- Brown rice
- Buckwheat
- Buckwheat flour
- Bulgur (cracked wheat)
- Millet
- Popcorn
- Quinoa
- Sorghum
- Triticale
- Whole farro
- Whole-grain barley
- Whole-grain corn/cornmeal
- Whole oats/oatmeal
- Whole rye
- Whole-wheat flour
- Wild rice

Most rolls, breads, cereals, and crackers labeled as "made with" or "containing" whole grains do not have whole grain as the first ingredient. Terms like "multigrain" on a label can be tricky as well; "multigrain" means that a product contains more than one type of grain, but it could be referring to multiple whole grains or multiple refined

THE WHOLE GRAIN STAMP

When shopping for whole grains and whole-grain products, it can sometimes be tricky to identify which products are actually a good source of whole grains. Not every product that mentions "whole grain" or "multigrain" on the label provides a significant amount of whole grains. Luckily, the Oldways Whole Grains Council has developed a tool to make it easier for shoppers to find whole-grain foods—the Whole Grain Stamp.

The Whole Grain Stamp shows a sheaf of grain on a yellow background with a black border; it features the words "Whole Grain" and shows how many grams of whole grain ingredients are in one serving of the food. There are three

For a wealth of healthy eating information, visit oldwayspt.org and wholegrainscouncil.org.

versions of the Whole Grain Stamp: the Basic Stamp, the 50% Stamp, and the 100% Stamp. Use these stamps to your advantage when looking for whole-grain products to incorporate into your eating plan.

- The Basic Stamp is used on products that contain a significant amount of whole grains but are primarily made with refined grains. The product must contain at least 8 grams (one-half serving) of whole grains per serving of the food.

- The 50% Stamp is used for products in which at least 50% of the grain used is whole grain. The product must contain at least 8 grams (one-half serving) of whole grains per serving of the food.

- The 100% Stamp is used on products where all of the grain is whole grain. The product must contain at least 16 grams (a full serving) of whole grains per serving of the food.

grains. Always read labels carefully to find the most nutritious grain products available. For cereals, pick those with at least 3 grams of fiber per serving and less than 6 grams of sugar per serving.

WHAT ARE OTHER CARBOHYDRATE FOODS?

In addition to whole grains and grain products, starchy foods also include starchy vegetables, legumes, and pulses, such as dried beans, peas, and lentils. Starchy vegetables are great sources of vitamins, minerals, and fiber. The best choices do not have added fats, sugar, or sodium. While these foods can be part of healthy eating plan, they do raise blood glucose, so aim for smaller portions.

STARCHY VEGETABLE OPTIONS

Try a variety of starchy vegetables, including:

- Acorn squash
- Butternut squash
- Corn
- Green peas
- Parsnip
- Plantain
- Potato
- Pumpkin

Legumes and pulses, such as beans, peas, and lentils, are also starchy foods. Both legumes and pulses contain both carbohydrates and protein. They also have a lower glycemic index and can help manage blood glucose better than foods containing carbs alone. Pulses also contain

fiber, vitamins, and minerals, making them a wonderful addition to many plates. Try to include these foods in several of your meals each week.

LEGUMES AND PULSE OPTIONS

Examples of these foods include:

- Bean products (for example, baked beans and refried beans)
- Beans (such as black, kidney, and pinto)
- Edamame
- Hummus and falafel
- Lentils (such as brown, green, or yellow)
- Nuts and nut spreads (such as almonds, almond butter, peanuts, peanut butter, cashews, cashew butter, walnuts, or pistachios)
- Peas (such as black-eyed or split peas)
- Products like meatless "chicken" nuggets, "beef" crumbles, "burgers," "bacon," "sausage," and "hot dogs"
- Soy nuts
- Tempeh, tofu

FRUIT

Wondering if you can eat fruit? Yes! Fruits are loaded with vitamins, minerals, and fiber just like vegetables. Fruit contains carbohydrate and can raise your blood glucose, so count it as part of your meal plan. Having a piece of fresh fruit or fruit salad for dessert is a great way to satisfy your sweet tooth and get the extra nutrition you're looking for.

FRUIT OPTIONS

Examples of common fruits include:

- Apples

- Applesauce
- Apricots
- Banana
- Blackberries
- Blueberries
- Cantaloupe
- Cherries

- Dried fruit (such as cherries, cranberries, dates, figs, prunes, raisins)
- Fruit cocktail
- Grapefruit
- Grapes

- Honeydew melon
- Kiwi
- Mango
- Nectarines
- Oranges
- Papaya
- Peaches

- Pears
- Pineapple
- Plums
- Raspberries
- Strawberries

- Tangerines
- Watermelon

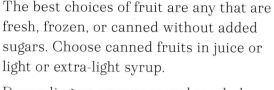

The best choices of fruit are any that are fresh, frozen, or canned without added sugars. Choose canned fruits in juice or light or extra-light syrup.

Depending on your personal meal plan and carb goals, you can enjoy a small piece of fruit as a snack between meals, or with breakfast or lunch. In the Diabetes Plate Method, having a small piece of whole fruit or 1/2 cup of fruit salad is a nice way to complement a vegetable omelet at breakfast or a green salad topped with salmon for lunch.

MILK AND DAIRY

Including sources of milk and dairy in your eating plan is a great way to get calcium and high-quality protein. But remember, some dairy products, like milk and yogurt, do contain carbohydrate and can raise your blood glucose. When choosing milk and dairy foods, keep in mind that low-fat and nonfat milk and dairy have fewer overall calories and less saturated fat compared to full-fat milk and dairy foods. Depending on your health goals and the other foods you include in your meal plan, the lower-fat dairy options may be right for you. Examples of low-fat and nonfat dairy products include nonfat milk (also called fat-free or skim milk), low-fat (1%) milk, low-fat or nonfat yogurt or Greek yogurt, low-fat or nonfat cottage cheese, and reduced-fat cheeses. If you're lactose intolerant or don't like milk, you may want to try lactose-free milk and dairy foods (like lactose-free cheese, cottage cheese, ice cream, and yogurt) or fortified soy milk.

A WORD ABOUT DESSERTS

Desserts are not specifically mentioned in the five steps of the Diabetes Plate Method, but that doesn't mean that people with diabetes can't enjoy a sweet treat from time to time. If you would like to enjoy dessert with a meal, there are a few things to keep in mind:

- Consider dessert a part of your plate. Most desserts are high in carbohydrate, so if you're planning on eating dessert, cut back on other carbohydrate foods in your meal.
- Choose desserts that are based on whole fruit and/or whole grains and limit added sugars.
- Keep portion sizes small.

CARBOHYDRATE FOODS RECAP

Every time you choose to eat a carbohydrate food, make it count! Choose from whole grains, starchy vegetables, and legumes. Leave the processed, white flour–based products, especially the ones with added sugar, on the shelves or use them only for a special occasion treat.

Carbohydrate foods include:

- Grains and grain-based products
- Starchy vegetables
- Beans and legumes
- Fruit
- Dairy (specifically milk and yogurt; other dairy products, like cheese, are considered protein foods because they are lower in carbohydrate and higher in protein)

All of these foods contain carbohydrate and can raise your blood glucose. The Diabetes Plate Method encourages smaller portions of carbohydrate foods, so plan to fill only one-quarter of your plate with any of the foods listed here.

Step 4
To complete your meal, add water or another very low-calorie or zero-calorie drink

Food is often a focus when it comes to diabetes. But don't forget that the beverages you drink can also have an effect on your weight and blood glucose! It's important to stay hydrated, and water is simply your best choice when it comes to hydration.

Avoid sugary drinks like regular soda, fruit punch, fruit drinks, energy drinks, sports drinks, sweet tea, and other sugary drinks. Juice, even 100% fruit or vegetable juice, can quickly raise blood glucose and should be avoided. All of these drinks will raise blood glucose and can provide several hundred calories in just one serving! See for yourself:

- One 12-ounce can of regular soda has about 150 calories and 40 grams of carbohydrate. This is the same amount of carbohydrate as in 10 teaspoons of sugar!
- One cup of fruit punch or other sugary fruit drinks has about 100 calories (or more) and 30 grams of carbohydrate.

Water is always the best beverage choice. But if you are tired of plain water there are other zero-calorie options to choose from. Mix it up by choosing unsweetened teas. Hot or cold, black, green, and herbal teas provide lots of flavor variety. You could also try sparkling water or making your own infused water at home. To make infused water, simply put a container of water with cucumbers, strawberries, fresh mint, or other fresh, flavorful ingredients in the fridge for a refreshing low-calorie drink. Get creative and invent your own natural fruit or herbal infusion, or buy one of the many zero-calorie drinks on the market.

Most diet drinks (like diet soda or diet tea) have 0 grams of carbohydrate per serving, so they will not raise blood glucose on their own. These diet drinks are sweetened with sugar substitutes instead of added sugars.

Removing the added sugars and replacing them with low-calorie sweeteners removes most of the calories and carbohydrate. It is important to consider that these products may help reduce calorie and carbohydrate intake only if they are used in place of other higher-calorie or higher-carbohydrate drinks.

Other low-calorie drinks and drink mixes are available in several flavors. These drinks also use low-calorie sweeteners in place of sugar, so they may be a good alternative to added sugar-sweetened drinks like regular lemonade, iced tea, and fruit punch. They are very low in calories (usually about 5-10 calories per 8-ounce portion) and have less than 5 grams of carbohydrate per serving.

COFFEE AND TEA

Plain coffee and tea contain very few calories and grams of carbohydrate and can be part of a healthy eating plan. Things added to coffee such as cream, sugar, sweetener, and non-dairy creamer can all add calories and carbohydrates, so using only a small amount of these additives or none at all will have the least impact on your blood glucose. Keep in mind that coffee drinks with flavors and syrups can contain excessive calories and carbohydrate.

There have been several large research studies indicating that drinking coffee may play a role in preventing type 2 diabetes. However, other research has also shown that coffee intake can increase blood glucose in the short term. People with type 1 diabetes may see a rise in blood glucose after drinking coffee alone. More research is needed on the effects of coffee in individuals with diabetes, but it can be enjoyed in moderation.

A WORD ABOUT SUGAR SUBSTITUTES

Drinks like coffee, tea, and homemade water infusions can be sweetened using sugar substitutes. Sometimes sugar substitutes are called low-calorie sweeteners, artificial sweeteners, or nonnutritive sweeteners. They can be used to sweeten drinks, baked goods, dressings, and marinades for fewer calories and grams of carbohydrate when they are used to replace sugar.

The sweetening power of most sugar substitutes is at least 100 times more intense than regular sugar, so only a small amount is needed when you use these products. Also, with the exception of aspartame, these sugar substitutes (see list below) cannot be broken down by the body. They pass through our systems without being digested so they provide no extra calories.

There are six artificial sweeteners that have been tested and approved by the FDA. These sweeteners include:

- Acesulfame potassium or ace-K (Sunett and Sweet One)
- Advantame
- Aspartame (Nutrasweet, Equal, and Sugar Twin)
- Neotame (Newtame)
- Saccharin (Sweet 'N Low, Sweet Twin, and Necta Sweet)
- Sucralose (Splenda)

Two other low-calorie sweeteners you may have heard of are stevia—also referred to as rebaudioside A, reb-A, or rebiana—and *luo han guo* or monk fruit. Stevia and *luo han guo* are generally recognized as safe (GRAS) sugar substitutes. When something is generally recognized as safe by the FDA, it means that experts have agreed that it is safe for use by the public in appropriate amounts. Sweetener brands that use stevia include Truvia, PureVia, and Enliten. Brands that include *luo han guo* include Nectresse, Monk Fruit in the Raw, and PureLo.

MILK

To reduce calories and saturated fat, choose low-fat (1%) or nonfat milk. Some early research is indicating that whole-milk dairy products may help reduce diabetes risk, but there is not strong enough evidence to recommend drinking it regularly for that purpose. One cup of nonfat milk provides about 12 grams of carbohydrate and 80 calories, plus calcium, vitamin D, and seven more essential nutrients. If you are lactose intolerant or don't like milk, other options include lactose-free milk or fortified soy milk. Remember, milk is considered a carbohydrate food, so make sure to consider what other carbohydrate foods you are having with your meal when including milk.

JUICE

Juice provides a lot of carbohydrates in a small portion. Usually about 4 ounces or less of juice contain at least 15 grams of carbohydrate and 50 or more calories. To quench your thirst, zero-calorie beverages, especially water, are the better choice over juice. If you're craving something sweet, choose a small piece of fresh or canned fruit (canned in their own juices or in light or extra-light syrup) instead. Just make sure to work that fruit into your eating plan for the day.

A WORD ABOUT ALCOHOL

Wondering if alcohol is off limits with diabetes? Research has shown that there can be some health benefits associated with alcohol such as reducing the risk for heart disease. But there are also risks. Drinking alcohol can cause a drop in blood glucose levels because alcohol blocks the production of glucose in the liver. (The liver contains "emergency stores" of glucose to raise your blood glucose if it drops too low.) Once the liver's stores of glucose are used up, a person who has been drinking alcohol can't make more right away, and that can lead to dangerously low blood glucose, which (in severe cases) can result in a coma or even death.

Also, alcohol is processed by your liver, which is responsible for removing toxins (like alcohol or drugs) and processing medication, so if you are taking medications, drinking too much alcohol can cause damage to your liver. If you have any questions about whether alcohol is safe for you, check with your doctor. People with diabetes need to use the same guidelines as those without diabetes if they choose to drink:

- Women: If you choose to drink, limit it to no more than 1 drink per day

- Men: If you choose to drink, then limit it to no more than 2 drinks per day.

One drink is equal to a 12-ounce beer, a 5-ounce glass of wine, or 1 1/2 ounces of distilled spirits (such as vodka, whiskey, gin, or rum).

If you have diabetes and choose to drink, then it's smart to:

- Not drink on an empty stomach or when your blood glucose is low, since your risk of low blood glucose increases after drinking.

- Consume alcohol with food. This is mainly important for those on insulin and other diabetes medications that can lower blood glucose by making more insulin.

- Not skip a meal if you are going to drink.

- Wear an I.D. that notes that you have diabetes. If you are in a setting where people are drinking alcohol, the symptoms of low blood glucose (hypoglycemia) may be mistaken for being drunk.

- Watch out for craft beers, which can have twice or even three times the alcohol and calories of a light beer.

- Choose calorie-free drink mixers like diet soda, club soda, diet tonic water, or water when having mixed drinks.

- As with anyone with or without diabetes, do not drive or plan to drive for several hours after you drink alcohol.

- If you are pregnant, with or without diabetes, refrain from consuming any alcohol.

Alcohol can cause hypoglycemia shortly after drinking and for up to 24 hours after drinking. If you are going to drink alcohol, check your blood glucose:

- Before you drink
- While you're drinking
- Before bed and throughout the night
- More often for up to 24 hours

After drinking alcohol, be sure your blood glucose is at a safe level–between 100 and 140 mg/dL–before you go to sleep. If your blood glucose is low, eat something to raise it and be sure to check it again before you go to sleep and overnight to be sure it's not dropping too low.

The symptoms of drinking too much alcohol and hypoglycemia can be similar–feeling sleepy, dizzy, and/or confused; nausea or hunger; irritability or impatience; headaches; and coordination problems. The one way to get the help you need if you experience a hypoglycemia emergency is to always wear an I.D. that says "I have diabetes." Also, be sure that your family and friends know to be aware of your symptoms of hypoglycemia and what to do to treat it.

Wondering if drinking a glass of wine or beer might help lower your blood glucose if it is high? The effects of alcohol can be unpredictable, and it is not recommended as a treatment for high blood glucose. The risks likely outweigh any benefit that may be seen in blood glucose levels alone.

Step 5
Choose healthy fats in small amounts

Healthy fats may be added to any part of your plate. For cooking, use plant-based oils like canola or olive oil. For salads, some healthy fat additions are nuts, seeds, avocado, and vinaigrettes. Try to choose protein foods that naturally contain healthy fats, like fatty fish (including salmon and tuna).

There is no doubt that carbohydrates get a lot of the attention when it comes to diabetes nutrition and management. However, fat is another macronutrient that needs attention. More important than total fat is the type of fat you eat. There are "healthy fats" and "unhealthy fats."

Unhealthy fats include saturated and trans fat. In order to help lower you risk of heart disease, try to eat less of these unhealthy fats. At the same time, you can protect your heart by eating more monounsaturated and polyunsaturated fats including omega-3 fatty acids, all of which are the healthy fats. See the Types of Fat table below for examples of healthy and unhealthy fats.

TYPES OF FAT	EXAMPLES
Saturated fat 	• Butter • Chocolate • Coconut and coconut oil • Cream sauces • Fatback and salt pork • Gravy made with meat drippings • High-fat meats like regular ground beef, bologna, hot dogs, sausage, bacon, and spareribs • High-fat dairy products like full-fat cheese, cream, ice cream, whole milk, 2% milk, and sour cream • Lard • Palm oil and palm kernel oil • Poultry (chicken and turkey) skin

TYPES OF FAT	EXAMPLES
Trans fat  	• Doughnuts • Fried foods • Some baked goods including cakes, pie crusts, biscuits, cookies • Some frozen pizzas • Some crackers • Some stick margarines and other spreads *Note: You can check if a food contains trans fat by reading the ingredient list on the package and looking for the ingredient "partially hydrogenated oils"
Unsaturated fat (mono-unsaturated and poly-unsaturated)  	• Avocado • Canola oil • Cottonseed oil • Nuts like almonds, cashews, pecans, and peanuts • Olive oil and olives • Peanut butter and peanut oil • Pumpkin or sunflower seeds • Safflower oil • Salad dressings • Sesame seeds • Corn oil • Soybean oil • Sunflower oil • Walnuts

TYPES OF FAT	EXAMPLES
Omega-3 fatty acids	• Albacore tuna • Herring • Mackerel • Rainbow trout • Salmon • Sardines • Tuna **Plant sources of omega-3s:** • Canola oil • Flaxseed and flaxseed oil • Tofu and other soybean products • Walnuts

SATURATED FAT

Saturated fat is unhealthy because it raises blood cholesterol levels. High blood cholesterol is a risk factor for heart disease. People with diabetes are at high risk for heart disease, so limiting your saturated fat intake can help lower your risk of having a heart attack or stroke.

The goal for people with and without diabetes is to eat less than 10% of calories from saturated fat. For most people, this is about 20 grams of saturated fat per day. That is not much when you consider that just 1 ounce of cheese can have 8 grams of saturated fat. For more information on the saturated fat content of certain foods, see the Amount of Saturated Fat in Various Foods table on page 15. Many adults, especially women or sedentary men, may need less.

AMOUNT OF SATURATED FAT IN VARIOUS FOODS

Food	Serving Size	Saturated Fat
Butter	1 tablespoon	7.3 g
Heavy cream	1 tablespoon	3.5 g
Alfredo sauce	1/2 cup	8 g
Coconut oil	1 tablespoon	11.2 g
Palm oil	1 tablespoon	6.7 g
Bacon grease	1 tablespoon	5.1 g
Roasted chicken with skin	3 ounces	3.2 g
Broiled hamburger (made with 80% lean/20% fat ground beef)	3 ounces	5.7 g
Hot dog	1 dog	6 g
Ice cream, chocolate	1/2 cup	4.5 g

*Data from the USDA's website FoodData Central, available at https://fdc.nal.usda.gov/.

HEALTHY FAT SWAPS

Instead of...	Choose...
Butter on baked potatoes	A drizzle of olive oil
Cream cheese on whole-wheat bread	Almond butter, peanut butter, or sunflower seed butter
Ground beef that is 80% lean/20% fat	Ground beef that is at least 90% lean/10% fat
Chicken with the skin	Chicken without the skin
Heavy cream to thicken soups	A combination of cornstarch or flour and low-sodium chicken or vegetable broth
Creamy dressings (like ranch) for dipping vegetables	Hummus or guacamole
An omelet made with 3 whole eggs	An omelet made with 1 whole egg and 3 egg whites
Coffee with whole milk	Coffee with nonfat milk
Chocolate ice cream	Chocolate frozen yogurt made with nonfat or low-fat milk
Coconut oil	Olive or canola oil

To find out a specific saturated fat goal for you, talk with your registered dietitian nutritionist (RDN) or healthcare provider. Saturated fat grams are listed on the Nutrition Facts food label under total fat. As a general rule, compare foods to find options with less saturated fat. Foods with 1 gram or less of saturated fat per serving are considered low in saturated fat.

It is true that all fat is high in calories so it is important to watch portion sizes in addition to paying attention to the type of fat you're eating. But you can keep your calories the same by cutting back on the sources of saturated and trans fats, while substituting healthy fats in their place. See the Healthy Fat Swaps table on page 23 for examples of how to make healthy fat substitutions.

TRANS FAT

Like saturated fat, trans fat increases blood cholesterol levels. It is actually worse for you than saturated fat; you want to eat as little trans fat as possible, especially if you're following a heart-healthy eating plan, by avoiding all foods that contain it.

Trans fat is produced when liquid oil is made into a solid fat. This process is called hydrogenation. Trans fat acts like saturated fats and can raise your cholesterol level. Trans fat is listed on the Nutrition Facts label, making it easier to identify these foods.

Stick margarines contain trans fat; however, you can now find trans fat-free margarines (like Smart Balance, for example) available in grocery stores. When selecting margarine, read the label to make sure that it says "trans fat free."

HEALTHY FAT

"Good" or "healthy" fats include monounsaturated fats, polyunsaturated fats, and omega-3 fatty acids.

Unsaturated Fat

Unsaturated fats are called "good" or "healthy" fats because they can lower your bad (LDL) cholesterol. It's recommended for people with and without diabetes to eat more unsaturated fats (both monounsaturated and polyunsaturated fats) than saturated or trans fats in their diet. To include more unsaturated fats, try to substitute olive or canola oil for butter, margarine, or shortening when cooking, if possible. Sprinkling a few chopped walnuts, almonds, or sunflower seeds on a salad, yogurt, or cereal is another way to eat more monounsaturated fats. But be careful! Nuts and oils are high in calories, like all fats. If you are trying to lose or maintain your weight, keep in mind that the serving size of these foods is small. For example, 6 almonds or 4 pecan halves have the same number of calories as 1 teaspoon of oil or butter. And 1 tablespoon of any oil–olive, canola, peanut, etc.–contains 120 calories per tablespoon. Even salad dressing can contain a lot of calories. If you make a salad dressing with 1/4 cup of olive oil, that's 480 calories–the amount of calories in one meal! You can get plenty of dressing by using half the amount of oil. Although it is not required to list unsaturated fats on food labels, many foods that are a good source of unsaturated fats do list them.

Omega-3 Fatty Acids

Omega-3 fatty acids are a type of polyunsaturated fatty acids (also called PUFA). Omega-3s have many functions in your heart, blood vessels, lungs, immune system, and brain. There are three main types of omega-3s including alpha-linolenic acid (ALA), eicosapentaenoic acid (EPA) and docosahexaenoic acid (DHA). ALA is found in land-based sources of omega-3s, whereas EPA and DHA come from the sea or marine-based sources. Foods that contain ALA include chia seeds and flaxseed. EPA and DHA are found in fatty fish like salmon, tuna, and mackerel, and also in some sea algae. EPA and DHA are the primary types of omega-3s known for

supporting heart, brain, and eye health at all stages of life. Your brain and the retinas of the eyes actually contain the highest amounts of omega-3s compared to other parts of your body.

ALA is also a healthy type of omega-3 fatty acids, but most people tend to get enough of it in their diets. The body is actually able to convert ALA to EPA and DHA, but the rate of conversion is very low. Only about 1-5% of ALA Is converted to EPA and DHA, which makes the process very inefficient. It's best to get EPA and DHA directly from fatty fish, if possible. Enjoy a non-fried serving of fish two or three times a week. (See the Types of Fat table on page 14 for examples of the sources of omega-3s.)

Diabetes-Friendly Eating Plans

You may be surprised to hear that when it comes to diabetes nutrition there is no "one-size-fits-all" approach–no "diabetes diet" or perfect amount of nutrients (protein, fat, or even carbohydrate) that is right for every person with diabetes. Diabetes affects people of all ages, across all cultures, with all different health backgrounds, eating preferences, and budgets. So, it makes sense that there is a variety of eating patterns that can help people manage diabetes. The eating pattern you follow should be personalized to meet your needs, fit your lifestyle, and help you achieve your health goals. With the help of your healthcare team, you can create an eating plan that will work best for you. A registered dietitian nutritionist (RDN) or certified diabetes educator (CDE) in particular can help you manage your diabetes or prediabetes through diet and lifestyle changes. Ask your primary care provider for a referral if an RDN or CDE is not already a part of your care team. In most cases, appointments with an RDN or CDE are covered by insurance.

What Is an Eating Plan?

"Eating plan" is simply a term used to describe the foods or groups of foods that a person chooses to eat (and the beverages he or she chooses to consume) on a daily basis over time. Examples of eating plans include vegetarian, vegan, low-carb, low-fat, and Mediterranean-style. This section covers the basics of a few of the eating plans that are appropriate for a diabetes-friendly lifestyle.

When choosing an eating plan with the help of your diabetes care team, look for a plan that you feel you can incorporate into your lifestyle and follow long term. It is important for your eating plan to fit your needs. You can stick to one plan or implement strategies from a variety of different plans. Remember to take your food likes and dislikes, time constraints, food access, and budget into account as well.

Guidelines for Vegetarian Eating Plans

If you follow a vegetarian eating plan, you can still "create your plate" using the same five steps I've outlined. All vegetarians include plant foods, such as whole grains, fruits, vegetables, legumes, nuts, seeds, and healthy fats, in their eating plans. As a general rule of thumb, people who follow a vegetarian eating plan do not eat any red meat, poultry, or products made with these foods. However, the term vegetarian is a broad term, and some vegetarians independently choose to include foods like eggs, milk and dairy, and fish in their meals. There are many different types of vegetarian eating plans. The most common types are:

- **Vegan:** People who follow a vegan eating plan do not eat any animal-derived food including meat, poultry, eggs, fish, or dairy products, or any food made from animals (like honey). It is a 100% plant-based eating plan. People with diabetes can choose to follow this type of vegetarian eating plan too. If you choose to follow a vegan eating plan, proper planning is essential to ensure you're getting all the nutrients your body needs.

In addition, you also may find yourself cooking more at home in order to ensure your dietary needs are met.

- **Lacto-vegetarian:** People who follow a lacto-vegetarian eating plan do not eat meat, poultry, fish, or eggs. However, they will consume milk and dairy products.

- **Lacto-ovo-vegetarian:** People who follow a lacto-ovo-vegetarian eating plan do not eat any meat, poultry, or fish. However, they will eat both dairy products and eggs.

- **Pescatarian:** People who follow a pescatarian eating plan do not eat meat, poultry, eggs, or milk and dairy products. They will eat fish and seafood.

If you choose to follow a vegetarian eating plan, be sure to eat a wide variety of fruits, vegetables, whole grains, legumes (beans, peas, and lentils), nuts, seeds, and healthy fats. If you choose to include milk and dairy products in your eating plan, low-fat and nonfat milk and dairy products may be the right choice for you.

A vegetarian eating plan can be a healthy option, even if you have diabetes. Research suggests that following this type of eating plan can help prevent and manage diabetes. In fact, research on vegan eating plans has found that carbohydrate and calorie restrictions were not necessary and that a vegan plan still promoted weight loss and lowered participants' A1C.

A well-planned vegan eating plan tends to be naturally higher in fiber, much lower in saturated fat, and cholesterol-free when compared with a traditional American diet. The high amount of fiber in this kind of eating plan may help you feel full for a longer time after eating and may help you eat less overall. When fiber intake is greater than 50 grams per day on a vegan eating plan, it may help lower blood glucose levels. In addition, a vegan eating plan may be less expensive than a traditional American diet because you are cutting out meat, poultry, and fish, which tend to be more expensive foods.

KEY NUTRIENTS ON A VEGETARIAN DIET

If you choose to go vegetarian or vegan, there are some nutrients that may be of concern when meal planning. The key nutrients to consider when planning your meals include vitamin B-12, omega-3 fatty acids, calcium, vitamin D, and iron. Eating a variety of plant-based foods is important for ensuring that you get the nutrients your body needs. Fortified foods can be another source of these important nutrients for vegetarians. Fortification is a process where extra nutrients are added to a food. Also, many people take a multivitamin to make sure they get enough of all nutrients. Always check with your doctor before choosing a multivitamin or supplement, as too much of certain nutrients can be harmful and supplements can interact with other medications you may be taking.

Here is a list of the nutrients that vegan and vegetarian eating plans may lack and the foods to eat so you get enough of them:

- **Vitamin B-12:** This vitamin is only found in animal products and fortified foods, so it can be difficult for those who follow a vegan diet to get enough of it. You can get some vitamin B-12 from fortified soy and rice beverages, fortified breakfast cereals, fortified meat substitutes, and nutritional yeasts. If you choose to go vegan, talk to your doctor about monitoring your vitamin B-12 levels (it is just a simple blood test) as you may need to take a vitamin B-12 supplement. Most multivitamins have vitamin B-12, but check the label to make sure. It should be listed as "cobalamin" or "cyanocobalamin." Milk and dairy products, eggs, and fish are good sources of vitamin B-12 for lacto-ovo-vegetarians and pescatarians.

- **Omega-3 fatty acids:** This healthy fat can be found in plant foods including walnuts, ground flaxseed or flaxseed oil, soybeans, soybean oil, canola oil, or wheat germ. Fatty fish like tuna, sardines, and salmon, which can be included in a pescatarian eating plan, also have omega-3 fatty acids. If you choose to follow a vegan or vegetarian diet without fatty fish, you can find omega-3 supplements made from marine algae, which contain high levels of EPA and DHA (the types of omega-3s found in fatty fish). These supplements can be found at your local grocery and health food stores. Before you start taking any supplement, make sure it is recommended by your diabetes care team.

- **Calcium:** This mineral is found in milk and dairy products, if you decide to include them in your eating plan. Calcium can also be found in lesser amounts in leafy green vegetables (like bok choy, Chinese cabbage, collards, kale, mustard greens, and turnip greens), broccoli, Brussels sprouts, fortified fruit juices, calcium-set tofu, fortified soy milk or rice milk, and fortified breakfast cereals. Note that some greens like spinach are not a good source of calcium even though they are leafy green vegetables. Other compounds in spinach prevent the calcium it has from being absorbed and used in the body. If you're unsure if you're taking in enough calcium, an RDN can evaluate your diet to see if a calcium supplement is necessary.

- **Vitamin D:** This vitamin can be found in fortified milk, fortified yogurt, cheese, or egg yolks, if you decide to include them in your diet. It is also in some brands of fortified soy milk and rice milk, fortified orange juice, and some fortified breakfast cereals and margarines. Sun exposure can also help your body make its own vitamin D. Recent research is finding that many more people are deficient in vitamin D than was once thought. A simple blood test can check your vitamin D levels, and a doctor may recommend that you take a vitamin D supplement if your levels are low.

- **Iron:** Iron-deficiency anemia is the most common deficiency in the world. It is as common with vegetarian eating plans as it is with non-vegetarian eating plans. Plant sources of iron include beans, lentils, dried fruits, enriched grain products, tofu, and cooked green vegetables. To help your body better absorb the iron, eat these foods with a good source of vitamin C such as citrus fruits (oranges, lemon or lemon juice, and grapefruit), tomatoes, broccoli, potatoes, kiwi, or strawberries.

PROTEIN IN VEGETARIAN EATING PLANS

In the past, many people thought those who followed a vegetarian eating plan were not getting enough protein. However, research has shown that Americans in general are already getting more protein than they need. While those who follow a vegetarian eating plan do not eat any beef, pork, lamb, or poultry, some people may include eggs, milk and dairy, or fish in their eating plans, all which are high-protein foods. Even without these foods, getting enough protein is not a problem with a vegan or vegetarian eating plan if you eat a variety of the many plant foods that provide protein. These foods include:

- Dried beans or canned beans that have been rinsed (such as black, pinto, navy, or kidney beans or chickpeas)

- Other bean products (such as bean spreads, hummus, fat-free refried beans, baked beans, or falafel)

- Lentils

- Peas (black-eyed or split peas)

- Nuts and nut spreads (such as almonds, almond butter, peanuts, peanut butter, cashews, cashew butter, walnuts, or pistachios)

- Soy and soy products (such as soy milk, edamame, soy nuts, tofu, or tempeh)

- Meat substitutes (such as veggie burgers, black bean burgers, meatless "chicken" nuggets, or "beef" crumbles. These can be found in most grocery stores.)

Plant-based proteins tend to be higher in carbohydrate compared to animal-based proteins, such as chicken, fish, or meat. If you choose to follow a vegetarian or plant-based eating plan, you may find yourself filling your plate with higher-carbohydrate sources of plant-based proteins, like beans or lentils, and a carbohydrate side dish too, like brown rice, whole-grain pasta, or quinoa. This means that your vegetarian plate will likely be slightly higher in carbohydrate than the plate of someone who eats animal proteins. However, you can make some simple swaps from higher- to lower-carbohydrate starches or plant-based proteins to help keep total carbohydrates in check:

- If you choose a higher-carbohydrate protein, like beans, lentils, or another similar food, try to choose a lower-carb vegetable (see the list of nonstarchy vegetables on page 2) to add to the quarter of your plate reserved for carbohydrate foods. For example, if you choose lentils for one-quarter of your plate (as your protein serving), pair it with spinach (as your carbohydrate food serving) and another nonstarchy vegetable.

- Opt for nuts or nut butters as a protein choice as nuts are a lower-carb protein. For example, try creating a vegetarian stir-fry with tofu and vegetables in peanut sauce.

Guidelines for a Mediterranean-Style Eating Plan

The "Mediterranean Diet" is an eating plan rich in fish, fruits, vegetables, whole grains, and healthy fats. Many studies have found that a Mediterranean-style eating plan may help lower the risk of stroke, heart attacks, and cancer. Researchers hypothesize that this way of eating may help lower LDL (bad) cholesterol, blood pressure, and damaging inflammation in the body.

The Mediterranean-style eating plan emphasizes:

- **Eating fruits, vegetables, and whole grains:** Plant-based foods make up the bulk of the Mediterranean eating plan. Opt for low-carbohydrate (nonstarchy) vegetables in order to feel full and to help maintain target blood glucose ranges.

- **Eating fish and poultry at least twice a week:** Tuna, salmon, trout, mackerel, and herring are all healthy fish choices. Choose healthy cooking methods to cook your fish, including grilling and baking, and avoid frying.

- **Choosing healthy fats:** Mediterranean-style eating plans are filled with sources of healthy unsaturated fat, such as olive oil, canola oil, and olives. Olive oil is used in cooked dishes and also used to flavor salad or make salad dressings.

- **Enjoying nuts and seeds in moderation:** Nuts and seeds are filled with healthy unsaturated fats. Whether you choose almonds, pistachios, walnuts, cashews, nut butters (like peanut, almond, or sunflower butter), or seeds, eat these in moderation because nuts and seeds are high in calories. Try using sesame seed paste (or tahini) as a condiment on chicken breast sandwiches or in other sandwiches or sprinkling chopped almonds on vegetables like string beans.

- **Choosing lean and extra-lean proteins from beef, pork, lamb, and poultry:** The Mediterranean-style eating plan focuses on fish as a source of animal protein and includes smaller amounts of meat and poultry. If you choose meat or poultry, choose leaner cuts (see examples on page 5) in small portions (about 3 ounces). Avoid high-fat cuts of meat like sausage, bacon, and other processed meats.

- **Using plenty of fresh herbs and spices:** Herbs and spices help add flavor to food for few calories and grams of carbohydrate. For example, add cinnamon to your oatmeal, chopped fresh cilantro to salads, or chopped parsley to rice dishes. The options are limitless.

- **Enjoying meals together with family and friends:** The Mediterranean lifestyle is more relaxed compared to a typical American lifestyle. Oftentimes meals are enjoyed outside or at leisure, with many family and friends. Take the time to put away electronic devices and enjoy the company of those around you.

- **Exercising regularly:** Physical activity is part of a Mediterranean lifestyle. This includes walking, riding a bike, playing soccer, or any other activities you love to do.

A Mediterranean-style eating plan tends to be lower in salt and butter than a traditional American diet. Butter is replaced with healthy fats like olive oil and canola oil, the fresh herbs and spices help displace salt. Wine is also consumed in a Mediterranean eating plan, but in moderation. In order to manage your blood glucose, be careful when consuming alcohol because its effects on your blood glucose can be unpredictable. For more guidelines on alcohol consumption, see pages 12-13.

A Mediterranean eating plan tends to include less milk and dairy foods. This means that you need to pay close attention to getting enough calcium and vitamin D if you follow this meal plan. Other sources of calcium include canned salmon with soft edible bones, fortified juices and cereals, calcium-set tofu, beans, broccoli, and egg yolks. Vitamin D is found in a limited amount of foods including salmon, tuna, fortified juice and cereal, and egg yolks. If you are following a Mediterranean-style eating plan, speak with your doctor if you think you aren't getting enough calcium or vitamin D. He or she can determine if a supplement is necessary.

If you choose to follow a Mediterranean-style eating plan, build your plate using the same five steps outlined on page 1. Some Mediterranean-style plates you can try include:

- Poached salmon with whole-wheat couscous and roasted asparagus
- Greek salad topped with grilled chicken and whole-wheat pita

Guidelines for a Gluten-Free Eating Plan

Gluten is a protein found in wheat, rye, barley, and all foods that are made with these grains. Some people have celiac disease, which is an autoimmune digestive disorder. Celiac disease is genetic and runs in families.

When folks with celiac disease eat a food containing gluten, their body's immune system attacks the small intestine. The attack on the small intestine leads to damage on the villi (small fingerlike projections that line the small intestine), which help absorb nutrients into the body. Once the villi get damaged, nutrients cannot be absorbed

properly into the body. This means that although people with celiac disease are taking in the food (and nutrients) they need, the body cannot use the nutrients. The symptoms of celiac disease can be painful and uncomfortable and include abdominal bloating and pain, fatigue, chronic diarrhea, vomiting, and constipation.

According to the Celiac Disease Foundation, 1% of the total population worldwide is affected by celiac disease. It is more common in people with type 1 diabetes than in the general population. An estimated 10% of people with type 1 diabetes also have celiac disease. The only way to manage celiac disease is to completely avoid all foods that have gluten. Following a gluten-free eating plan will prevent permanent damage to your body and will help you feel better. An individual with celiac disease can easily follow the steps of the Diabetes Plate Method—just make sure the carbohydrate foods selected on the plate are gluten free (see the list of gluten-free grains on page 24) .

GLUTEN INTOLERANCE

There are also people who have a gluten intolerance. When these people eat foods that contain gluten, they also experience uncomfortable symptoms. However, they test negative for celiac disease and actual damage to their small intestine does not occur. More research about gluten intolerance is needed, but avoiding foods with gluten can help to relieve these symptoms.

FOLLOWING A GLUTEN-FREE EATING PLAN

Taking gluten out of your diet can be a difficult and frustrating change to make in your life, especially if you already feel limited by your diabetes. But once you get the hang of it, you'll find the things that work for you! Whole grains can be an important part of an eating plan for diabetes. There are some grains that you may not realize contain gluten. Here is a list of grains that should be avoided if you have celiac disease or cannot eat gluten:

- Barley
- Bulgur
- Durum
- Farro
- Kamut
- Oats made in a facility that also processes wheat and wheat products (look for oats specifically labeled "gluten free")
- Rye
- Semolina
- Spelt
- Triticale
- Wheat

However, even if you must cut gluten out of your eating plan, there are still many grains that are gluten free. These include:

- Amaranth
- Buckwheat
- Corn
- Millet
- Oats (processed in a facility that does not also process wheat and wheat products)
- Quinoa
- Rice (including brown rice)
- Sorghum
- Teff
- Wild Rice

You can also find many foods that are labeled "gluten free." However, just because a food is gluten free, that doesn't mean it is low in calories or carbohydrate or healthy. You can find cookies, cakes, and other unhealthy foods labeled "gluten free." These foods are still unhealthy and contain carbohydrates and sugar that can raise your blood glucose. When shopping for gluten-free foods, choose foods that provide nutrients to your body.

GLUTEN CLAIMS ON FOOD LABELS

Since 2014, the FDA has been regulating the term "gluten free" on food labels. The FDA requires that any foods that have a label saying, "gluten free," "no gluten," "free of gluten," or "without gluten" must meet clear standards to ensure that the product is gluten free. Foods that carry these labels must contain less than 20 parts per million of gluten (a very small amount that is generally fine for people with celiac disease). Any manufacturer using the term "gluten free" must also ensure that the food does NOT contain:

- An ingredient that is any type of wheat, rye, barley, or a crossbreed of these grains,
- An ingredient derived from these grains (unless it has been processed to remove gluten), or
- An ingredient derived from these grains that has been processed to remove gluten but still contains more than 20 parts per million of gluten.

These regulations mean that, if you're following a gluten-free eating plan, you can shop with confidence knowing that "gluten free" claims on products are consistent and accurate.

Tips for Holiday Meal Planning

Holidays are an opportunity to spend time with family and friends. The focus on food and traditions during the holidays can be very stressful, especially if you have diabetes. Advanced planning and preparation make holiday time much more enjoyable.

The most practical way to approach managing diabetes during the holiday season is to plan ahead. Advanced planning can help minimize stress during the holidays so that you can keep your diabetes management on track and enjoy your time with family and friends. Here are several things to plan in advance for the holidays:

- **Stick to the Diabetes Plate Method:** To help balance your meals and control portions of the holiday foods you love, use the Diabetes Plate Method during any holiday. Remember, if you don't have room on your plate for all your holiday favorites, you can always use leftovers to create another plate for your next meal.

- **Timing of meals:** During the holidays many families eat large feasts during odd times. For example, Thanksgiving dinner may be served starting at 3:00 or 4:00 pm. Plan in advance for how you will handle making changes if your holiday meal does not line up with your regular meal schedule. If you take insulin injections or a pill that lowers blood glucose, speak with your doctor or certified diabetes educator (CDE) so you can plan the best way to handle the meal time changes.

- **Be physically active:** With all the food being served during the holidays, many people forget to move around. Start a new tradition that involves physical activity away from the food. For example, before Thanksgiving many towns hold a "turkey trot," a race or long walk that usually takes place on Thursday morning. You can get the whole family and even the neighbors involved in activities like a friendly game of touch football, soccer, or Frisbee. It can also be as simple as a family walk around the neighborhood.

- **Lighten up healthier versions of your favorite holiday foods:** There are many simple ways to lighten up favorite holiday dishes. Oftentimes simply reducing the amount of carbohydrate in a food can be helpful. For example, if you're using oats for a crunchy topping for an apple crisp, cut the amount in half. Added sugar can also be minimized in desserts like fruit pies. Fruits are naturally sweet and you do not need to add a lot of sugar in order to taste its delicious flavor. You can also make swaps to cut back on the unhealthy saturated fat. For example, use nonfat or light sour cream instead of the regular version in casseroles. Or swap out butter with oil, where possible, and use a lesser amount.

- **Plan your snacks:** During the holidays, you may head to a party and have to wait a little while before the food is served. If possible, check with the party host in advance to see if there will be food to nibble on and what foods will be available. Make sure the food that is available will not sabotage your blood glucose levels before the meals. The last thing you want to do is indulge on high-calorie or fried appetizers. If the foods being offered are not appropriate for your eating plan, or if there will be no food for a period of time, ask the host if you can bring your own. Offer to bring a platter of raw or blanched vegetables with your favorite low-calorie dip, or pack a few small pieces of low-fat cheese.

- **Be selective:** Many traditional foods served over the holidays are high in carbohydrate. For example, traditional Thanksgiving fare includes mashed potatoes, sweet potatoes, stuffing, dinner rolls, cranberry sauce, pumpkin pie, and other desserts. For the 4th of July, you will find high-carbohydrate foods like potato salad, pasta salad, hot dog and hamburger buns, ice cream, and a variety of other sugary desserts. There are often so many options that even just a spoonful of each dish could be too much. Use "Toby's 2 Tablespoon Rule": scout everything that is available (you can always ask the host what is going to be served), then choose two or three of your favorites high-carbohydrate options and take 2 tablespoons of each. The rest you can skip, or you can always have some the next day as leftovers.

- **Eat smaller portions:** Most holidays offer plentiful options for carbohydrate-based foods. Your best bet is to watch portion sizes. If you cannot decide on one or two carbohydrate foods to eat, then take very small portions or "samples" of several. To keep your blood glucose trends in your normal ranges, try to keep your total carbohydrate intake the same as it would be on a regular day.

- **Eat your vegetables:** During the holidays the vegetable selection tends to be limited. However, just a few simple vegetable dishes can add beautiful colors—and a lot of nutrients—to the table. Offer to bring a green salad or a side of steamed or roasted vegetables seasoned with delicious herbs or spices. If you choose to bring a vegetable dish, opt for nonstarchy vegetables (see page 2 for a list of popular nonstarchy vegetable options), which are low in carbohydrate and calories. This will help fill you up and keep you from overeating other high-calorie, high-carbohydrate, and high-fat foods that are being offered.

Fitting in Sweets

Holidays and other special occasions can be tough when it comes to desserts. Whether it is cake for a birthday, pie for Thanksgiving, or ice cream on the 4th of July, sweets are everywhere. Holidays are special times to spend with family and friends, and for many people, enjoying sweet treats is part of the experience. Most people with diabetes can enjoy a small serving of their favorite dessert now and then.

It is important to remember that most sweets have a lot of calories and many grams of carbohydrate in a small serving, so pay attention to your serving size. You can work a sweet treat into your meal plan by substituting a small portion of dessert for other carbohydrate foods already in your meal plan. For example, if you want a small serving of apple pie for dessert, pass on eating a dinner roll and sweet potatoes during the main course. Incorporating desserts into your eating plan once in a while is about making a few smart carbohydrate swaps within your meal.

If you choose to eat dessert during the holidays, keep the following in mind:

- Decide ahead of time what and how much you will eat and how you will handle social pressure. For example, if Aunt Mary always insists on serving you large portions of every pie offered, choose to sit at the other end of the table from Aunt Mary. It is also okay to politely decline seconds or turn down food when it is offered. A simple "No, thank you" or "I'm too full" can do the trick.

- Share one portion of dessert with one or two other people at the table. Also, scrape off high-calorie whipped cream topping or extra frosting, and opt for cakes and pie without ice cream (or do not order it à la mode).

- Oftentimes there is at least one other person at the party or dinner who is trying to watch what they eat. You can excuse yourselves together from the table or party for a breath of fresh air or take a walk together while dessert is served.

- Offer to bring a lighter dessert option. There are ways to revise many dessert recipes so they are healthier and still taste great. Many times, you can use less sugar or replace up to half of the sugar in a recipe with a sugar substitute. Ask the host if you can bring a lighter version of your favorite dessert. This way you can have the most control over what you eat for dessert.

Chapter 2
Heart-Healthy Cooking

Turkey and Mozzarella Snack Skewers, p. 95

Cooking and preparing heart-healthy (and diabetes-friendly) food can help decrease your risk of developing heart disease. The most common cause of death for people with both type 1 and type 2 diabetes is cardiovascular disease (CVD), a disease of the heart and blood vessels. It is sometimes referred to as macrovascular disease, which refers to large blood vessels, like those in the heart. This chapter will explain how to prepare and cook foods that are heart healthy. These foods can be used with the Diabetes Plate Method approach to meal planning and can also help you keep your blood glucose within your target ranges.

What Is Cardiovascular Disease?

Lipids and cholesterol can build up along the walls of your blood vessels and lead to atherosclerosis, the narrowing, hardening, or clogging of blood vessels. Atherosclerosis is a common cause of CVD in people with diabetes and can lead to a heart attack or stroke.

The risk of CVD can be reduced by careful monitoring and regulating of blood pressure and blood lipids such as triglycerides, LDL (bad) cholesterol, and HDL (good) cholesterol. The recommended levels of blood pressure and blood lipids for people with diabetes are listed below. Eating a heart-healthy diet can help people with diabetes reduce the risk of CVD. Smoking also increases CVD risk, so quitting smoking also is an important step to help reduce the risk.

Healthy ABCs

Taking care of diabetes and other health conditions that can come along with it can help lower your risk of CVD. Even if you have heart disease, every step you take to keep your ABCs in your target range can help lower your risk of future heart attacks or a stroke. When I say "ABCs" I mean:

- **A1C:** Know your A1C, which tells you your average blood glucose for the past 2-3 months. Your healthcare provider can check your A1C with a blood test.

- **Blood pressure:** High blood pressure makes your heart work harder than it should. Goals for systolic and diastolic pressure for people with diabetes are listed below.

- **Cholesterol:** Your cholesterol numbers tell you about the amount of fat in your blood. Some forms of cholesterol, like HDL cholesterol, are healthy or "good," and help protect your heart. Others,

RECOMMENDED LEVELS OF BLOOD PRESSURE AND BLOOD LIPIDS FOR PEOPLE WITH DIABETES

Systolic blood pressure	< 130 mmHg	LDL cholesterol	< 100 mg/dL
Diastolic blood pressure	< 80 mmHg	HDL cholesterol	> 40 mg/dL (men); > 50 mg/dL (women)
Triglycerides	< 150 mg/dL		

like LDL cholesterol, are unhealthy or "bad," and can clog your arteries. High triglyceride levels increase your risk for a heart attack or stroke. Goals for cholesterol and triglycerides for people with diabetes are listed on page 29.

Why Choose Heart-Healthy Foods?

Because people with diabetes are at a higher risk for CVD, it is important to follow a heart-healthy eating plan. You can protect your heart and blood vessels by eating less unhealthy fat (saturated fat and trans fat) and by choosing the types of fat that help lower your cholesterol numbers (unsaturated fat). You can also protect your heart and blood vessels by maintaining a healthy weight. To do so, keep portions in perspective and make healthy food choices. You can also reduce your sodium intake, which can help many people with blood pressure control. Ask your healthcare team what your personal goals for fat and sodium intake should be.

Selecting Heart-Healthy Ingredients

The ingredients you use and the way you cook can make a big difference in your health. Heart-healthy foods include fresh, frozen, and canned fruits and vegetables, nuts, seeds, whole grains, low- and nonfat dairy, and lean proteins.

FRUITS AND VEGETABLES

Fruits and vegetables are an important part of heart-healthy eating. Choose a variety of fruits and vegetables in a range of different colors. The different colors provide different nutrients. Choose from fresh, canned, and frozen fruits and vegetables. The advantage of canned and frozen fruits and vegetables is that they can be stored for longer in your pantry or freezer. When purchasing canned fruit, make sure it is packed in water or light or extra-light syrup. For canned vegetables, drain and rinse them before using to remove any excess sodium, or look for no-added-salt or low-sodium varieties.

Frozen fruits should contain no added sugar and only consist of one ingredient–the fruit. Frozen vegetables should not contain sodium and should not be smothered in any sauces, like butter or cheese sauce. Buy them plain and dress them up with heart-healthy ingredients in your kitchen.

NUTS AND SEEDS

Nuts and seeds provide protein and healthy fat. Both nuts and seeds, and their corresponding nut and seed butters, can be part of a heart-healthy eating plan. Choose unsalted varieties whenever possible. Also, look for raw or dry-roasted nuts and seeds, as opposed to those roasted in oil. Nuts and seeds are healthy, but do contain a lot of calories. Keeping an eye on portions is important when it comes to nuts, seeds, and their butters. For example, 1 ounce of unsalted raw almonds (about 23 almonds) provides 161 calories, while 2 tablespoons of peanut butter provide 188 calories. When sprinkling chopped nuts on a salad or side dish, aim for 1-2 tablespoons per serving. When snacking on nuts, aim for no more than a small handful–about 1/4 cup.

WHOLE GRAINS

Whole grains can be an important part of heart-healthy eating. Refined grains/grain products (like white bread) contain little or no fiber, while whole grains are brimming with it. Fiber is important when eating heart healthy as it can help you improve blood cholesterol levels and lower your risk of heart disease and stroke. Fiber can also help you feel full, so you may feel more satisfied after eating it. Whole grains provide a variety of nutrients including thiamin, riboflavin, niacin, folate, iron, magnesium, and selenium. It is important to include a variety of whole grains in your eating plan because they can differ in their nutrient content. You can find a list of whole-grain ingredients on page 6.

LOW-FAT AND NONFAT MILK AND DAIRY

Milk and dairy foods can also be an important part of eating heart healthy. Milk provides nine essential nutrients, including three that are underconsumed by Americans—vitamin D, calcium, and potassium. Choose from a variety of low-fat and nonfat milk and dairy products. Full- and reduced-fat dairy products have a higher amount of saturated fat, which has been linked to heart disease. That is why low-fat and nonfat varieties may be a better choice for some people with diabetes. Here is a list of some of the more popular products you can choose from:

- Nonfat, low-fat, or 1% milk
- Nonfat or low-fat dry milk powder
- Evaporated nonfat milk
- Buttermilk made from nonfat or 1% milk
- Nonfat or low-fat yogurt or Greek yogurt
- Nonfat or low-fat frozen yogurt

- Low-fat cheeses including: low-fat cottage cheese, low-fat natural cheeses, or processed cheeses made with nonfat or low-fat milk with no more than 3 grams of fat per ounce and no more than 2 grams of saturated fat per ounce

If you do not drink milk or eat dairy products, then opt for soy milk. Other alternative plant-based beverages (like almond and rice milk) do not measure up to the nutrients in milk or soy milk.

LEAN PROTEIN

Both plant-based proteins and lean meat and poultry, along with fish and eggs, can be enjoyed as sources of lean protein. A list of plant-based proteins and lean meat, poultry, fish, and eggs can be found on pages 3-5. When preparing meat and poultry, always remove the skin and trim any visible fat. This is where a majority of the artery-clogging saturated fat is found.

HEALTHY FATS IN MODERATION

Unhealthy fat includes saturated fat and trans fat, which can be found in processed snacks and sweets, baked goods, fried foods, high-fat dairy products, solid fats, and high-fat meats. Instead of choosing these sources of unhealthy fats, choose lean protein foods and low-fat or nonfat milk and dairy foods, and limit the amount of processed snacks and baked goods you buy and eat. Choose more whole, nutritious foods to include in your snacks and meals, such as vegetables, whole grains, nuts, seeds, and fruit. When cooking, avoid using butter and margarine, and instead opt for vegetable-based oils, such as olive, canola, sunflower, safflower, and avocado oils.

Choose foods high in omega-3 fatty acids. Research has shown that omega-3s can help reduce the risk of heart disease. A list of foods high in omega-3 fatty acids can be found on page 14.

The Benefits of Healthy Home Cooking

Dining out may be easy, especially on busy nights, but portions in most restaurants tend to be oversized and the food is usually high in calories, sodium, and unhealthy fats. These are all the nutrients you want to minimize when you are eating heart healthy. Cooking at home gives you the most control over the fresh, healthy ingredients that go into your food. Throughout this cookbook you will find delicious, diabetes-friendly, and heart-healthy recipes that you can easily whip up at home. With this cookbook, cooking and meal planning for heart health and diabetes management have never been easier.

Tips for Meal Planning and Meal Prepping

In order to get heart-healthy, diabetes-friendly meals on the table, it is important to plan and prepare your meals in advance. This will ensure that you are not scrambling last minute to cook and end up ordering in pizza or driving to the nearest drive through. In order to efficiently plan and prepare your meals, follow these four steps:

1. Chose when to prepare your food

If you like to prepare your meals every night of the week, then make sure your schedule allows it. Some people like to meal prep numerous meals over the weekend so they have them ready to heat and eat throughout the busy work week. You can also opt to prepare meals for the week in batches on 2 days of the week, like Sunday and Wednesday. This can also help save you time during the busy work week, but still enable you to get healthy meals on the table. Regardless of when you like to prepare your food, make sure to schedule the meals you will prepare in advance.

2. Choose which meals to prepare

Whenever you choose to prepare your meals, you need to select the recipes you will cook. Keep variety in mind when it comes to fruit, vegetables, lean protein, low-fat and nonfat milk and dairy, whole grains, and healthy fats. This will enable you to take in a wider variety of nutrients.

This cookbook provides 125 healthy, tasty recipes to choose from. Once you try a recipe and you like it, tag it so you can make it again. After preparing a recipe several times it will start to feel easier each time. You can also find recipes on the American Diabetes Association's recipe website, DiabetesFoodHub.org, that can also be used when following the Diabetes Plate Method meal planning approach.

3. Go food shopping

To make the most of your time and money, after selecting your recipes, make a shopping list. If you like to cook every night of the week, then go food shopping for the ingredients you need for at least half the week. If you plan on cooking all your meals in one day, then you will need to make a more extensive shopping list.

Choosing recipes that use some of the same ingredients can help make your grocery list shorter, save you money, and prevent food waste. Take stock of what you already have on hand as you start selecting recipes for the week.

When writing a shopping list, sit down in your kitchen and check each recipe's ingredient list. Evaluate what you already have and what you need to buy. Jot it down on a list according to the flow of the supermarket. For example, supermarkets usually have you enter in the produce department so fruits and vegetables should be the first categories on your list. Also include how much you need of each ingredient in order to prevent overbuying and overspending.

4. Prepare and cook

If you plan on cooking every night of the week, then a little advanced preparing can help shave off prep time. You can chop vegetables or nuts or marinate meat or poultry the night before or in the morning before you head to work. Then when you get home, all you have to do is toss the ingredients together and cook. If you plan on taking leftovers to work, pack them the night before so you can just grab and go in the morning.

Eight Ways to Boost the Flavor

Classic French cooking uses three ingredients to boost flavor: butter, sugar, and salt. These are three ingredients that are still used today to add flavor to dishes—and a little goes a long way! But there are numerous other ways you can add flavor to your meals without adding much fat, sodium, or sugar. These include using herbs and spices, juices, vinegars, stocks, rubs and marinades, aromatic vegetables, sauce alternatives, alcohol, and extracts.

HERBS AND SPICES

Herbs are the leafy parts of certain plants that grow in temperate climates, and spices are the root, bark, seeds, flowers, buds, and fruits of certain plants. You can use fresh or dried herbs and spices to add flavor for few calories and minimal sodium. When using dried herbs, it's best to add them during the cooking process so their flavor has time to be infused into the dish. Fresh herbs, on the other hand, are best when added at the end of the cooking process or to finish off a dish, like sprinkling chopped cilantro over finished tacos.

If your recipe calls for fresh herbs and you only have dried or you have extra of a fresh herb and want to substitute it for dried–it's possible. Dried herbs have a more concentrated flavor so you want to use less of the dried variety than fresh, which will have a more delicate flavor. As a general rule of thumb, use about 1 1/2 times the amount of fresh herbs versus dried. You can play around with the flavor to see what suits your palate best.

COMMON HERBS AND SPICES

HERBS

- Basil
- Bay leaves
- Chervil
- Chives
- Cilantro
- Dill
- Mint
- Oregano
- Parsley
- Rosemary
- Saffron
- Sage
- Tarragon
- Thyme

SPICES

- Allspice
- Anise seed
- Caraway seed
- Cardamom
- Cayenne pepper
- Celery seed
- Cinnamon
- Cloves
- Coriander
- Cumin
- Curry powder
- Fennel seed
- Fenugreek
- Ginger
- Mustard seed
- Nutmeg
- Paprika
- Peppercorns
- Star anise
- Turmeric

JUICES

One hundred-percent fruit or vegetable juice can be used to add flavor or can be reduced to get a more intense flavor. To "reduce" a juice means to boil or simmer it down to a smaller volume until it gets a thicker or syrupy texture and vibrant color. Lemon and lime juice are common juices used in dishes. A small amount of juice can add a good amount of flavor to a dish. Common juices used in heart-healthy cooking include:

- Beet juice
- Cranberry juice
- Grapefruit juice
- Orange juice
- Pomegranate juice
- Tomato juice

A small amount of juice has a concentrated amount of sugar, so it's always important to be mindful of portions.

VINEGARS

The word "vinegar" originates from the French words *vin aigre*, which mean "sour wine." Vinegars are made by introducing bacteria into a fermented liquid like wine, beer, or cider. This creates the sour flavor you taste in vinegar. The acidity of vinegar makes it a perfect addition to marinades, where the acidity helps break down the protein fibers and softens the protein. Vinegars can also be used to balance the flavor of a dish or cut down on bitterness. Use vinegars to make vinaigrette–for example, sprinkle a few drops of balsamic vinegar over part-skim mozzarella cheese and tomatoes.

Below is a table with common types of vinegars and the best uses of each.

COMMON VINEGARS AND HOW TO USE THEM

Type of vinegar	Description	Best for...
Balsamic vinegar	Typically made from red or white wine from Trebbiano grapes, this vinegar is aged in wooden barrels for up to 50 years. The longer this vinegar ages, the sweeter and thicker (and pricier) it gets. Many balsamic vinegars are made with the addition of sulfites, which some asthmatics may be allergic to.	Dishes with tomatoes or strawberries, salad dressings, sauces, marinades, soups, grilled meats, chicken, and vegetables, and poached fruit
Cider vinegar	Also called apple cider vinegar, it has a rich and fruity flavor and pale brown color. Cider vinegar is made from fermented apple cider, unpasteurized apple juice, or pulp and is rather affordable.	Chutneys, stews, chilis, marinades, and coleslaw dressing
Red and white wine vinegar	Made from either red or white wine, these vinegars are typically aged in wooden barrels. Both vinegars are typically used in French and Mediterranean cuisines and are much less acidic than cider or distilled vinegar.	Red wine vinegar: Hearty dishes like stews, sauces, marinades, and salad dressings White wine vinegar: Vinaigrette, vegetable dishes, soups, and stews
Rice vinegar	Also called rice wine vinegar, rice vinegar is made from fermented rice. It has a mild, sweet flavor and is much less acidic than other vinegars.	Seafood dishes, marinades, salad dressings, along with Japanese and Chinese cuisine, like sushi and pickled ginger
White vinegar	Also called distilled vinegar or distilled white vinegar, white vinegar is colorless. It is made from grain alcohol and has a high acidity and overpowering sour flavor. It is inexpensive.	Preserving and pickling

STOCKS

Stocks are flavored liquids used to make soups and sauces. Stocks are made by simmering water, bones, and a combination of vegetables, usually celery, onion, and carrots (also called a *mirepoix*). As the ingredients simmer in the pot, the flavors from the bones and vegetables dissolve into the water to create the stock. To make a stock fat-free, skim off the fat that floats to the top of the pot after it is cooked. You can also refrigerate the stock, and the fat will separate and harden on the top, making it easier to skim off.

Making your own stock is a great way to save money and use up scraps of meat, bones, and vegetables that would otherwise be thrown away. Stocks do take several hours to prepare. You can also purchase them premade at the store. Choose low-sodium stocks or broths to use for cooking.

RUBS AND MARINADES

Rubs combine dry ground spices and chopped herbs and are classified as dry or wet. A dry rub combines dry ingredients only. A wet rub, also called a paste, adds a liquid ingredient like mustard, oil, or vinegar to the mixture. Dry and wet rubs work well to flavor meat, poultry, fish, and tofu. Rubs can be placed on the food right before cooking. The rub flavors the exterior part of the protein as it cooks.

Marinades are seasoned liquids in which foods are immersed before cooking. Marinades always have an acidic ingredient like vinegar, citrus juice, or wine. This acidic ingredient helps tenderize the meat, poultry, or fish; adds flavor; and also helps makes it a bit tougher for bacteria to grow. In order

for a marinade to do its job, the food must be immersed for at least 30 minutes or up to overnight.

AROMATIC VEGETABLES

Aromatic vegetables add strong flavors and aromas to foods. They can be used in both cooked and uncooked foods. For example, sautéing onions and garlic before cooking string beans punches up the flavor. Or you can fold scallions into light cream cheese, which adds depth to the flavor of the cream cheese. Aromatic vegetables include:

- Chives
- Garlic
- Leeks
- Onion
- Scallions
- Shallots

SAUCE ALTERNATIVES

Many classic sauces, such as Alfredo or other cream- or butter-based sauces, are high in fat. Instead of these high-fat sauces, there is a variety of sauce alternatives you can use that impart a delicious flavor without much salt, sugar, and saturated fat.

Coulis

Coulis is a French term that refers to a sauce made of puréed fruits or vegetables. Coulis can be served warm or cold. The consistence of a coulis is typically thin, like the texture of tomato sauce, but it can vary depending on the fruit or vegetable used. An example of a fruit coulis is blended blueberry purée served over part-skim ricotta cheese or poached pears. An example of a vegetable coulis is puréed bell peppers served over fish.

Salsa

Salsas are chopped vegetables or fruit, combined with herbs and spices. They tend to be vibrant in color and low in fat. When you make them at home, you can control the sodium content, too. You can make a chunky salsa by leaving chopped vegetable or fruit chunks as is, or you can blend them until smooth. Salsa can add flavor to fish, chicken, soups, and many Mexican-inspired dishes. It can also be used as a dip.

Alcohol

Wine, liqueurs, brandy, cognac, beer, and other forms of alcohol can be used to impart flavor to a dish. Usually a small amount of alcohol is added during the cooking process. Once the alcohol comes in contact with heat, the alcohol begins to burn off. The longer it is cooked, the more alcohol is removed, but the delicious flavor is left behind.

EXTRACTS

Extracts are derived from aromatic plants and are used in small amounts to add flavor. Common extracts include vanilla, almond, and lemon. Vanilla extract is commonly used in baked goods like cookies, pancakes, and muffins (all of which can be made heart healthy and diabetes-friendly using the right ingredients) and to add flavor in dishes like oatmeal and poached pears.

Choosing Healthy Cooking Methods

You can cut down on the calories and fat in your meals by using healthy cooking methods. It is okay to use some fat when cooking. Just make sure to use oils that are high in unsaturated fat and monitor your portions. Remember, all oils contain 120 calories per tablespoon, so the calories can add up quickly. You will see in all the recipes in this cookbook that only a few tablespoons of oil at most are used in any recipe that is cooked. Unsaturated oils that can be used when cooking include olive, peanut, corn, canola, safflower, avocado, sunflower, and flaxseed oil. Nonstick pans and cooking sprays also work well if you are trying to reduce the calories in a dish.

There are two categories of cooking methods–dry heat and moist heat. Dry-heat cooking methods use little or no fat. Excess fat is allowed to drip away from the food being cooked with dry-heat techniques. Dry-heat methods include roasting, broiling or grilling, sautéing, and stir-frying. Moist-heat cooking methods use water or liquids in order to transfer heat to cook the food. There are several moist-heat methods that can be used in heart-healthy cooking, including steaming, poaching, and braising or stewing.

DRY-HEAT COOKING TECHNIQUES

Roasting

With roasting, the food is cooked in the oven using heated dry air. A few tips for heart-healthy roasting include:

- When roasting meat and poultry, trim excess fat before cooking.

- Roast meat or poultry on a rack uncovered. Cook to the appropriate minimum internal temperature to prevent the food from drying out. Basting, or adding liquid to the meat, helps prevent drying.

- Use marinades and rubs to add flavor to meats, poultry, and fish before roasting.

Broiling and Grilling

Broiling cooks food using radiant heat from above, usually the top of the oven. It is a good cooking method for single servings of fish, poultry, and meat that will be served immediately. Grilling cooks food using radiant heat from below and is a good cooking method for meat, poultry, fish, vegetables, fruits, and tofu. To add flavor to food that will be broiled or grilled, use marinades, rubs, herbs, or spices.

Sautéing

Sautéing cooks food quickly over high heat using a small amount of fat. This technique can be used to cook small pieces of food. It also can be used as a step in a recipe to add flavor. When sautéing, use a shallow pan and allow the moisture to escape. Also, allow space between the food items inside the pan. For best results when sautéing:

- Use marinades, herbs, or spices to add flavor.
- Use high or medium-high heat to cook the food.
- Pound pieces of meat or poultry before sautéing to increase the surface area and ensure the food will be cooked through. It also helps reduce the cooking time.

Stir-Frying

This is when you cook small pieces of foods over high heat in a very small amount of oil–usually only a few teaspoons. This helps maintain the texture, crispiness, and bright color of any vegetables you're cooking. It also cooks strips of meat, poultry, or chunks of tofu quickly. Typically stir-frying is done in a wok, but you can also do it in a nonstick sauté pan. For best results when stir-frying:

- Coat the surface of the wok or sauté pan with a small layer of oil.
- Have all the ingredients prepared and ready to use as stir-frying is done quickly.
- Preheat the wok or sauté pan to a high temperature before adding the ingredients.
- Foods that take the longest to cook, like meat or poultry, should be cooked first. After they are cooked, they can be removed while the vegetables are being cooked.
- Use aromatic vegetables (see the examples on page 36), rice vinegar, reduced-sodium/lite soy sauce, ginger, or low-sodium stocks to add flavor.

MOIST-HEAT COOKING TECHNIQUES

Steaming

Steaming cooks vegetables quickly and retains the moisture, flavor, and nutrients in the food. Although the most common food to steam is vegetables, you can also steam shellfish, fish, chicken breasts, and fruits.

Poaching

Poaching is a technique where food cooks while it is submerged in water or liquid like a broth. Foods that are commonly poached include some fruits and vegetables, eggs, fish, and chicken.

Braising or Stewing

This cooking method typically involves cooking food in two steps. First the food is browned in a small amount of fat (like oil), and then a liquid is added and the food is simmered until it is done. Braising uses larger cuts of meat, while stewing uses smaller pieces of meat or poultry.

Microwaving

Although not a cooking method preferred by many, microwaving uses moist heat and is very convenient as it cooks food quickly. Microwaving vegetables in a small amount of liquid helps retain their nutrients, color, flavor, and texture.

There are several cooking methods that you want to avoid when preparing heart-healthy, diabetes-friendly meals including frying. With frying, the oil adds many unwanted calories. Also, boiling foods tends to destroy the vitamins and can make food rather mushy.

Tips for Lightening Up Your Favorite Dishes

There are many simple swaps you can make to lighten up your favorite dishes. The chart below suggests easy swaps that can help you cut calories, saturated fat, sodium, and/or added sugar.

SIMPLE SWAPS TO LIGHTEN DISHES

Instead of...	Use...	Best Dishes for Swap
Regular ground beef	At least 90% lean ground beef or lean ground turkey breast	• Lasagna • Meatballs • Meatloaf
Sour cream	Nonfat plain yogurt, regular or Greek	• Tacos • Baked potatoes • Dips
Butter or margarine (when cooking)	Oils like olive oil, canola oil, peanut oil, avocado oil	• Vegetable dishes, like sautéed asparagus • Sautéed chicken breasts
Butter or margarine (when baking)	Substitute half the butter or margarine with a fruit or vegetable purée like zucchini or carrot purée	• Cookies • Cupcakes • Cakes
Cream, whole milk, or reduced-fat or 2% milk	Low-fat or 1% milk or nonfat milk	• Pancake batters • Hot beverages like hot cocoa • Creamy soups
Regular mayonnaise	• Light mayonnaise, mustard, or hummus • A 50:50 combination of light mayonnaise and nonfat plain Greek yogurt	• Sandwiches • Pasta or potato salad (mayo–Greek yogurt mixture) • Dips or dressings (mayo–Greek yogurt mixture)
High-fat deli meats like bologna, salami, or pastrami	• Low-sodium turkey or roast beef • Cooked fresh chicken or turkey	• Sandwiches and wraps

Putting It All Together

Step 1

Fill half of your plate with nonstarchy vegetables. Nonstarchy vegetables are very nutrient dense, meaning they are high in healthy nutrients like vitamins, minerals, and fiber, but low in calories, fat, and carbohydrate. See page 2 for a list of nonstarchy vegetable options.

Step 2

Fill one of the small sections (one-quarter) of your plate with lean protein foods, such as lean meat, fish and seafood, eggs, or plant-based proteins. The biggest difference among foods in this group is how much fat they contain and, for the plant-based proteins, how much carbohydrate they contain. See page 3 for a list of plant-based protein options.

Step 5

Choose healthy fats in small amounts. Healthy fats can be added to any part of your plate. For cooking, use plant-based oils like canola or olive oil. For salads, some healthy fat additions are nuts, seeds, avocado, and vinaigrettes. Try to choose protein foods that naturally contain healthy fats, like fatty fish (including salmon and tuna). Minimize the amount of saturated fat and trans fat in your eating plan.

Step 4

To complete your meal, add water or another zero-calorie beverage. Water is always the best beverage choice. But if you are tired of plain water, there are other zero-calorie options to choose from, including unsweetened coffees and tea, sparkling water or infused water, and diet sodas sweetened with sugar substitutes instead of added sugars. Avoid sugary drinks like regular soda, fruit punch, fruit drinks, energy drinks, sports drinks, and sweet tea.

Step 3

Fill the other small section (one-quarter) of your plate with carbohydrate foods. When you choose to eat carbohydrate foods, make them count! Choose from whole grains, starchy vegetables and legumes, fruit, milk, and yogurt. Leave the processed, white flour-based products, especially the ones with added sugar, on the shelves, or enjoy them only for a special occasion treat.

Chapter 3
Sample Plates

This chapter shows you how to put it all together! These sample plates pair several recipes from the book together (and add a few other simple, healthy foods) to demonstrate how you can use the Diabetes Plate Method to create meals. In this chapter you will find a 7-day meal plan, which includes three meals plus two snacks per day and features delicious, diabetes-friendly dishes that can be found in this cookbook. As you're building these plates, keep in mind that you should add a single serving of each recipe listed on the plate unless otherwise specified.

Each day of the meal plan provides 1,500–1,700 calories, 130–165 total grams of carbohydrate, and at least 25 grams of fiber. Once you get the hang of meal planning with the Diabetes Plate Method, you can build your own daily and weekly meal plans. After the 7-day meal plan, you'll find some additional sample plates—five breakfast plates, six lunch plates, and six dinner plates—that you can incorporate into your own meal plans.

Monday

BREAKFAST PLATE

	Calories	Carb	Fiber	Fat	Sat. Fat	Protein	Sodium
Avocado Toast with Turkey Bacon (p. 69)	230	20 g	7 g	14 g	2.5 g	8 g	450 mg
1/2 cup nonfat plain Greek Yogurt	65	4 g	0 g	0.5 g	0.1 g	11 g	40 mg
1/2 cup fresh blueberries	40	11 g	2 g	0 g	0 g	0 g	0 mg
Breakfast Plate Total	335	35 g	9 g	14.5 g	2.6 g	19 g	490 mg

SNACK 1

	Calories	Carb	Fiber	Fat	Sat. Fat	Protein	Sodium
Date Nut Bar (1 serving, p. 87)	160	21 g	3 g	8 g	1.9 g	3 g	30 mg

LUNCH PLATE

	Calories	Carb	Fiber	Fat	Sat. Fat	Protein	Sodium
Beef Barley Soup with Sweet Potatoes (p. 144)	380	38 g	8 g	12 g	3 g	29 g	400 mg
Simple Side Salad with Balsamic Vinaigrette (p. 188)	70	7 g	1 g	4 g	0.6 g	1 g	50 mg
Lunch Plate Total	450	45 g	9 g	16 g	3.6 g	30 g	450 mg

SNACK 2

	Calories	Carb	Fiber	Fat	Sat. Fat	Protein	Sodium
Peanut Butter, Cranberry, and Walnut Apple Slices (p. 88)	140	13 g	3 g	9 g	2.3 g	3 g	50 mg

DINNER PLATE

	Calories	Carb	Fiber	Fat	Sat. Fat	Protein	Sodium
Sheet Pan Tuna with Asparagus (p. 162)	320	5 g	2 g	18 g	3.3 g	36 g	310 mg
Charred Cabbage with Cilantro-Lime Sauce (p. 199)	60	5 g	2 g	5 g	0.7 g	2 g	50 mg
Red Quinoa and Farro (p. 207)	180	28 g	5 g	5 g	0.7 g	5 g	220 mg
Dinner Plate Total	560	38 g	9 g	28 g	4.7 g	43 g	580 mg

	Calories	Carb	Fiber
TOTAL FOR THE DAY	1,645	152 g	33 g

When you "create your plate," don't forget to include all parts of your meal, even if a food is served on a different plate or at a different time. For example, if you have a serving of dessert after your dinner, you should still count that as part of your meal, just as if it was on your dinner plate.

Tuesday

BREAKFAST PLATE

	Calories	Carb	Fiber	Fat	Sat. Fat	Protein	Sodium
Veggie Egg Scramble (p. 70)	130	6 g	2 g	6 g	2 g	14 g	330 mg
1 slice whole-wheat toast	70	12 g	2 g	1 g	0.2 g	3 g	130 mg
2 teaspoon trans fat-free margarine	60	0 g	0 g	8 g	2.2 g	0 g	80 mg
1 small apple	75	20 g	4 g	0 g	0 g	0 g	0 mg
Breakfast Plate Total	335	38 g	8 g	15 g	4.4 g	17 g	540 mg

SNACK 1

	Calories	Carb	Fiber	Fat	Sat. Fat	Protein	Sodium
Savory Snack Mix (p. 92)	190	17 g	3 g	12 g	1.5 g	4 g	230 mg

LUNCH PLATE

	Calories	Carb	Fiber	Fat	Sat. Fat	Protein	Sodium
Greek-Style Salad with Tuna and Farro (p. 152)	210	26 g	6 g	4.5 g	1.2 g	19 g	360 mg
Lemon-Parsley Vinaigrette (p. 224)	60	1 g	0 g	7 g	0.9 g	0 g	75 mg
1/2 cup nonfat plain Greek yogurt	65	4 g	0 g	0.5 g	0.1 g	12 g	40 mg
1/2 cup diced cantaloupe	25	6 g	1 g	0 g	0 g	1 g	10 mg
1 tablespoon slivered almonds	40	1 g	1 g	3 g	0.2 g	1 g	0 mg
Lunch Plate Total	400	38 g	8 g	15 g	2.4 g	33 g	485 mg

SNACK 2

	Calories	Carb	Fiber	Fat	Sat. Fat	Protein	Sodium
Lemon Hummus (p. 210)	100	8 g	2 g	6 g	0.9 g	3 g	105 mg
8 baby carrots	30	7 g	2 g	0 g	0 g	0 g	60 mg
Snack 2 Total	130	15 g	4 g	6 g	0.9 g	3 g	165 mg

DINNER PLATE

	Calories	Carb	Fiber	Fat	Sat. Fat	Protein	Sodium
Skillet Tofu and Cabbage (p. 156)	210	11 g	2 g	15 g	1.9 g	11 g	290 mg
Red Beans and Rice (p. 205)	150	27 g	4 g	2.5 g	0.4 g	5 g	110 mg
Frozen Blueberries with Cinnamon-Almond Drizzle (p. 102)	110	7 g	2 g	9 g	0.7 g	3 g	0 mg
Dinner Plate Total	470	45 g	8 g	26.5 g	3.0 g	19 g	400 mg

	Calories	Carb	Fiber
TOTAL FOR THE DAY	1,525	153 g	31 g

You can still use the Diabetes Plate Method for mixed or combination foods like spaghetti and meatballs. Roughly one-quarter of the plate should be protein (meatballs) and one-quarter should be carbohydrate foods (whole-wheat spaghetti).

Wednesday

BREAKFAST PLATE

	Calories	Carb	Fiber	Fat	Sat. Fat	Protein	Sodium
Funky Monkey Yogurt Bowls (p. 86)	200	21 g	3 g	7 g	1.4 g	15 g	80 mg
3 turkey breakfast-sausage links	90	0 g	0 g	5 g	1.5 g	10 g	350 mg
1 cup nonfat milk	80	12 g	0 g	0 g	0 g	8 g	100 mg
Breakfast Plate Total	**370**	**33 g**	**3 g**	**12 g**	**2.9 g**	**33 g**	**530 mg**

SNACK 1

	Calories	Carb	Fiber	Fat	Sat. Fat	Protein	Sodium
4-Layer Stuffed Avocado (p. 100)	160	12 g	6 g	12 g	2 g	5 g	180 mg

LUNCH PLATE

	Calories	Carb	Fiber	Fat	Sat. Fat	Protein	Sodium
Turkey, Walnut, and Pomegranate Salad (p. 151)	290	22 g	5 g	14 g	3.3 g	21 g	440 mg
Pomegranate Vinaigrette (p. 223)	70	3 g	0 g	7 g	0.9 g	0 g	90 mg
1 medium whole-wheat roll	75	14 g	2 g	1 g	0.2 g	3 g	130 mg
1 teaspoon trans fat-free margarine	30	0 g	0 g	4 g	1.1 g	0 g	40 mg
Lunch Plate Total	**465**	**39 g**	**7 g**	**26 g**	**5.5 g**	**24 g**	**700 mg**

SNACK 2

	Calories	Carb	Fiber	Fat	Sat. Fat	Protein	Sodium
Cajun-Spiced Eggplant Chips (p. 91)	70	13 g	6 g	1.5 g	0.2 g	2 g	140 mg

DINNER PLATE

	Calories	Carb	Fiber	Fat	Sat. Fat	Protein	Sodium
Blended Beef and Mushroom Meatballs (p. 180)	160	9 g	1 g	8 g	2.1 g	13 g	160 mg
1/2 cup low-sodium tomato sauce	40	9 g	1 g	0 g	0 g	2 g	20 mg
1 cup cooked whole-wheat spaghetti	175	35 g	5 g	2 g	0.3 g	7 g	0 mg
1/2 cup chopped zucchini and red bell pepper	20	5 g	1 g	0 g	0 g	1 g	200 mg
Simple Side Salad with Balsamic Vinaigrette (p. 188)	70	7 g	1 g	4 g	0.6 g	1 g	50 mg
Dinner Plate Total	**465**	**65 g**	**9 g**	**14 g**	**3 g**	**24 g**	**430 mg**

	Calories	Carb	Fiber
TOTAL FOR THE DAY	**1,530**	**162 g**	**31 g**

An easy way to fill half your plate with vegetables is to double the serving size of your nonstarchy vegetable side dish!

Thursday

BREAKFAST PLATE

	Calories	Carb	Fiber	Fat	Sat. Fat	Protein	Sodium
Open-Faced Egg Sandwich (p. 73)	250	20 g	5 g	13 g	2.8 g	16 g	470 mg
1 small apple	75	20 g	4 g	0 g	0 g	0 g	0 mg
Breakfast Plate Total	325	40 g	9 g	13 g	2.8 g	16 g	470 mg

SNACK 1

	Calories	Carb	Fiber	Fat	Sat. Fat	Protein	Sodium
PB&J Smoothie (p. 131)	180	24 g	3 g	6 g	1.2 g	9 g	100 mg

LUNCH PLATE

	Calories	Carb	Fiber	Fat	Sat. Fat	Protein	Sodium
Tomato, Shrimp, and Orzo Soup (p. 143)	190	23 g	4 g	4 g	0.6 g	17 g	380 mg
Mediterranean Stuffed Pitas (p. 99)	140	21 g	3 g	5 g	1.1 g	5 g	260 mg
Lunch Plate Total	330	44 g	7 g	9 g	1.7 g	22 g	640 mg

SNACK 2

	Calories	Carb	Fiber	Fat	Sat. Fat	Protein	Sodium
Basil-Thyme Popcorn (p. 94)	180	13 g	3 g	14 g	2 g	2 g	220 mg

DINNER PLATE

	Calories	Carb	Fiber	Fat	Sat. Fat	Protein	Sodium
Lemon Chicken with Rosemary and Garlic (p. 172)	230	3 g	0 g	10 g	1.9 g	30 g	190 mg
1/2 small sweet potato with skin	50	12 g	2 g	0 g	0 g	1 g	70 mg
1 teaspoon trans fat-free margarine	30	0 g	0 g	4 g	1.1 g	0 g	40 mg
Collard Greens and Yellow Squash (2 servings, p. 194)	200	10 g	4 g	16 g	2.6 g	6 g	260 mg
Dinner Plate Total	510	25 g	6 g	30 g	5.6 g	37 g	560 mg

	Calories	Carb	Fiber
TOTAL FOR THE DAY	1,525	146 g	28 g

Friday

BREAKFAST PLATE

	Calories	Carb	Fiber	Fat	Sat. Fat	Protein	Sodium
Blueberry Soy Smoothie (p. 126)	140	18 g	3 g	4 g	0.6 g	8 g	30 mg
22 almonds	170	6 g	3 g	15 g	1.2 g	6 g	0 mg
1 hard-boiled egg	80	0 g	0 g	5 g	1.6 g	6 g	60 mg
Breakfast Plate Total	390	24 g	6 g	24 g	3.4 g	20 g	90 mg

SNACK 1

	Calories	Carb	Fiber	Fat	Sat. Fat	Protein	Sodium
Pineapple Spinach Smoothie (p. 127)	150	23 g	3 g	2 g	0.2 g	14 g	130 mg

LUNCH PLATE

	Calories	Carb	Fiber	Fat	Sat. Fat	Protein	Sodium
Simple Grilled Steaks (p. 182)	190	1 g	0 g	8 g	2.4 g	28 g	150 mg
Brown Rice with Scallions (p. 206)	140	25 g	2 g	3.5 g	0.5 g	3 g	230 mg
Weeknight Vegetable Stir-Fry (p. 202)	80	10 g	3 g	4 g	0.5 g	3 g	150 mg
Lunch Plate Total	410	36 g	5 g	15.5 g	3.4 g	34 g	530 mg

SNACK 2

	Calories	Carb	Fiber	Fat	Sat. Fat	Protein	Sodium
Antipasto Skewers (2 servings, p. 107)	180	10 g	4 g	14 g	4.4 g	10 g	340 mg

DINNER PLATE

	Calories	Carb	Fiber	Fat	Sat. Fat	Protein	Sodium
Pork Chops with Fennel and Shallots (p. 177)	270	5 g	2 g	18 g	4 g	22 g	350 mg
Simple Side Salad with Balsamic Vinaigrette (p. 188)	70	7 g	1 g	4 g	0.6 g	1 g	50 mg
Red Quinoa and Farro (p. 207)	180	28 g	5 g	5 g	0.7 g	5 g	220 mg
Dinner Plate Total	520	40 g	8 g	27 g	5.3 g	28 g	620 mg

	Calories	Carb	Fiber
TOTAL FOR THE DAY	1,650	133 g	26 g

Saturday

BREAKFAST PLATE	Calories	Carb	Fiber	Fat	Sat. Fat	Protein	Sodium
Whole-Grain Waffles with Peaches and Cinnamon Yogurt (p. 82)	500	56 g	9 g	26 g	2.5 g	19 g	550 mg
Breakfast Plate Total	500	56 g	9 g	26 g	2.5 g	19 g	550 mg

SNACK 1	Calories	Carb	Fiber	Fat	Sat. Fat	Protein	Sodium
Whole-Grain Vegetable Tortilla Pizza (p. 98)	130	16 g	3 g	5 g	2.1 g	5 g	240 mg

LUNCH PLATE	Calories	Carb	Fiber	Fat	Sat. Fat	Protein	Sodium
Turkey Vegetable Soup with Quinoa (p. 145)	350	32 g	5 g	12 g	1.9 g	27 g	410 mg
Creamy Avocado Dip (p. 211)	40	3 g	2 g	3 g	0.5 g	1 g	45 mg
8 slices zucchini	15	3 g	1 g	0 g	0 g	1 g	0 mg
Lunch Plate Total	405	38 g	8 g	15 g	2.4 g	29 g	455 mg

SNACK 2	Calories	Carb	Fiber	Fat	Sat. Fat	Protein	Sodium
Curried Chicken Salad Lettuce Cups (p. 111)	100	3 g	1 g	5 g	0.7 g	12 g	140 mg

DINNER PLATE	Calories	Carb	Fiber	Fat	Sat. Fat	Protein	Sodium
Easy Broccoli and Shrimp Stir-Fry (p. 165)	270	10 g	3 g	11 g	1.5 g	34 g	400 mg
Brown Rice with Scallions (p. 206)	140	25 g	2 g	3.5 g	0.5 g	3 g	230 mg
Whipped Goat Cheese–Stuffed Strawberries (p. 110)	70	4 g	1 g	4.5 g	1.7 g	4 g	90 mg
Dinner Plate Total	480	39 g	6 g	19 g	3.7 g	41 g	720 mg

	Calories	Carb	Fiber
TOTAL FOR THE DAY	1,615	152 g	27 g

Sunday

BREAKFAST PLATE

	Calories	Carb	Fiber	Fat	Sat. Fat	Protein	Sodium
Mexican-Style Scrambled Eggs (p. 72)	140	4 g	1 g	8 g	2 g	11 g	270 mg
1 (8-inch) whole-wheat tortilla	130	22 g	3 g	3.5 g	1 g	4 g	320 mg
1/4 cup fresh baby spinach	5	0 g	0.5 g	0 g	0 g	0 g	10 mg
Almost Smooth Salsa (p. 215)	15	1 g	0 g	1 g	0.2 g	0 g	45 mg
1 clementine	35	9 g	1 g	0 g	0 g	1 g	0 mg
Breakfast Plate Total	325	36 g	5.5 g	12.5 g	3.2 g	16 g	645 mg

SNACK 1

	Calories	Carb	Fiber	Fat	Sat. Fat	Protein	Sodium
Turkey and Mozzarella Snack Skewers (p. 95)	110	4 g	1 g	7 g	2.6 g	9 g	260 mg

LUNCH PLATE

	Calories	Carb	Fiber	Fat	Sat. Fat	Protein	Sodium
Salmon and White Bean Salad with Fennel and Orange (p. 149)	310	30 g	8 g	7 g	1.5 g	32 g	85 mg
Lighter Italian Dressing (p. 222)	40	1 g	0 g	3.5 g	0.3 g	0 g	105 mg
Roasted Beets with Lemon and Dill (p. 201)	70	12 g	2 g	2 g	0.2 g	2 g	150 mg
Lunch Plate Total	420	43 g	10 g	12.5 g	2 g	34 g	340 mg

SNACK 2

	Calories	Carb	Fiber	Fat	Sat. Fat	Protein	Sodium
Cinnamon Roasted Nuts (p. 93)	160	7 g	3 g	13 g	1.1 g	4 g	35 mg

DINNER PLATE

	Calories	Carb	Fiber	Fat	Sat. Fat	Protein	Sodium
Turkey and Black Bean Sloppy Joes (p. 167)	380	30 g	7 g	16 g	3.5 g	30 g	170 mg
1 whole-wheat hamburger bun	130	22 g	3 g	4 g	1.5 g	0 g	190 mg
Chopped Romaine Salad (p. 190)	35	4 g	1 g	2 g	0.3 g	1 g	65 mg
Dinner Plate Total	545	56 g	11 g	22 g	5.3 g	31 g	425 mg

	Calories	Carb	Fiber
TOTAL FOR THE DAY	1,560	146 g	31 g

More Sample Plates

Breakfasts

BREAKFAST PLATE 1

	Calories	Carb	Fiber	Fat	Sat. Fat	Protein	Sodium
Peanut Butter-Banana Bran Muffins (p. 78)	240	28 g	3 g	12 g	2.2 g	9 g	200 mg
1/2 cup nonfat plain Greek yogurt	65	4 g	0 g	0.5 g	0.1 g	12 g	40 mg
3/4 cup sliced strawberries	40	10 g	2.5 g	0 g	0 g	1 g	0 mg
1 tablespoon chopped pecans	45	1 g	1 g	5 g	0.4 g	1 g	0 mg
Breakfast Plate 1 Total	**390**	**43 g**	**6.5 g**	**17.5 g**	**2.7 g**	**23 g**	**240 mg**

BREAKFAST PLATE 2

	Calories	Carb	Fiber	Fat	Sat. Fat	Protein	Sodium
Apple Pie Parfaits (p. 66)	380	26 g	5 g	25 g	3.3 g	17 g	70 mg
Breakfast Plate 2 Total	**380**	**26 g**	**5 g**	**25 g**	**3.3 g**	**17 g**	**70 mg**

BREAKFAST PLATE 3

	Calories	Carb	Fiber	Fat	Sat. Fat	Protein	Sodium
Pear and Almond Overnight Oats (p. 76)	310	49 g	8 g	6 g	0.9 g	17 g	65 mg
Breakfast Plate 3 Total	**310**	**49 g**	**8 g**	**6 g**	**0.9 g**	**17 g**	**65 mg**

BREAKFAST PLATE 4

	Calories	Carb	Fiber	Fat	Sat. Fat	Protein	Sodium
Mushroom and Leek Frittata (p. 74)	200	8 g	1 g	13 g	3.4 g	14 g	340 mg
1 slice whole-wheat toast	70	12 g	2 g	1 g	0.2 g	3 g	130 mg
1 teaspoon trans fat-free margarine	30	0 g	0 g	4 g	1.1 g	0 g	40 mg
Breakfast Plate 4 Total	**300**	**20 g**	**3 g**	**18 g**	**4.7 g**	**17 g**	**510 mg**

BREAKFAST PLATE 5

	Calories	Carb	Fiber	Fat	Sat. Fat	Protein	Sodium
Whole-Wheat Almond French Toast Strips (p. 80)	230	26 g	5 g	8 g	1.7 g	13 g	240 mg
1/2 cup low-fat cottage cheese	80	3 g	0 g	1 g	0.7 g	14 g	460 mg
Breakfast Plate 5 Total	**310**	**29 g**	**5 g**	**9 g**	**2.4 g**	**27 g**	**700 mg**

Lunches

LUNCH PLATE 1

	Calories	Carb	Fiber	Fat	Sat. Fat	Protein	Sodium
Slow-Cooker Mexican Chicken Soup (p. 142)	240	35 g	5 g	2 g	0.4 g	22 g	360 mg
Simple Side Salad with Balsamic Vinaigrette (p. 188)	70	7 g	1 g	4 g	0.6 g	1 g	50 mg
1/2 small sweet potato with skin	50	12 g	2 g	0 g	0 g	1 g	70 mg
1 teaspoon trans fat-free margarine	30	0 g	0 g	4 g	1.1 g	0 g	40 mg
Lunch Plate 1 Total	**390**	**54 g**	**8 g**	**10 g**	**2.1 g**	**24 g**	**520 mg**

LUNCH PLATE 2

	Calories	Carb	Fiber	Fat	Sat. Fat	Protein	Sodium
Sheet Pan Chicken with Artichokes and Onions (p. 170)	270	13 g	5 g	10 g	1.9 g	32 g	290 mg
Mashed Red Potatoes (p. 203)	100	19 g	2 g	1.5 g	1 g	3 g	100 mg
Mushroom Soup (p. 141)	100	10 g	2 g	4 g	0.6 g	5 g	190 mg
Lunch Plate 2 Total	**470**	**42 g**	**9 g**	**15.5 g**	**3.5 g**	**40 g**	**580 mg**

LUNCH PLATE 3

	Calories	Carb	Fiber	Fat	Sat. Fat	Protein	Sodium
Barley Salad with Warmed Chicken, Mushrooms, and Brussels Sprouts (p. 146)	370	28 g	7 g	14 g	2.4 g	33 g	290 mg
Crudité Cups (p. 106)	60	7 g	2 g	3 g	1.3 g	4 g	100 mg
Lunch Plate 3 Total	**430**	**35 g**	**9 g**	**17 g**	**3.7 g**	**37 g**	**390 mg**

LUNCH PLATE 4

	Calories	Carb	Fiber	Fat	Sat. Fat	Protein	Sodium
Slow-Cooker Ratatouille with White Beans (p. 157)	180	30 g	10 g	3.5 g	0.5 g	10 g	230 mg
Side Greek Salad with Red Wine Vinaigrette (p. 189)	120	7 g	2 g	11 g	1.3 g	1 g	170 mg
Lunch Plate 4 Total	**300**	**37 g**	**12 g**	**14.5 g**	**1.8 g**	**11 g**	**400 mg**

LUNCH PLATE 5

	Calories	Carb	Fiber	Fat	Sat. Fat	Protein	Sodium
Caprese Quinoa Salad with Steak (p. 153)	360	29 g	4 g	13 g	3.6 g	31 g	220 mg
Zucchini Fritters with Lemon-Yogurt Sauce (p. 120)	140	16 g	3 g	5 g	1 g	8 g	200 mg
Lunch Plate 5 Total	**500**	**45 g**	**7 g**	**18 g**	**4.6 g**	**39 g**	**420 mg**

LUNCH PLATE 6

	Calories	Carb	Fiber	Fat	Sat. Fat	Protein	Sodium
Lamb and Chickpea Curry (p. 183)	390	35 g	10 g	12 g	3 g	33 g	300 mg
Steamed Green Beans with Cashews (p. 197)	90	9 g	3 g	5 g	0.9 g	3 g	105 mg
Lunch Plate 6 Total	**480**	**44 g**	**13 g**	**17 g**	**3.9 g**	**36 g**	**405 mg**

THE CREATE-YOUR-PLATE DIABETES COOKBOOK

Dinners

DINNER PLATE 1

	Calories	Carb	Fiber	Fat	Sat. Fat	Protein	Sodium
Roasted Salmon with Chimichurri Sauce (p. 158)	280	2 g	1 g	17 g	3.3 g	28 g	240 mg
Zucchini with Basil, Mint, and Pine Nuts (2 servings, p. 196)	160	10 g	4 g	14 g	1.6 g	4 g	320 mg
Crostini with Pan-Roasted Strawberries and Ricotta (p. 122)	140	18 g	2 g	4.5 g	1.8 g	6 g	140 mg
Dinner Plate 1 Total	**580**	**30 g**	**7 g**	**35.5 g**	**6.7 g**	**38 g**	**700 mg**

DINNER PLATE 2

	Calories	Carb	Fiber	Fat	Sat. Fat	Protein	Sodium
Mediterranean Chicken and Vegetable Bake (p. 171)	270	10 g	4 g	12 g	3.2 g	30 g	400 mg
Tabbouleh with Cucumber, Strawberries, and Mint (p. 204)	150	28 g	7 g	3.5 g	0.4 g	5 g	130 mg
Dinner Plate 2 Total	**420**	**38 g**	**11 g**	**15.5 g**	**3.6 g**	**35 g**	**530 mg**

DINNER PLATE 3

	Calories	Carb	Fiber	Fat	Sat. Fat	Protein	Sodium
Boiled Shrimp with Green Goddess Sauce (p. 159)	120	4 g	0 g	3.5 g	0.4 g	19 g	240 mg
Simple Side Salad with Balsamic Vinaigrette (2 servings, p. 188)	140	14 g	2 g	8 g	1.2 g	2 g	100 mg
Red Quinoa and Farro (p. 207)	180	28 g	5 g	5 g	0.7 g	5 g	220 mg
Dinner Plate 3 Total	**440**	**46 g**	**7 g**	**16.5 g**	**2.3 g**	**26 g**	**560 mg**

DINNER PLATE 4

	Calories	Carb	Fiber	Fat	Sat. Fat	Protein	Sodium
Easy Beef Chili (p. 184)	290	34 g	9 g	8 g	2.3 g	22 g	180 mg
2 tablespoons nonfat plain Greek yogurt	15	1 g	0 g	0 g	0 g	3 g	10 mg
Almost Smooth Salsa (p. 215)	15	1 g	0 g	1 g	0.2 g	0 g	45 mg
Kale Apple Slaw (p. 192)	100	13 g	3 g	4 g	0.5 g	5 g	210 mg
Dinner Plate 4 Total	**420**	**49 g**	**12 g**	**13 g**	**3 g**	**30 g**	**445 mg**

Dinners continued on page 63

Dinners

Dinners continued from page 61

DINNER PLATE 5

	Calories	Carb	Fiber	Fat	Sat. Fat	Protein	Sodium
Southwest-Style Turkey Meatloaf (p. 169)	220	15 g	2 g	8 g	2.4 g	20 g	400 mg
Mashed Red Potatoes (p. 203)	100	19 g	2 g	1.5 g	1 g	3 g	100 mg
Green Salad with Orange, Avocado, and Onion (p. 191)	140	14 g	5 g	9 g	1.3 g	2 g	135 mg
Dinner Plate 5 Total	**460**	**48 g**	**9 g**	**18.5 g**	**4.7 g**	**25 g**	**635 mg**

DINNER PLATE 6

	Calories	Carb	Fiber	Fat	Sat. Fat	Protein	Sodium
Grilled Chicken and Vegetable Skewer (p. 174)	260	10 g	2 g	10 g	1.9 g	32 g	140 mg
Kale Apple Slaw (p. 192)	100	13 g	3 g	4 g	0.5 g	5 g	210 mg
1 grilled corn on the cob	75	17 g	2 g	1 g	0 g	3 g	10 mg
1 teaspoon trans fat-free margarine	30	0 g	0 g	4 g	1.1 g	0 g	40 mg
Dinner Plate 6 Total	**465**	**40 g**	**7 g**	**19 g**	**3.5 g**	**40 g**	**400 mg**

Chapter 4
Breakfasts

How Breakfast Fits on Your Plate

When using the Diabetes Plate Method, breakfast is one meal where you don't always divide your plate the same way you do for lunch and dinner. It's typically a smaller meal, and as such, you don't need to fill your whole plate or include all three food groups. At breakfast, you can choose to fill only half your dinner plate (or use a smaller plate) and include at least two of the three food groups. Choose carb foods that are high in fiber like oatmeal, whole-grain bread, or fruit. Choose leaner proteins like eggs, turkey bacon, Greek yogurt, or cottage cheese. Include vegetables whenever you can. For example, add chopped veggies to scrambled eggs, add fresh greens to a breakfast sandwich, or add spinach or kale to a smoothie. Adding healthy fats at breakfast can help you feel more satisfied since fat takes longer to digest. For a healthy fat boost, try adding avocado slices on the side of your scrambled eggs, or a tablespoon of nut butter to your smoothie, or top your oatmeal or Greek yogurt with chopped nuts.

TOTAL TIME 31 minutes plus
10 minutes cooling time
PREP TIME 20 minutes
COOK TIME 11 minutes

SERVES 4
SERVING SIZE 1 parfait

COMPLETE THE PLATE
This recipe: Lean Protein,
Carbohydrate Food
Pair with: A serving of
Nonstarchy Vegetables such as
freshly sliced cucumbers

2 tablespoons canola oil

2 teaspoons stevia brown
    sugar blend (such as Truvia)

2 tablespoons sunflower or
    almond butter

Nonstick cooking spray

1/4 cup quick-cooking
    rolled oats

1/4 cup raw walnuts, chopped

1/4 cup sunflower seeds

1 1/2 tablespoons flaxseed

1/3 cup water

2 teaspoons lemon juice

1 teaspoon vanilla

1 teaspoon ground cinnamon

1/8 teaspoon ground nutmeg

2 medium apples, peeled,
    cored, and diced

2 teaspoons unsalted butter

2 cups nonfat plain Greek
    yogurt

Zest of 1 lemon (1 tablespoon)

APPLE PIE PARFAITS

*Enjoy the flavors of the all-American dessert, apple pie, in
a healthy, balanced breakfast parfait. These parfaits are
made with sautéed apples, sprinkled with delicious fall
flavors, and topped with a crunchy oat blend.*

1 Line a baking sheet with aluminum foil or parchment paper.

2 In a small bowl, whisk together the canola oil, brown sugar
blend, and sunflower butter until smooth. Set aside.

3 Coat a medium saucepan with nonstick cooking spray and
heat over medium-low heat. Add the oats, walnuts, sunflower
seeds, and flaxseed and toast until slightly brown and fragrant,
stirring regularly, about 5 minutes. Remove the toasted oat
mixture from the saucepan and place in a small bowl.

4 Add the oil mixture into the saucepan and bring to a boil.
Then quickly turn the heat to low and whisk regularly, until the
mixture has slightly thickened, about 1 minute. Remove the
saucepan from the heat and then add the toasted oat mixture.
Stir to evenly coat.

5 Spread the oat mixture in a single layer on the prepared
baking sheet and allow to cool for 10 minutes. Wipe the
saucepan clean with a paper towel.

6 In a medium bowl, whisk together the water, lemon juice,
vanilla, cinnamon, and nutmeg. Add the apples and toss to
evenly coat.

Choices/Exchanges 1 Fruit, 1/2 Carbohydrate, 2 Lean Protein, 4 1/2 Fat

Calories 380
Calories from Fat 220
Total Fat 25.0 g
Saturated Fat 3.3 g
Trans Fat 0.1 g

Cholesterol 10 mg
Sodium 70 mg
Potassium 440 mg
Total Carbohydrate 26 g
Dietary Fiber 5 g

Sugars 15 g
Added Sugars 1 g
Protein 17 g
Phosphorus 380 mg

7 In the same saucepan, heat the butter over a medium heat. Once the butter has melted, add the apple mixture and cook until the apples have slightly softened, about 5 minutes. Set aside to slightly cool.

8 While the apples are cooking, mix the yogurt and lemon zest together in a small bowl. In each of 4 parfait glasses, layer 1/4 cup of the yogurt, 1/3 cup of the apple mixture, another 1/4 cup of yogurt, and top with 1/4 cup of the granola.*

Chef's note: The parfaits can be made ahead of time and stored in the refrigerator for up to 3 days. Store the granola separately and add just before eating.

Choose Honeycrisp, Pink Lady, Braeburn, or Jonagold varieties of apples, which all hold up well when the apples are cooked.

TOTAL TIME 33 minutes
PREP TIME 15 minutes
COOK TIME 18 minutes

SERVES 4
SERVING SIZE 1 parfait

COMPLETE THE PLATE
This recipe: Lean Protein, Carbohydrate Food
Pair with: A serving of Nonstarchy Vegetables such as freshly sliced tomatoes

1/2 cup shelled unsalted pistachios, chopped

3 tablespoons water

1 1/2 tablespoons stevia brown sugar blend (such as Truvia), divided

Juice of 1 orange (about 3 tablespoons)

Zest of 1 lemon (1 tablespoon)

4 cups strawberries, diced

3/4 cup part-skim ricotta cheese

1 1/4 cups nonfat plain Greek yogurt

1 teaspoon vanilla extract

STRAWBERRY-RICOTTA PARFAITS WITH PISTACHIOS

Strawberries and ricotta make an oh-so-delicious combination. In this recipe, I whip the ricotta with nonfat plain Greek yogurt, which helps keep the saturated fat low while adding a boost of protein.

1 Heat a medium skillet over medium-low heat. Add the pistachios and toast until slightly brown and fragrant, tossing regularly, about 3 minutes. Remove the pistachios from the saucepan and set aside to cool. Wipe the saucepan with a paper towel.

2 In a medium bowl, whisk together the water, 1 tablespoon of the brown sugar blend, orange juice, and lemon zest. Add the strawberries and toss to evenly coat.

3 Add the strawberries with the sauce to the same skillet and bring the mixture to a boil. Lower the heat and simmer until the mixture thickens, about 15 minutes. Spoon the strawberry sauce into a small bowl and set aside to cool.

4 In a medium bowl, add the ricotta, yogurt, vanilla extract, and remaining 1/2 tablespoon of the brown sugar blend. Whisk quickly until the ingredients are well incorporated, about 30–45 seconds.

5 In each of 4 parfait glasses, spoon 1/2 cup of the whipped ricotta mixture, top with 1/2 cup of the strawberry sauce, and sprinkle with 2 tablespoons of the pistachios.

 To properly store fresh strawberries, refrigerate them as soon as possible in their original clamshell (or plastic container) or in a container layered with a dry paper towel at the bottom. Wash under cool water just before preparing or eating.

Choices/Exchanges 1 Fruit, 1/2 Fat-Free Milk, 1/2 Carbohydrate, 2 Lean Protein, 1 Fat

Calories 270
Calories from Fat 100
Total Fat 11.0 g
Saturated Fat 3.2 g
Trans Fat 0.0 g

Cholesterol 20 mg
Sodium 90 mg
Potassium 600 mg
Total Carbohydrate 26 g
Dietary Fiber 5 g

Sugars 15 g
Added Sugars 2 g
Protein 17 g
Phosphorus 295 mg

AVOCADO TOAST WITH TURKEY BACON

Avocado toast is a quick and easy go-to breakfast that incorporates healthy fat, whole grains, and protein. Change things up by substituting the turkey bacon with an easy over egg or sliced hard-boiled egg.

1 Coat a medium skillet with nonstick cooking spray and place it over medium heat until hot. Add the turkey bacon and cook until crispy, 8 minutes, flipping the slices over halfway through. Transfer the bacon to a paper towel-lined plate. Set aside to cool for 10 minutes.

2 Scoop out the flesh from each avocado half onto a slice of toasted bread. Mash the avocado with a fork until flattened. Sprinkle with sea salt and black pepper.

3 Top each avocado toast with 1 slice of turkey bacon and half of the tomato slices.

 When purchasing whole-grain bread, look for the words "100% whole grain" on the label. This means they use every part of the grain when making the bread.

TOTAL TIME 10 minutes
PREP TIME 5 minutes
COOK TIME 8 minutes

SERVES 2
SERVING SIZE 1 avocado toast

COMPLETE THE PLATE
This recipe: Lean Protein, Carbohydrate Food
Pair with: A serving of Nonstarchy Vegetables such as freshly sliced cucumbers, tomatoes, and bell peppers

Nonstick cooking spray

2 slices lean turkey bacon (look for one with 35 calories per slice)

1 ripe avocado, pitted and halved

2 slices 100%-whole-wheat bread, toasted

1/8 teaspoon sea salt

1/8 teaspoon ground black pepper

1 plum tomato, thinly sliced

Choices/Exchanges 1 Starch, 1/2 Fruit, 1 Lean Protein, 2 Fat

Calories 230
Calories from Fat 130
Total Fat 14.0 g
Saturated Fat 2.5 g
Trans Fat 0.0 g

Cholesterol 10 mg
Sodium 450 mg
Potassium 540 mg
Total Carbohydrate 20 g
Dietary Fiber 7 g

Sugars 3 g
Added Sugars 0 g
Protein 8 g
Phosphorus 145 mg

TOTAL TIME 14 minutes
PREP TIME 5 minutes
COOK TIME 9 minutes

SERVES 4
SERVING SIZE About 1 cup

COMPLETE THE PLATE
This recipe: Nonstarchy
Vegetable, Lean Protein
Pair with: A serving of
Carbohydrate Foods such as
whole-wheat bread or a whole-
wheat English muffin

4 large eggs

6 large egg whites

1/4 teaspoon salt

1/4 teaspoon ground black
  pepper

Nonstick cooking spray

2 plum tomatoes, chopped

1 green bell pepper, chopped

1 red bell pepper, chopped

2 tablespoons reduced-fat
  shredded cheddar cheese

VEGGIE EGG SCRAMBLE

*Don't toss those golden yolks! Egg yolks are also brimming
with many good-for-you nutrients, such as riboflavin,
vitamin D, and vitamin B-12. Plus, the yolk is home to
nutrients including choline and selenium. The antioxidant
selenium is a trace mineral and is involved in the immune
system and hormone balance. Studies have shown that
selenium may also help protect against certain forms of
cancer. So, don't get rid of all of them. Egg yolks do contain
some saturated fat, so try keeping just one in the recipe
and bulk it up using 2 egg whites.*

1 In a small bowl, whisk together the eggs, egg whites, salt,
and black pepper.

2 Coat a medium skillet with nonstick cooking spray
and heat over medium heat. Once the skillet is hot, add
the tomato and bell peppers and cook until slightly
softened, about 3–4 minutes. Pour the egg mixture over
the vegetables. Using a spatula, fold and invert the eggs
until large, soft curds form, about 4 minutes. Sprinkle
with cheese and cook an additional 30 seconds until the
cheese is slightly melted.

*Use any low-carb vegetables you have in your
refrigerator, such as mushrooms, spinach, or broccoli,
in this scramble.*

Choices/Exchanges 1 Nonstarchy Vegetable, 2 Lean Protein, 1/2 Fat

Calories 130	**Cholesterol** 190 mg	**Sugars** 4 g
Calories from Fat 50	**Sodium** 330 mg	**Added Sugars** 0 g
Total Fat 6.0 g	**Potassium** 370 mg	**Protein** 14 g
Saturated Fat 2.0 g	**Total Carbohydrate** 6 g	**Phosphorus** 150 mg
Trans Fat 0.0 g	**Dietary Fiber** 2 g	

TOTAL TIME 20 minutes
PREP TIME 15 minutes
COOK TIME 5 minutes

SERVES 4
SERVING SIZE 2/3 cup

COMPLETE THE PLATE
This recipe: Lean Protein
Pair with: A serving of Nonstarchy Vegetables such as Simple Side Salad with Balsamic Vinaigrette (page 188) and Carbohydrate Foods such as a whole-wheat tortilla

1/4 cup canned low-sodium black beans, drained and rinsed

1/4 small red onion, chopped

1/4 red bell pepper, chopped

4 large eggs

4 large egg whites

1/2 teaspoon dried parsley

1/4 teaspoon salt

1/8 teaspoon ground black pepper

1 tablespoon olive oil

MEXICAN-STYLE SCRAMBLED EGGS

When wrapped in a whole-wheat tortilla, this recipe provides whole grains, protein, and veggies—it's an all-in-one breakfast that's quick and easy. To round out your plate, you can add a serving of your favorite fruit on the side.

1 In a small bowl, toss together the beans, onion, and bell pepper.

2 In a separate medium bowl, whisk together the eggs, egg whites, salt, and black pepper.

3 Heat the olive oil in a medium skillet over medium heat. When the oil is shimmering, add the bean and pepper mixture and cook until slightly softened, 3 minutes. Add the egg mixture and, using a spatula, fold and invert the eggs until large, soft curds form, about 3 minutes. Serve warm.

 If you can't find low-sodium canned beans, just rinse them well. Studies show that rinsing canned beans can lower the sodium by up to 40%.

Choices/Exchanges 2 Lean Protein, 1 Fat

Calories 140	**Cholesterol** 185 mg	**Sugars** 1 g
Calories from Fat 70	**Sodium** 270 mg	**Added Sugars** 0 g
Total Fat 8.0 g	**Potassium** 200 mg	**Protein** 11 g
Saturated Fat 2.0 g	**Total Carbohydrate** 4 g	**Phosphorus** 125 mg
Trans Fat 0.0 g	**Dietary Fiber** 1 g	

OPEN-FACED EGG SANDWICH

Eggs contain lutein, a natural plant compound that helps maintain your skin's elasticity and hydration. It has been linked to preventing plaque buildup in your arteries, which is very important for a healthy heart.

---

1 To keep the yolk intact, carefully crack the egg into a small glass bowl or wine glass.

2 Coat a small skillet with nonstick cooking spray and heat over medium heat. Once the skillet is hot, carefully add the cracked egg so as not to break open the yolk. Cook until the whites are completely set and yolk is still runny, about 2 minutes. Sprinkle with black pepper.

3 Spread the margarine onto half of a toasted English muffin. Top with the ham, tomato slices, and avocado slice, then carefully top with the cooked egg. Sprinkle with the chopped scallions.

Pasteurized eggs are heat treated to destroy any pathogenic bacteria. If you use a regular, unpasteurized egg, then cook your egg over hard or scrambled.

TOTAL TIME 7 minutes
PREP TIME 5 minutes
COOK TIME 2 minutes

SERVES 1
SERVING SIZE 1 sandwich

COMPLETE THE PLATE
This recipe: Nonstarchy Vegetable, Lean Protein, Carbohydrate Food
Pair with: A serving of Nonstarchy Vegetables such as Sautéed Mushroom Medley (page 198)

1 large pasteurized egg

Nonstick cooking spray

1/8 teaspoon ground black pepper

1 teaspoon trans fat-free margarine (such as Benecol)

1/2 whole-wheat English muffin, toasted

1 ounce reduced-sodium deli ham

2 slices tomato

3 slices avocado (about 1/5 avocado)

1 scallion (green part only), chopped, for garnish

Choices/Exchanges 1 Starch, 1 Nonstarchy Vegetable, 2 Lean Protein, 1 1/2 Fat

Calories 250
Calories from Fat 120
Total Fat 13.0 g
Saturated Fat 2.8 g
Trans Fat 0.0 g

Cholesterol 200 mg
Sodium 470 mg
Potassium 490 mg
Total Carbohydrate 20 g
Dietary Fiber 5 g

Sugars 5 g
Added Sugars 0 g
Protein 16 g
Phosphorus 280 mg

TOTAL TIME 40 minutes
PREP TIME 15 minutes
COOK TIME 25 minutes

SERVES 4
SERVING SIZE 1 slice

COMPLETE THE PLATE
This recipe: Nonstarchy Vegetable, Lean Protein
Pair with: A serving of Nonstarchy Vegetables such as freshly sliced cucumbers and tomatoes and Carbohydrate Foods such as 100%-whole-wheat bread

4 large eggs

4 large egg whites

1/4 cup nonfat milk

1 teaspoon ground thyme

1/4 teaspoon salt

1/8 teaspoon ground black pepper

2 tablespoons olive oil

1/2 medium leek, sliced lengthwise and thinly sliced (1 cup)

1 clove garlic, minced

1 (8-ounce) package crimini or baby bella mushrooms, thinly sliced (3 cups)

1/4 cup reduced-fat shredded cheddar cheese

MUSHROOM AND LEEK FRITTATA

This flavorful frittata is perfect for a Sunday brunch. Round out the plate by serving with a slice of 100%-whole-wheat bread and one serving of your favorite fruit on the side.

---

1 Preheat broiler.

2 In a medium bowl, whisk together the eggs, egg whites, milk, thyme, salt, and black pepper.

3 Heat the olive oil in a medium skillet over medium heat. Once the skillet is hot, add the leeks and cook until softened, about 2 minutes. Add the garlic and cook until fragrant, 30 seconds more. Add the mushrooms and cook until softened and the mushrooms release their liquid, about 8 minutes.

4 Pour the egg mixture over the cooked vegetables and cook until the eggs solidify, about 8 minutes.

5 Sprinkle the top evenly with the cheese and carefully place the skillet in the broiler until the cheese has melted and the eggs have set, about 5 minutes.

6 Allow the frittata to cool for 10 minutes before cutting into 4 even slices.

 Switch things up by substituting 1 cup of chopped onion or shallot for the leeks.

Choices/Exchanges 1 Nonstarchy Vegetable, 2 Lean Protein, 2 Fat

Calories 200	**Cholesterol** 190 mg	**Sugars** 3 g
Calories from Fat 120	**Sodium** 340 mg	**Added Sugars** 0 g
Total Fat 13.0 g	**Potassium** 450 mg	**Protein** 14 g
Saturated Fat 3.4 g	**Total Carbohydrate** 8 g	**Phosphorus** 240 mg
Trans Fat 0.0 g	**Dietary Fiber** 1 g	

BLUEBERRY OATMEAL

Healthy, diabetes-friendly meals don't have to be complicated. This warm cup of oatmeal takes less than 10 minutes to whip up and provides a balance of food groups including dairy, whole grains, and fruit.

1 Combine the oats and milk in a medium saucepan and bring to a boil. Lower the heat and simmer, stirring frequently, until the oats begin to soften and the liquid thickens, about 5 minutes. Stir in the brown sugar blend and cinnamon. Remove the pot from the heat.

2 Spoon the oatmeal into a medium bowl. Top with blueberries and chopped walnuts.

Boost the protein of this recipe by mixing 1 tablespoon of peanut butter into your oatmeal.

TOTAL TIME 7 minutes
PREP TIME 2 minutes
COOK TIME 5 minutes

SERVES 1
SERVING SIZE 1 cup

COMPLETE THE PLATE
This recipe: Lean Protein, Carbohydrate Food
Pair with: A serving of Nonstarchy Vegetables such as baby carrots

1/2 cup old-fashioned oats

1 cup nonfat milk

1 teaspoon stevia brown sugar blend (such as Truvia)

1/8 teaspoon ground cinnamon

1/2 cup fresh blueberries

4 raw walnut halves, roughly chopped

Choices/Exchanges 2 Starch, 1 Fruit, 1 Fat-Free Milk, 1 Fat

Calories 340
Calories from Fat 70
Total Fat 8.0 g
Saturated Fat 1.1 g
Trans Fat 0.0 g

Cholesterol 8 mg
Sodium 105 mg
Potassium 620 mg
Total Carbohydrate 54 g
Dietary Fiber 7 g

Sugars 22 g
Added Sugars 2 g
Protein 15 g
Phosphorus 450 mg

TOTAL TIME 10 minutes plus at least 8 hours refrigeration time
PREP TIME 10 minutes
COOK TIME 0 minutes

SERVES 1
SERVING SIZE 1 jar

COMPLETE THE PLATE
This recipe: Lean Protein, Carbohydrate Food
Pair with: A serving of Nonstarchy Vegetables such as freshly sliced celery and bell peppers

1/2 cup old-fashioned oats

1/3 cup nonfat milk

1/3 cup nonfat plain Greek yogurt

1 teaspoon zero-calorie sweetener (such as stevia sugar) or 1/2 teaspoon Truvia nectar

1/4 teaspoon vanilla extract

1/8 teaspoon ground cinnamon

1/2 medium pear, finely diced

1 tablespoon roasted, chopped almonds

PEAR AND ALMOND OVERNIGHT OATS

Pear is an underappreciated fruit that combines beautifully with almonds and other nuts. To make sure your pear is perfectly ripe check the neck. Gently press at the neck of the pear using your thumb and forefinger and it should give slightly.

1 Combine the oats, milk, Greek yogurt, stevia sugar, vanilla extract, and cinnamon in a jar or bowl with a tight-fitting lid and stir to combine. Add the pear and stir to combine. Cover with the lid and place in the refrigerator for at least 8 hours or up to overnight. When ready to eat, remove the jar from the refrigerator and stir to combine. If you like it warm, place in the microwave (without the lid) for 2 minutes.

2 Top with the almonds before eating.

When making overnight oats, use old-fashioned oats (not quick-cooking oats) as they hold up best overnight in the fridge.

You can make several servings of overnight oats and store in the refrigerator for up to 3 days. Top with the almonds right before eating.

Choices/Exchanges 2 Starch, 1 Fruit, 1/2 Fat-Free Milk, 1 Lean Protein, 1/2 Fat

Calories 310
Calories from Fat 50
Total Fat 6.0 g
Saturated Fat 0.9 g
Trans Fat 0.0 g

Cholesterol 5 mg
Sodium 65 mg
Potassium 520 mg
Total Carbohydrate 49 g
Dietary Fiber 8 g

Sugars 16 g
Added Sugars 0 g
Protein 17 g
Phosphorus 390 mg

CARROT-RAISIN MUFFINS

Store-bought muffins tend to be oversized and brimming with added sugar and saturated fat. Make your own muffins so you can control the portion and ingredients. This recipe contains healthy omega-3 fatty acids because it uses canola oil and nonfat plain Greek yogurt instead of any butter. Plus, the stevia-based brown sugar blend works beautifully in baked goods like muffins, to help keep added sugar low. The result is moist, delicious muffins that you can enjoy on your diabetes-friendly diet.

TOTAL TIME 33 minutes plus 20 minutes cooling time
PREP TIME 15 minutes
COOK TIME 18 minutes

SERVES 12
SERVING SIZE 1 muffin

COMPLETE THE PLATE
This recipe: Carbohydrate Food
Pair with: A serving of Nonstarchy Vegetables such as celery and carrot sticks and Lean Protein such as peanut butter or almond butter

1 Preheat the oven to 375°F. Coat a muffin tin with nonstick cooking spray.

2 In a medium bowl, sift together the all-purpose flour, whole-wheat flour, oat bran, baking powder, baking soda, cinnamon, salt, and nutmeg.

3 In a large bowl, whisk together the canola oil and brown sugar blend. Add the Greek yogurt, beaten eggs, and vanilla extract.

4 Gently fold the dry ingredients into the wet ingredients being careful not to overmix the batter. Gently fold in the carrots, raisins, and walnuts making sure to evenly distribute throughout the batter.

5 Evenly scoop the batter into each cup of a 12-muffin tin. Tap the muffin tin on the counter a few times to get rid of any bubbles in the batter.

6 Bake until the muffins are golden brown on top and a toothpick inserted into the center comes out clean, about 18 minutes. Remove the muffin tin from the oven and allow to cool for 10 minutes before transferring muffins to a wire rack to finish cooling for another 10 minutes.

Nonstick cooking spray

1 cup unbleached all-purpose flour

1 cup whole-wheat flour

1/4 cup oat bran

2 teaspoons baking powder

1 teaspoon baking soda

1 teaspoon ground cinnamon

1/2 teaspoon salt

1/8 teaspoon ground nutmeg

1/2 cup canola oil

1/3 cup stevia brown sugar blend (such as Truvia)

1 cup nonfat plain Greek yogurt

2 large eggs, beaten

1 teaspoon vanilla extract

2 medium carrots, peeled and shredded (1 cup)

1/2 cup seedless golden raisins

1/3 cup walnut pieces

Toby Tip *You can use a mini-muffin tin with this recipe to make 24 mini muffins. Two mini muffins equal 1 serving.*

Choices/Exchanges 1 Starch, 1/2 Fruit, 2 1/2 Fat

Calories 240
Calories from Fat 120
Total Fat 13.0 g
Saturated Fat 1.2 g
Trans Fat 0.0 g

Cholesterol 30 mg
Sodium 290 mg
Potassium 190 mg
Total Carbohydrate 27 g
Dietary Fiber 3 g

Sugars 8 g
Added Sugars 3 g
Protein 7 g
Phosphorus 200 mg

TOTAL TIME 33 minutes plus 20 minutes cooling time
PREP TIME 15 minutes
COOK TIME 18 minutes

SERVES 12
SERVING SIZE 1 muffin

COMPLETE THE PLATE
This recipe: Carbohydrate Food
Pair with: A serving of Nonstarchy Vegetables such as grape tomatoes and Lean Protein such as a hard-boiled egg

Nonstick cooking spray

1 cup unbleached all-purpose flour

1 cup whole-wheat flour

1/4 cup oat bran

1 teaspoon baking powder

1/2 teaspoon baking soda

1/8 teaspoon salt

3/4 cup creamy peanut butter or sunflower seed butter, at room temperature

1/4 cup nonfat plain Greek yogurt

1/2 cup nonfat milk

2 ripe bananas, mashed

1/3 cup stevia brown sugar blend (such as Truvia)

2 tablespoons canola oil

2 large eggs, beaten

1 teaspoon vanilla extract

PEANUT BUTTER-BANANA BRAN MUFFINS

There's very little saturated fat in this recipe. In addition to providing sweetness, bananas replace part of the fat in the muffin recipe, resulting in a simple, delicious baked good without any butter. Plus, you can use those overripe bananas, which is a good way to reduce food waste.

1 Preheat oven to 350°F. Coat a standard 12-muffin tin with nonstick cooking spray and set aside.

2 In a medium bowl, sift together the all-purpose flour, whole-wheat flour, oat bran, baking powder, baking soda, and salt.

3 In a large bowl, whisk together the peanut butter, yogurt, and milk until the mixture is smooth. Add the mashed bananas, brown sugar blend, and oil and whisk until combined. Add the eggs and vanilla extract, whisking until completely incorporated.

4 Gently fold the dry ingredients into the wet ingredients, being careful not to overmix the batter.

5 Evenly scoop the batter into each cup of the 12-muffin tin. Tap the muffin tin on the counter a few times to get rid of any bubbles in the batter.

6 Bake until the tops are browned and a toothpick inserted into the center of a muffin comes out clean, about 18 minutes. Remove the muffin tin from the oven and allow to cool for 10 minutes, then transfer muffins to a wire rack to finish cooling for another 10 minutes. Sprinkle a little additional oat bran on top of the muffins for texture, if desired.

 Muffins are a fabulous recipe to prep in advance. Make a double batch over the weekend and freeze half for up to 2 months to save for a week when you're really busy.

Choices/Exchanges 1 Starch, 1/2 Fruit, 1/2 Carbohydrate, 1 High-Fat Protein

Calories 240	**Cholesterol** 30 mg	**Sugars** 8 g
Calories from Fat 110	**Sodium** 200 mg	**Added Sugars** 3 g
Total Fat 12.0 g	**Potassium** 280 mg	**Protein** 9 g
Saturated Fat 2.2 g	**Total Carbohydrate** 28 g	**Phosphorus** 195 mg
Trans Fat 0.0 g	**Dietary Fiber** 3 g	

HUMMINGBIRD BREAKFAST COOKIES

You can have cookies for breakfast! The combination of pineapple, coconut, and pecans in this recipe add fat and fruit to these whole-grain morning cookies. Pair with nonfat plain Greek yogurt and a scrambled egg on the side. You can also make a batch and store half in the freezer for up to 2 months.

TOTAL TIME 33 minutes plus 10 minutes cooling time
PREP TIME 15 minutes
COOK TIME 18 minutes

SERVES 15
SERVING SIZE 1 cookie

COMPLETE THE PLATE

This recipe: Carbohydrate Food
Pair with: A serving of Nonstarchy Vegetables such as freshly sliced celery and Lean Protein such as peanut butter

1 Preheat the oven to 350°F. Line two baking sheets with parchment paper.

2 In a medium bowl, sift together the flour, oats, cinnamon, baking soda, ginger, salt, nutmeg, and allspice.

3 In a large bowl, whisk together the applesauce, almond butter, and brown sugar blend until well combined. Add the eggs and vanilla extract and whisk until smooth.

4 Gently fold the dry ingredients into the wet ingredients and stir until just combined. Fold in the pineapple, pecans, and shredded coconut, making sure to evenly distribute them throughout the batter.

5 For each cookie, spoon 2 tablespoons of batter into clean hands and roll into a ball. Place onto the baking sheet leaving about 1 inch around each cookie. Gently press down on the top of each cookie to slightly flatten it.

6 Bake until the cookies are soft and golden brown and a toothpick inserted into the center of 1 or 2 cookies comes out clean, 18 minutes. Remove the baking sheet from the oven and allow the cookies to cool for about 10 minutes before eating.

- 1 1/2 cups whole-wheat flour
- 1/2 cup rolled oats
- 1 teaspoon ground cinnamon
- 1 teaspoon baking soda
- 1/4 teaspoon ground ginger
- 1/4 teaspoon salt
- 1/8 teaspoon ground nutmeg
- 1/8 teaspoon ground allspice
- 1/2 cup unsweetened applesauce
- 1/2 cup almond butter
- 1/3 cup stevia brown sugar blend (such as Truvia)
- 2 eggs, beaten
- 1 teaspoon vanilla extract
- 1 cup finely diced fresh pineapple
- 1 cup pecans, roughly chopped
- 1/4 cup unsweetened shredded coconut

Toby Tip *If you find the batter sticking to your hands as you're rolling the cookies, wet your hands slightly in cool water and then handle the batter.*

Choices/Exchanges 1/2 Starch, 1/2 Carbohydrate, 2 1/2 Fat

Calories 190
Calories from Fat 110
Total Fat 12.0 g
Saturated Fat 1.9 g
Trans Fat 0.0 g

Cholesterol 25 mg
Sodium 135 mg
Potassium 190 mg
Total Carbohydrate 19 g
Dietary Fiber 4 g

Sugars 5 g
Added Sugars 2 g
Protein 5 g
Phosphorus 135 mg

TOTAL TIME 35 minutes
PREP TIME 15 minutes
COOK TIME 20 minutes

SERVES 6
SERVING SIZE 4 pieces and 1/2 cup strawberries

COMPLETE THE PLATE
This recipe: Medium-Fat Protein, Carbohydrate Food
Pair with: A serving of Nonstarchy Vegetables such as freshly sliced tomatoes

8 slices 100%-whole-wheat bread

1/2 cup unsalted raw or dry-roasted almonds

1 1/3 cups nonfat milk or almond milk

6 large eggs

1 teaspoon vanilla extract

1 teaspoon ground cinnamon

Nonstick cooking spray

3 cups strawberries, sliced

WHOLE-WHEAT ALMOND FRENCH TOAST STRIPS

To balance your plate, serve these high-fiber French toast strips with a scrambled egg or a slice of turkey bacon on the side.

———————————————

1 Cut each slice of bread into 3 even pieces. Set aside.

2 In a food processor, finely chop almonds.

3 In a medium bowl, whisk together the milk, eggs, vanilla extract, and cinnamon. Add the almonds and toss to combine.

4 Coat a large skillet with nonstick cooking spray. Heat it over a medium-low heat.

5 Submerge half the slices of bread in the egg mixture, being sure to moisten both sides. Then place the soaked slices on the heated skillet and cook until golden brown, about 5 minutes. Flip and cook on the other side until browned, about 4–5 minutes. Remove from the skillet and keep warm. Spray the skillet again with nonstick cooking spray and repeat the process with the remaining slices of bread.

6 Top the French toast strips with the sliced strawberries. Drizzle with sugar-free maple syrup, if desired.

 Swap the strawberries for the sautéed apples from the Apple Pie Parfaits recipe (page 66) or the cooked strawberries from the Strawberry-Ricotta Parfaits with Pistachios recipe (page 68).

Choices/Exchanges 1 Starch, 1/2 Fruit, 1 Medium-Fat Protein, 1/2 Fat

Calories 230
Calories from Fat 70
Total Fat 8.0 g
Saturated Fat 1.7 g
Trans Fat 0.0 g

Cholesterol 140 mg
Sodium 240 mg
Potassium 380 mg
Total Carbohydrate 26 g
Dietary Fiber 5 g

Sugars 8 g
Added Sugars 0 g
Protein 13 g
Phosphorus 245 mg

WHOLE-WHEAT BUTTERMILK PANCAKES WITH ORANGE-RASPBERRY SAUCE

Instead of store-bought sauces that are high in added sugar, you can whip up your own in less than 5 minutes with minimal added sugar—and it tastes fantastic!

1 In a medium bowl, sift together the all-purpose flour, whole-wheat flour, baking powder, and sea salt.

2 In a large bowl, whisk together the buttermilk, canola oil, brown sugar blend, and eggs.

3 Add the dry mixture into the wet mixture and stir to combine.

4 Spray a large skillet with nonstick cooking spray and heat it over a medium heat. For each pancake, drop 1/4 cup of the batter onto the hot skillet. Repeat leaving about 2 inches between the pancakes. Cook until the tops are bubbly and the edges are set, about 4 minutes. Flip the pancakes over and cook until the pancakes are golden and crisp, about 3 more minutes. Transfer pancakes to a plate and cover with a paper towel or aluminum foil to keep warm. Repeat with the remaining batter.

5 To make the sauce, add the Orange-Raspberry Sauce ingredients to a blender and blend until smooth.

6 To serve, place 2 pancakes on a plate and top with 2 tablespoons of the sauce.

 When using whole-wheat flour in some baked goods, use it in a 1:1 ratio with all-purpose flour like in this recipe.

TOTAL TIME 30 minutes
PREP TIME 15 minutes
COOK TIME 15 minutes

SERVES 4
SERVING SIZE 2 pancakes with 2 tablespoons sauce

COMPLETE THE PLATE

This recipe: Lean Protein, Carbohydrate Food
Pair with: A serving of Nonstarchy Vegetables such as freshly sliced tomatoes

3/4 cup unbleached all-purpose flour

3/4 cup whole-wheat flour

1 teaspoon baking powder

1/2 teaspoon sea salt

1 cup low-fat buttermilk

3 tablespoons canola oil

2 tablespoons stevia brown sugar blend (such as Truvia)

2 large eggs, beaten

Nonstick cooking spray

ORANGE-RASPBERRY SAUCE

1 cup raspberries

2 tablespoons freshly squeezed orange juice

1 teaspoon orange zest

1 teaspoon stevia brown sugar blend (such as Truvia)

Choices/Exchanges 2 Starch, 1 Carbohydrate, 1 Lean Protein, 2 Fat

Calories 350
Calories from Fat 130
Total Fat 14.0 g
Saturated Fat 2.0 g
Trans Fat 0.1 g

Cholesterol 95 mg
Sodium 460 mg
Potassium 310 mg
Total Carbohydrate 46 g
Dietary Fiber 5 g

Sugars 9 g
Added Sugars 4 g
Protein 11 g
Phosphorus 330 mg

TOTAL TIME 30 minutes
PREP TIME 15 minutes
COOK TIME 15 minutes

SERVES 4
SERVING SIZE 1 (8-inch) waffle,
1/4 cup yogurt mixture, 6 peach
wedges, 1 tablespoon walnuts

COMPLETE THE PLATE
This recipe: Lean Protein,
Carbohydrate Food
Pair with: A serving of
Nonstarchy Vegetables such
as freshly sliced cucumbers
and tomatoes

Nonstick cooking spray

1 1/3 cups whole-wheat flour

1/4 cup oat bran

2 teaspoons baking powder

1/2 teaspoon salt

1 1/4 cups nonfat milk

1/3 cup canola oil

2 tablespoons zero-calorie
   stevia sweetener (such as
   Truvia or Splenda)

1 large egg, beaten

1/4 cup raw walnuts, chopped

1 cup nonfat plain Greek yogurt

1 tablespoon sugar-free maple-
   flavored syrup

1/2 teaspoon vanilla extract

1/2 teaspoon ground cinnamon

1/8 teaspoon ground nutmeg

4 fresh peaches, pitted and
   sliced into 6 wedges each

WHOLE-GRAIN WAFFLES WITH PEACHES AND CINNAMON YOGURT

Topped with the right ingredients, you can make your waffles into a full plate–like in this recipe, which provides fruit, dairy, and whole grains.

1 Preheat an electric waffle iron and coat with nonstick cooking spray.

2 In a medium bowl, sift together the whole-wheat flour, oat bran, baking powder, and salt.

3 In a large bowl, whisk together the milk, canola oil, sweetener, and egg.

4 Add the dry mixture to the wet mixture and stir to combine.

5 For each waffle, scoop 1 1/4 cups of the batter onto a standard 8-inch waffle iron.* Cook for 3 minutes on each side or according to the manufacturer's instructions. Transfer the cooked waffle to a plate, and repeat for the remaining batter to make a total of 2 (8-inch) waffles.

6 Heat a small skillet over medium-low heat and add the chopped walnuts. Toast until the walnuts are fragrant and slightly browned, about 3 minutes. Set aside to slightly cool.

7 In a small bowl, stir together the yogurt, sugar-free maple syrup, vanilla extract, cinnamon, and nutmeg.

8 Cut each 8-inch waffle into 4 equal wedges. Place 2 wedges of an 8-inch waffle (or one 4-inch waffle) onto a plate. Top with 1/4 cup of the yogurt, 6 peach wedges, and sprinkle with 1 tablespoon of the walnuts.

Chef's note: If using a 4-inch waffle iron, scoop about 2/3 cup (1/4 of the batter) per waffle onto a 4-inch waffle iron, to make a total of 4 (4-inch) waffles.

Choices/Exchanges 2 Starch, 1 Fruit, 1/2 Fat-Free Milk, 1 Lean Protein, 4 1/2 Fat

Calories 500	**Cholesterol** 50 mg	**Sugars** 20 g
Calories from Fat 230	**Sodium** 550 mg	**Added Sugars** 1 g
Total Fat 26.0 g	**Potassium** 730 mg	**Protein** 19 g
Saturated Fat 2.5 g	**Total Carbohydrate** 56 g	**Phosphorus** 645 mg
Trans Fat 0.1 g	**Dietary Fiber** 9 g	

Want a warm topping for your waffles? Coat a skillet with nonstick cooking spray and toss the peaches in a touch of cinnamon and vanilla extract and cook until soft.

Make the waffles ahead of time, slice in half, and store in a resealable container or plastic bag in the freezer for up to 2 months. Reheat in a toaster oven or toaster (large enough to fit a bagel half) for a quick weekday breakfast.

Chapter 5
Snacks

How Snack Fits on Your Plate

Snacks are not an essential part of a meal plan. If you are trying to cut calories or lose weight, limiting snacks can be a good place to start. However, choosing snacks that are high in fiber, protein, and/or healthy fats—such as hummus and baby carrots or edamame—can help keep you feeling satisfied throughout the day. Including nonstarchy vegetables in your snack is a great way to get more fiber and more servings of vegetables. You can find a list of nonstarchy vegetable options on page 2. If you do choose a carbohydrate food as a snack, like whole-grain crackers or fruit, pair it with a protein food or healthy fat, like string cheese or nut butter, to reduce the carbohydrate's effect on your blood glucose.

Ruby Red Ice Pops, p. 103

TOTAL TIME 5 minutes
PREP TIME 5 minutes
COOK TIME 0 minutes

SERVES 2
SERVING SIZE 1 bowl
(1/2 cup yogurt, 1/2 banana,
1 1/2 teaspoons peanuts)

1 cup nonfat plain Greek yogurt

1 tablespoon creamy peanut
butter

1/2 teaspoon zero-calorie stevia
sweetener (such as Truvia or
Splenda)

1/8 teaspoon ground cinnamon

1/8 teaspoon ground nutmeg

1 medium banana, sliced
lengthwise and then cut into
half-moons

1 tablespoon unsalted dry-
roasted peanuts, roughly
chopped

FUNKY MONKEY YOGURT BOWLS

*Greek yogurt provides twice the amount of protein
compared to traditional yogurt and approximately 40%
less sodium and sugar. Greek yogurt also provides live
and active cultures, many of which act as tummy-pleasing
probiotics.*

---

1 In a small bowl, add the yogurt, peanut butter, sweetener,
cinnamon, and nutmeg. Stir to combine.

2 In 2 breakfast bowls, add about 1/2 cup of the yogurt and top
with half the banana pieces and 1 1/2 teaspoons of peanuts.

 *To make the peanut butter easy to mix into the
yogurt, place it in a microwave-safe bowl and
microwave for 45–60 seconds to soften. Allow it to
cool a few minutes before mixing it into the yogurt.*

Choices/Exchanges 1 Fruit, 1/2 Fat-Free Milk, 1 High-Fat Protein

Calories 200	**Cholesterol** 5 mg	**Sugars** 12 g
Calories from Fat 60	**Sodium** 80 mg	**Added Sugars** 0 g
Total Fat 7.0 g	**Potassium** 470 mg	**Protein** 15 g
Saturated Fat 1.4 g	**Total Carbohydrate** 21 g	**Phosphorus** 215 mg
Trans Fat 0.0 g	**Dietary Fiber** 3 g	

DATE NUT BARS

There's no baking involved in these fruit and nut bars. When you purée the dried fruit, it helps make all the ingredients stick together, resulting in these delicious, grab-and-go bars.

TOTAL TIME 15 minutes plus 20 minutes refrigeration time
PREP TIME 15 minutes
COOK TIME 0 minutes

SERVES 12
SERVING SIZE 1 bar

1 cup pitted dates

3/4 cup dried tart cherries

1 cup whole unsalted raw almonds, chopped

2 tablespoons water

1 teaspoon vanilla extract

1 teaspoon ground cinnamon

1/8 teaspoon salt

6 tablespoons unsweetened shredded coconut

1 Line an 8 × 8-inch baking pan with plastic wrap.

2 Place the dates, tart cherries, almonds, water, vanilla, cinnamon, and salt in a food processor and purée until mixture becomes a smooth paste.

3 Sprinkle 3 tablespoons of the coconut evenly along the bottom of the prepared pan.

4 Spoon the date mixture into the prepared baking pan and, using clean hands, spread evenly to about 1/2-inch thickness. Sprinkle the top of the mixture with the remaining 3 tablespoons of the coconut. Using a clean, flat-bottomed drinking glass, press the bars until they are an even thickness. Place the baking pan in the refrigerator for at least 20 minutes.

5 Remove the baking pan from the refrigerator. Using the plastic wrap, lift the bars out of the baking pan. Slice into 12 even bars. Enjoy immediately. Or individually wrap each bar or place them in an airtight container in the refrigerator for up to 5 days.

 Substitute raisins or dried cranberries for the tart cherries.

Choices/Exchanges 1 Fruit, 1/2 Carbohydrate, 1 1/2 Fat

Calories 160
Calories from Fat 70
Total Fat 8.0 g
Saturated Fat 1.9 g
Trans Fat 0.0 g

Cholesterol 0 mg
Sodium 30 mg
Potassium 210 mg
Total Carbohydrate 21 g
Dietary Fiber 3 g

Sugars 15 g
Added Sugars 1 g
Protein 3 g
Phosphorus 125 mg

TOTAL TIME 10 minutes
PREP TIME 10 minutes
COOK TIME 0 minutes

SERVES 6
SERVING SIZE 2 slices

2 medium apples, cored and cut into 6 even slices each

4 tablespoons creamy peanut butter, divided

3 tablespoons dried cranberries

3 tablespoons roughly chopped raw walnuts

2 tablespoons unsweetened coconut flakes

PEANUT BUTTER, CRANBERRY, AND WALNUT APPLE SLICES

Simple and delicious can go hand-in-hand! You can always tailor this recipe to your liking by substituting a pear for the apple, your favorite nut butter for the peanut butter, and raisins or dried cherries for the cranberries. The most important thing is to stick to the portions listed below.

1 Lay the 12 slices of apples on a flat surface. Spread each slice with 1 teaspoon of peanut butter.

2 In a small bowl, mix together the cranberries, walnuts, and coconut flakes.

3 Evenly sprinkle each apple with about 1 tablespoon of the cranberry mixture.

You can find coconut in different forms at the market. This recipe uses the large coconut flakes, which look like large snowflakes. You can also find shredded coconut, which is much smaller and works well as a mix in for yogurt or in recipes like my Date Nut Bars (page 87).

Choices/Exchanges 1 Fruit, 2 Fat

Calories 140
Calories from Fat 80
Total Fat 9.0 g
Saturated Fat 2.3 g
Trans Fat 0.0 g

Cholesterol 0 mg
Sodium 50 mg
Potassium 150 mg
Total Carbohydrate 13 g
Dietary Fiber 3 g

Sugars 9 g
Added Sugars 3 g
Protein 3 g
Phosphorus 60 mg

NO-BAKE OATMEAL-RAISIN BITES

TOTAL TIME 15 minutes plus
15 minutes refrigeration time
PREP TIME 15 minutes
COOK TIME 0 minutes

SERVES 12
SERVING SIZE 1 piece

1 cup quick-cooking rolled oats

1/4 cup flaxseed

1 teaspoon ground cinnamon

1/8 teaspoon sea salt

1/3 cup creamy almond butter

1/2 cup unsweetened
   applesauce

2 tablespoons canola oil

1 teaspoon vanilla extract

1/4 cup golden raisins

These bites have all the flavors of oatmeal raisin cookies without the flour or added sugar. They're perfect to make ahead for your busy week and package in individual containers or baggies for an easy, delicious snack that you can grab and go.

1 In a small bowl, combine the oats, flaxseed, cinnamon, and sea salt. Stir to combine.

2 Place the almond butter in a separate microwave-safe bowl. Place in the microwave to soften, about 45–60 seconds.

3 Add the melted almond butter, applesauce, canola oil, and vanilla to a medium bowl. Whisk to evenly combine. Add the dry ingredients into the wet ingredients and stir well to combine into a paste. Fold in the raisins until evenly distributed.

4 Using clean hands, scoop 2 tablespoons of batter and form into a 2-inch ball. Place it in a container or onto a platter. Repeat with the remaining batter, making a total of 12 balls. Cover the container or platter with plastic wrap and refrigerate for at least 15 minutes to allow the bites to set before eating. Store bites for up to 1 week in the refrigerator.

 For a creative spin, swap the flaxseed for oat bran, chia seeds, or hemp seeds.

Choices/Exchanges 1/2 Starch, 1 1/2 Fat

Calories 120
Calories from Fat 70
Total Fat 8.0 g
Saturated Fat 0.7 g
Trans Fat 0.0 g

Cholesterol 0 mg
Sodium 25 mg
Potassium 135 mg
Total Carbohydrate 11 g
Dietary Fiber 3 g

Sugars 3 g
Added Sugars 0 g
Protein 3 g
Phosphorus 90 mg

CAJUN-SPICED EGGPLANT CHIPS

Store-bought Cajun seasoning is delicious, but brimming with sodium. This homemade version takes minutes to make with only 105 milligrams of sodium per serving.

TOTAL TIME 55 minutes plus 10 minutes cooling time
PREP TIME 15 minutes
COOK TIME 40 minutes

SERVES 4
SERVING SIZE 3/4 cup

1 Preheat the oven to 400°F. Coat 3 baking sheets with nonstick cooking spray.

2 Using a mandolin or sharp knife, slice the eggplant into 1/8-inch slices.

3 In a small bowl, combine the paprika, garlic powder, oregano, thyme, onion powder, cayenne, black pepper, and salt.

4 Place the eggplant slices in a single layer on the prepared baking sheets. Coat the eggplant slices with nonstick cooking spray and sprinkle evenly with half the seasoning. Flip the eggplant slices and coat the other side of the eggplant slices with nonstick cooking spray and sprinkle with the remaining seasoning.

5 Place 2 baking sheets at a time into the preheated oven. Bake until the tops of the eggplant are browned, about 10 minutes, then remove the baking sheets from the oven and, using a spatula, flip the eggplant slices over. Place the baking sheets back in the oven and continue baking for an additional 10 minutes, until the eggplant slices are crispy and brown. Remove the baking sheets from the oven and allow to cool for 10 minutes before eating. Repeat with the remaining baking sheet.

Nonstick cooking spray

1 medium eggplant (about 1 1/2 pounds), unpeeled

2 teaspoons smoked paprika

2 teaspoons garlic powder

1 teaspoon ground oregano

1 teaspoon ground thyme

1 teaspoon onion powder

1/2 teaspoon cayenne pepper

1/4 teaspoon ground black pepper

1/4 teaspoon sea salt

 Use this homemade Cajun seasoning to punch up the flavor of baked fries or to rub on beef or chicken before cooking.

Choices/Exchanges 2 Nonstarchy Vegetable

Calories 70
Calories from Fat 15
Total Fat 1.5 g
Saturated Fat 0.2 g
Trans Fat 0.0 g

Cholesterol 0 mg
Sodium 140 mg
Potassium 440 mg
Total Carbohydrate 13 g
Dietary Fiber 6 g

Sugars 6 g
Added Sugars 0 g
Protein 2 g
Phosphorus 55 mg

TOTAL TIME 1 hour plus 10 minutes cooling time
PREP TIME 15 minutes
COOK TIME 45 minutes

SERVES 8
SERVING SIZE 1/2 cup

1 cup frozen peas, defrosted

1/4 cup plus 1 teaspoon canola oil, divided

1/4 teaspoon kosher salt, divided

1 cup wheat Chex cereal or another whole-grain crunchy cereal

2 cups whole-grain pretzel sticks (2 ounces)

1/3 cup unsalted dry-roasted cashews

1/4 cup unsalted pumpkin seeds

1/2 tablespoon Worcestershire sauce

1/4 teaspoon garlic powder

1/4 teaspoon onion powder

SAVORY SNACK MIX

This is a simple, delicious, and easy-to-tote snack that is perfect to bring to any gathering. The next time you're invited to an outing, offer to make it for everyone so you don't have to worry about finding diabetes-friendly snacks.

1 Preheat the oven to 375°F. Line a baking sheet with parchment paper.

2 Place the defrosted peas into a medium bowl. Add 1 teaspoon of the canola oil and 1/8 teaspoon of the salt and toss to evenly coat. Spread the peas in a single layer onto the prepared baking sheet. Roast in the oven until crispy, about 45 minutes. Remove the baking sheet from the oven and set aside to cool for at least 10 minutes.

3 In a large bowl, add the roasted peas, Chex, pretzels, cashews, and pumpkin seeds; toss to combine.

4 In a small bowl, whisk together the remaining 1/4 cup of oil, the remaining 1/8 teaspoon of salt, and the Worcestershire sauce, garlic powder, and onion powder. Drizzle over the snack mixture and toss to evenly coat. Serve immediately.

 Toby Tip *Planning on feeding a crowd with this snack mix? You can double or even triple the recipe!*

Choices/Exchanges 1 Starch, 2 1/2 Fat

Calories 190	**Cholesterol** 0 mg	**Sugars** 2 g
Calories from Fat 110	**Sodium** 230 mg	**Added Sugars** 0 g
Total Fat 12.0 g	**Potassium** 160 mg	**Protein** 4 g
Saturated Fat 1.5 g	**Total Carbohydrate** 17 g	**Phosphorus** 120 mg
Trans Fat 0.0 g	**Dietary Fiber** 3 g	

CINNAMON ROASTED NUTS

Nuts are a well-balanced snack providing healthy fat, protein, and carbohydrates. Spice up your favorite type of nuts with this sweet cinnamon blend made with minimal added sugar.

TOTAL TIME 20 minutes plus 10 minutes cooling time
PREP TIME 10 minutes
COOK TIME 10 minutes

SERVES 8
SERVING SIZE 1/4 cup

1 large egg white

1 tablespoon water

3 tablespoons stevia brown sugar blend (such as Truvia)

1 teaspoon ground cinnamon

1 teaspoon vanilla extract

1/8 teaspoon kosher salt

3/4 cup raw pecans

3/4 cup unsalted raw almonds

1 Preheat the oven to 350°F. Line a baking sheet with parchment paper.

2 In a medium bowl, whisk together the egg white, water, brown sugar blend, cinnamon, vanilla, and salt. Add the pecans and almonds and toss to coat.

3 Spread the nuts in a single layer onto the prepared baking sheet. Bake until the nuts are slightly browned and fragrant, about 8-10 minutes. Remove the baking sheet from the oven and set aside to cool for at least 10 minutes.

 Want a savory seasoning blend? Coat your nuts with nonstick cooking spray and sprinkle with the Cajun spice mixture used in the Cajun-Spiced Eggplant Chips recipe (page 91). Roast at 350°F for 8-10 minutes.

Choices/Exchanges 1/2 Carbohydrate, 2 1/2 Fat

Calories 160
Calories from Fat 120
Total Fat 13.0 g
Saturated Fat 1.1 g
Trans Fat 0.0 g

Cholesterol 0 mg
Sodium 35 mg
Potassium 140 mg
Total Carbohydrate 7 g
Dietary Fiber 3 g

Sugars 3 g
Added Sugars 2 g
Protein 4 g
Phosphorus 90 mg

TOTAL TIME 10 minutes
PREP TIME 5 minutes
COOK TIME 5 minutes

SERVES 4
SERVING SIZE 2 cups

1/4 cup olive oil, divided

1/4 cup popcorn kernels

1 teaspoon ground basil

1 teaspoon ground thyme

1/4 plus 1/8 teaspoon salt

BASIL-THYME POPCORN

There's no need to drown your popcorn in butter! Instead use very low-calorie herbs and spices to flavor your popcorn.

---

1 In a medium pot over medium-low heat, heat 3 tablespoons of the olive oil. Add 3 popcorn kernels, and when one of the kernels pops, add the rest. Cover and shake the pot occasionally to prevent the popcorn from burning. Once fully popped, transfer the popcorn to a large bowl. Alternatively, pop the popcorn kernels in a popcorn maker without the 3 tablespoons of oil.

2 Add the basil, thyme, and salt to a blender. Blend until a powder forms, about 1 minute.

3 Add the remaining tablespoon of olive oil to the popcorn; toss to evenly coat. Sprinkle with the spice powder, tossing to evenly coat, and serve.

 Invest in a hot air popcorn maker to make popcorn in minutes. You can find them at your local kitchen stores, where they run between $20 and $40. I bought mine 10 years ago and use it regularly!

Choices/Exchanges 1 Starch, 2 1/2 Fat

Calories 180	**Cholesterol** 0 mg	**Sugars** 0 g
Calories from Fat 130	**Sodium** 220 mg	**Added Sugars** 0 g
Total Fat 14.0 g	**Potassium** 65 mg	**Protein** 2 g
Saturated Fat 2.0 g	**Total Carbohydrate** 13 g	**Phosphorus** 60 mg
Trans Fat 0.0 g	**Dietary Fiber** 3 g	

MADE WITH 1 TBSP OIL IN AIR POPPER:

Choices/Exchanges 1 Starch, 1/2 Fat

Calories 90	**Cholesterol** 0 mg	**Sugars** 0 g
Calories from Fat 35	**Sodium** 220 mg	**Added Sugars** 0 g
Total Fat 4.0 g	**Potassium** 65 mg	**Protein** 2 g
Saturated Fat 0.6 g	**Total Carbohydrate** 13 g	**Phosphorus** 60 mg
Trans Fat 0.0 g	**Dietary Fiber** 3 g	

TURKEY AND MOZZARELLA SNACK SKEWERS

It's always more fun to eat food off skewers! This simple snack stacks protein, dairy, and veggies onto a small skewer or toothpick. Make them a day or two in advance, so you can quickly grab and enjoy when you're on the go.

TOTAL TIME 10 minutes
PREP TIME 10 minutes
COOK TIME 0 minutes

SERVES 4
SERVING SIZE 3 skewers

4 ounces lower-sodium turkey breast

12 small skewers

1/4 hothouse cucumber, sliced in half lengthwise then cut into half-moons

12 cherry tomatoes

24 mozzarella pearls (2 ounces)

1 tablespoon olive oil

1 tablespoon balsamic vinegar

1/8 teaspoon sea salt

1/8 teaspoon ground black pepper

1 Cut the turkey into 12 (1-inch) cubes.

2 Thread each skewer with 1 slice of cucumber, 1 turkey cube, 1 tomato, and 2 mozzarella pearls.

3 Place the skewers in a single layer on a large plate. Drizzle with the olive oil and balsamic vinegar and sprinkle with the salt and black pepper.

 Ask your deli counter to slice a 4-ounce-thick chunk of turkey so you can easily cube it for skewers.

Choices/Exchanges 1 Lean Protein, 1 1/2 Fat

Calories 110
Calories from Fat 60
Total Fat 7.0 g
Saturated Fat 2.6 g
Trans Fat 0.0 g

Cholesterol 20 mg
Sodium 260 mg
Potassium 230 mg
Total Carbohydrate 4 g
Dietary Fiber 1 g

Sugars 2 g
Added Sugars 0 g
Protein 9 g
Phosphorus 130 mg

ENDIVE TUNA BOATS

Endive is a member of the chicory family, which includes escarole, radicchio, and frisée. This vegetable has a crisp texture and nutty flavor with a mild bitterness. The crunchiness from the endive pairs beautifully with tuna in these two-bite boats.

TOTAL TIME 15 minutes
PREP TIME 15 minutes
COOK TIME 0 minutes

SERVES 6
SERVING SIZE 3 pieces

2 tablespoons nonfat plain Greek yogurt

1 1/2 tablespoons light mayonnaise

1 tablespoon Dijon mustard

1/2 teaspoon dried parsley

1/8 teaspoon ground black pepper

2 (5-ounce) cans chunk light tuna packed in water, drained

1 rib celery, finely chopped

1/4 medium red onion, finely chopped

18 leaves Belgium endive (about 2 heads)

1 In a medium bowl, whisk together the yogurt, mayonnaise, mustard, parsley, and black pepper until well combined. Add the tuna, celery, and onion and toss to evenly coat.

2 Rinse the endive and separate each leaf so you have 18 separate "boats." Spoon 1 1/2 tablespoons of the tuna mixture into each boat.

Instead of endive, try using romaine or Bibb lettuce to make the "boats."

Choices/Exchanges 1 Lean Protein

Calories 50
Calories from Fat 20
Total Fat 2.0 g
Saturated Fat 0.2 g
Trans Fat 0.0 g

Cholesterol 15 mg
Sodium 220 mg
Potassium 190 mg
Total Carbohydrate 3 g
Dietary Fiber 1 g

Sugars 1 g
Added Sugars 0 g
Protein 8 g
Phosphorus 80 mg

TOTAL TIME 20 minutes plus
10 minutes cooling time
PREP TIME 10 minutes
COOK TIME 10 minutes

SERVES 4
SERVING SIZE 2 pieces

2 (8-inch) whole-wheat tortillas

1/2 cup lower-sodium marinara
sauce (I like Amy's Organic)

1/2 cup baby spinach

4 medium button or white
capped mushrooms,
thinly sliced

1/4 cup shredded part-skim
mozzarella cheese

WHOLE-GRAIN VEGETABLE TORTILLA PIZZA

Pizza is one of the most popular foods, but many come with thick crusts and toppings high in artery-clogging saturated fat (hello, pepperoni!). You can easily make your own healthier, diabetes-friendly pizza using whole-grain tortillas as a super thin crust, low-sodium tomato sauce, lots of veggies, and a sprinkle of cheese.

1 Preheat the oven to 400°F. Line a baking sheet with parchment paper.

2 Place each of the tortillas on the baking sheet.

3 Pour 1/4 cup of the marinara sauce over each of the tortillas. Using the back of a spoon, evenly distribute on each tortilla.

4 Evenly distribute the baby spinach leaves over the marinara sauce and top with the mushrooms. Sprinkle 2 tablespoons of cheese over each tortilla.

5 Place the pizzas in the oven and bake until the cheese is bubbly and the tortilla edges are lightly browned, about 8–10 minutes. Remove the baking sheet from the oven and allow the pizza to cool for at least 10 minutes before slicing each into 4 quarters.

 Use leftover vegetables like chopped broccoli or bite-size pieces of cooked chicken to tailor these snack pizzas to your liking.

Choices/Exchanges 1 Starch, 1 Fat

Calories 130
Calories from Fat 45
Total Fat 5.0 g
Saturated Fat 2.1 g
Trans Fat 0.0 g

Cholesterol 5 mg
Sodium 240 mg
Potassium 250 mg
Total Carbohydrate 16 g
Dietary Fiber 3 g

Sugars 3 g
Added Sugars 0 g
Protein 5 g
Phosphorus 150 mg

MEDITERRANEAN STUFFED PITAS

During my childhood, I spent many summers living in Israel where the cuisine is very similar to the food enjoyed in the Mediterranean. These stuffed pitas were a quick snack my mom used to pack for us when we would head to the beach each morning.

---

1 Using a sharp knife, carefully cut the 6-inch pitas in half (or cut a slit at the top of each mini pita).

2 Spoon 1 tablespoon of the hummus into each pita half. Use the back of the spoon to spread it evenly inside the pita half. Next, stuff each pita half with 1/4 cup baby spinach, 2–3 tomato slices, and 2 teaspoons of feta cheese.

TOTAL TIME 10 minutes
PREP TIME 10 minutes
COOK TIME 0 minutes

SERVES 4
SERVING SIZE 1 stuffed pita half (or 1 stuffed mini pita)

2 (6-inch) whole-wheat pitas or 4 (4-inch) whole-wheat mini pitas, lightly toasted

1/4 cup Lemon Hummus (page 210) or store-bought hummus

1 cup baby spinach

2 plum tomatoes, thinly sliced

8 teaspoons crumbled feta cheese

Plum tomatoes are seedless and are perfect for sandwiches where you want to minimize those wet tomato seeds.

Choices/Exchanges 1 1/2 Starch, 1/2 Fat

Calories 140	**Cholesterol** 5 mg	**Sugars** 3 g
Calories from Fat 45	**Sodium** 260 mg	**Added Sugars** 0 g
Total Fat 5.0 g	**Potassium** 210 mg	**Protein** 5 g
Saturated Fat 1.1 g	**Total Carbohydrate** 21 g	**Phosphorus** 105 mg
Trans Fat 0.0 g	**Dietary Fiber** 3 g	

TOTAL TIME 10 minutes
PREP TIME 10 minutes
COOK TIME 0 minutes

SERVES 4
SERVING SIZE 1 avocado half

1/3 cup canned no-added-salt black beans, drained and rinsed

2 avocados, halved

4 tablespoons nonfat plain Greek yogurt

4 tablespoons Almost Smooth Salsa (page 215) or jarred salsa

4 teaspoons reduced-fat shredded sharp cheddar cheese

1/4 teaspoon sea salt

1 lime, quartered

4-LAYER STUFFED AVOCADO

Avocados are filled with heart-healthy monounsaturated fats. When these monounsaturated fats are eaten in moderation in place of saturated and trans fats, it can help reduce bad (LDL) cholesterol.

_____

1 Place the beans in a small bowl. Using the back of a fork, mash until they reach an almost smooth consistency.

2 Make sure the pits are removed from the avocado halves. In the center of each avocado, layer 1 tablespoon of the beans, 1 tablespoon of Greek yogurt, and 1 tablespoon of salsa and sprinkle with 1 teaspoon of cheese. Sprinkle the salt evenly over the avocados. Serve each avocado half with 1 slice of lime to squeeze over the dish.

 For a variation on this recipe, stuff the avocado halves with the tuna mixture from the Endive Tuna Boats (page 97).

Choices/Exchanges 1/2 Fruit, 1/2 Carbohydrate, 2 1/2 Fat

Calories 160
Calories from Fat 110
Total Fat 12.0 g
Saturated Fat 2.0 g
Trans Fat 0.0 g

Cholesterol 0 mg
Sodium 180 mg
Potassium 490 mg
Total Carbohydrate 12 g
Dietary Fiber 6 g

Sugars 2 g
Added Sugars 0 g
Protein 5 g
Phosphorus 95 mg

TOTAL TIME 15 minutes plus at least 2 hours 20 minutes freezing time
PREP TIME 15 minutes
COOK TIME 1 minute

SERVES 4
SERVING SIZE 4 skewers

80 fresh blueberries (about 4 ounces)

16 toothpicks or short skewers

1/4 cup creamy almond butter

1/4 teaspoon ground cinnamon

1/4 teaspoon vanilla extract

FROZEN BLUEBERRIES WITH CINNAMON-ALMOND DRIZZLE

To indulge my sweet tooth for frozen goodies, I love snacking on frozen berries, such as sliced strawberries, blueberries, or blackberries. These berries contain anthocyanins, which are what gives these berries their gorgeous hue. Anthocyanins are phytochemicals, or natural plant compounds, and are an anti-inflammatory antioxidant that may help protect the body's blood vessels and nervous system.

---

1 Thread 5 blueberries onto each of 16 toothpicks or short skewers. Place in the freezer for at least 2 hours or up to overnight.

2 Place the almond butter, cinnamon, and vanilla in a small microwave-safe bowl. Microwave until the almond butter is melted, about 45–60 seconds. Remove the bowl and stir to combine.

3 Line a small baking sheet with parchment paper.

4 Remove the blueberry skewers from the freezer and place in a single layer on the prepared baking sheet. Drizzle with the melted almond butter mixture. Place the baking sheet in the freezer until the almond butter freezes, at least 20 minutes.

Freezing blueberries is simple and easy. You can also freeze the berries off the skewers for a delicious, frozen snack. Just give the berries a quick rinse and pat dry, and then place them in a single layer on a sheet pan and pop them in the freezer. After 2 hours the blueberries are ready to eat.

Choices/Exchanges 1/2 Carbohydrate, 1 1/2 Fat

Calories 110	**Cholesterol** 0 mg	**Sugars** 4 g
Calories from Fat 80	**Sodium** 0 mg	**Added Sugars** 0 g
Total Fat 9.0 g	**Potassium** 140 mg	**Protein** 3 g
Saturated Fat 0.7 g	**Total Carbohydrate** 7 g	**Phosphorus** 85 mg
Trans Fat 0.0 g	**Dietary Fiber** 2 g	

RUBY RED ICE POPS

There are many flavorful ways to add vegetables to your popsicles. These pomegranate- and strawberry-flavored ice pops have cauliflower blended in (you can't even taste the cauliflower!). Carrots and beets are other veggies that work well in popsicles, plus they look gorgeous!

1 Place the pomegranate juice, strawberries, cauliflower, Greek yogurt, and lemon zest in a blender or food processor and blend until completely combined and smooth, about 1 minute.

2 Place 1 teaspoon of the pomegranate arils into each of 12 standard ice pop molds. Using a 1/3-cup scoop, pour 1/3 cup of the blended mixture into each of the popsicle molds, then insert a popsicle stick into each one. Freeze until the ice pops are set, at least 4 hours.

TOTAL TIME 10 minutes plus at least 4 hours freezing time
PREP TIME 10 minutes
COOK TIME 0 minutes

SERVES 9
SERVING SIZE 1 popsicle

1 1/2 cups 100% pomegranate juice

1 cup fresh or frozen strawberries

1/2 cup cauliflower florets, roughly chopped

1/2 cup nonfat plain Greek yogurt

Zest of 1 lemon (1 tablespoon)

1/4 cup pomegranate arils

Don't forget that liquid expands when frozen. Fill your molds by pouring the liquid mixture only three-quarters of the way up the mold. Some molds will have a fill line to help guide you.

Choices/Exchanges 1/2 Fruit

Calories 40
Calories from Fat 0
Total Fat 0.0 g
Saturated Fat 0.1 g
Trans Fat 0.0 g

Cholesterol 0 mg
Sodium 10 mg
Potassium 160 mg
Total Carbohydrate 8 g
Dietary Fiber 1 g

Sugars 7 g
Added Sugars 0 g
Protein 2 g
Phosphorus 30 mg

Chapter 6
Appetizers

How Appetizers Fit on Your Plate

Appetizers are not an essential part of a meal. If you choose to eat an appetizer before a meal, consider them part of your plate. For example, if you have an appetizer that is higher in carbs, then cut back on other carbohydrate foods in your meal. If you choose to make a meal out of appetizers or small plates (like when eating tapas), follow the same portions as the Diabetes Plate Method with 2 parts nonstarchy vegetables, 1 part lean protein, and 1 part carbohydrate foods.

Curried Chicken Salad Lettuce Cups, p. 111

18 grape tomatoes

6 toothpicks or short skewers

12 spears asparagus, washed
and trimmed

3/4 cup Herb Dip (page 212)

6 small cups or ramekins

1 endive head, washed and
leaves separated (about
12 leaves)

1 medium cucumber, sliced in
half crosswise then cut into
12 (1-inch) strips

1 yellow bell pepper, sliced
into 12 (1-inch) strips

CRUDITÉ CUPS

*Eye-appealing appetizers always draw in a crowd!
What's more gorgeous than starting a meal with individual
bouquets of vegetables? Feel free to swap in radishes,
carrots, purple cabbage, or any other vegetable you love.*

---

1 Thread 3 tomatoes onto each of 6 toothpicks or short skewers.

2 Fill a large pot with water and bring it to a boil over high
heat. Carefully plunge the asparagus spears into the water for
1 minute. Remove and immediately rinse under cold water.
Place the asparagus onto a baking sheet in a single layer to
allow them to cool.

3 Place 2 tablespoons of the dip into each of 6 small cups.
Arrange 2 endive leaves, 2 asparagus spears, 2 cucumber strips,
2 bell pepper strips, and a tomato skewer in each cup so they are
standing upright like a vegetable bouquet.

*Get creative with this recipe! Swap the Herb Dip
for the avocado cream from my Cherry Tomatoes
Stuffed with Avocado Cream recipe (page 112).*

Choices/Exchanges 1 Nonstarchy Vegetable, 1/2 Fat

Calories 60
Calories from Fat 25
Total Fat 3.0 g
Saturated Fat 1.3 g
Trans Fat 0.0 g

Cholesterol 5 mg
Sodium 100 mg
Potassium 370 mg
Total Carbohydrate 7 g
Dietary Fiber 2 g

Sugars 3 g
Added Sugars 0 g
Protein 4 g
Phosphorus 70 mg

ANTIPASTO SKEWERS

Reduced-fat and reduced-sodium cheeses aren't always easy to find. Head to your deli counter to ask if they carry it or check in the dairy aisle to see if they have a packaged variety. If you can't find provolone that is reduced-fat and reduced-sodium, use whatever you can find. If you can only find reduced-sodium provolone, then use half a slice of cheese for each skewer instead of a whole slice.

1 Thread 1 artichoke heart, 1 pepper, 1 slice of cheese (folded into quarters), and 1 tomato onto each of 8 skewers.

2 Place the 8 skewers in a single layer on a serving platter. Drizzle with the olive oil, oregano, and black pepper. Serve immediately.

TOTAL TIME 15 minutes
PREP TIME 15 minutes
COOK TIME 0 minutes

SERVES 8
SERVING SIZE 1 skewer

1 (14-ounce) can artichoke hearts, drained and rinsed

8 mini sweet peppers

8 slices reduced-fat provolone cheese (such as Alpine Lace; 4 ounces)

8 red or yellow cherry tomatoes

8 mini wooden skewers

2 tablespoons extra-virgin olive oil

1/2 teaspoon ground oregano

1/8 teaspoon ground black pepper

To make these skewers dairy free, swap out the cheese for radishes or a folded cabbage leaf.

Choices/Exchanges 1 Nonstarchy Vegetable, 1 1/2 Fat

Calories 90
Calories from Fat 60
Total Fat 7.0 g
Saturated Fat 2.2 g
Trans Fat 0.0 g

Cholesterol 10 mg
Sodium 170 mg
Potassium 160 mg
Total Carbohydrate 5 g
Dietary Fiber 2 g

Sugars 1 g
Added Sugars 0 g
Protein 5 g
Phosphorus 95 mg

TOTAL TIME 10 minutes
PREP TIME 10 minutes
COOK TIME 0 minutes

SERVES 6
SERVING SIZE 2 pieces

12 whole-grain crackers
(such as Wheat Thins)

2 ounces brie cheese, sliced
into 12 pieces

12 unsalted raw pecan halves
(about 3/4 ounce)

BRIE AND PECANS OVER WHOLE-GRAIN CRACKERS

This simple three-ingredient appetizer is perfect for an upscale cocktail party, a tailgating get-together, or just a quiet family night at home.

---

1 Place the 12 whole-grain crackers on a flat surface, like a cutting board or plate.

2 Gently top each cracker with 1 piece of the brie cheese and then place 1 pecan on top of the cheese. Serve at room temperature.

Whole-grain crackers vary in portion size and quality. Compare labels to choose a cracker made with 100% whole grains and select the one that is highest in fiber.

Choices/Exchanges 1 1/2 Fat

Calories 70	Cholesterol 10 mg	Sugars 0 g
Calories from Fat 50	Sodium 95 mg	Added Sugars 0 g
Total Fat 6.0 g	Potassium 45 mg	Protein 2 g
Saturated Fat 1.9 g	Total Carbohydrate 4 g	Phosphorus 40 mg
Trans Fat 0.0 g	Dietary Fiber 1 g	

CUCUMBER BITES WITH CREAMY SUN-DRIED TOMATOES

Sun-dried tomatoes provide an array of nutrients. A 1/4-cup serving has 2 grams of fiber, close to 2 grams of protein, and about 10% of the daily recommended amount of potassium. They also provide the antioxidants vitamins A and C plus lycopene, which may help protect your eyes from age-related diseases like cataracts and macular degeneration.

TOTAL TIME 20 minutes
PREP TIME 20 minutes
COOK TIME 0 minutes

SERVES 6
SERVING SIZE 4 pieces

24 raw walnuts pieces (1 1/2 ounces)

3/4 English or hothouse cucumber (8.5 ounces)

1/4 cup sun-dried tomatoes packed in oil, drained and roughly chopped

1/4 cup nonfat plain Greek yogurt

3 tablespoons whipped cream cheese

2 tablespoons light mayonnaise

1 tablespoon olive oil

1 clove garlic, crushed

1 scallion (green and white parts), roughly chopped

1/2 teaspoon sriracha

1/4 teaspoon salt

1 Place the walnuts in a small saucepan over medium-low heat. Cook, stirring frequently, until the walnuts are fragrant, about 3 minutes. Remove the walnuts from the pan and allow to cool.

2 Slice the cucumber into 24 (1/4-inch-thick) rounds. Arrange the cucumber slices on a serving platter.

3 In a blender or food processor, add the sun-dried tomatoes, yogurt, cream cheese, mayonnaise, olive oil, garlic, scallion, sriracha, and salt. Blend until the mixture is smooth.

4 Top each cucumber with 1 teaspoon of the sun-dried tomato mixture, then 1 toasted walnut piece. Serve immediately.

 Toby Tip

Swap out the cucumber slices for sliced carrots or zucchini if desired.

Choices/Exchanges 1 Nonstarchy Vegetable, 2 Fat

Calories 120	**Cholesterol** 5 mg	**Sugars** 2 g
Calories from Fat 90	**Sodium** 180 mg	**Added Sugars** 0 g
Total Fat 10.0 g	**Potassium** 190 mg	**Protein** 3 g
Saturated Fat 1.7 g	**Total Carbohydrate** 5 g	**Phosphorus** 60 mg
Trans Fat 0.0 g	**Dietary Fiber** 1 g	

TOTAL TIME 20 minutes
PREP TIME 20 minutes
COOK TIME 0 minutes

SERVES 6
SERVING SIZE 2 stuffed strawberries

12 medium strawberries, washed and trimmed

2 ounces soft goat cheese

1/4 cup nonfat plain Greek yogurt

1 tablespoon chopped fresh basil leaves

1/8 teaspoon salt

1/8 teaspoon ground black pepper

1/4 cup unsalted dry-roasted pistachios, chopped

WHIPPED GOAT CHEESE–STUFFED STRAWBERRIES

The red hue in strawberries is due to the phytochemical anthocyanins, which have been shown to be beneficial for both the brain and heart. Research suggests that strawberries help boost antioxidants in your blood around 30 minutes after munching on them.

---

1 Using a paring knife, create a cone-shaped pocket in each strawberry. Rinse the strawberries and pat dry on a paper towel.

2 In a blender or using a hand-held blender, beat the goat cheese, yogurt, basil, salt, and black pepper together until fluffy, about 1 minute. Place the cheese mixture into a resealable plastic bag and cut the bottom corner off of the bag using scissors. Pipe the cheese mixture into each strawberry.

3 Place the pistachios in a small bowl. Dip the top of the berry into the pistachio mixture. Serve immediately.

 Choose strawberries that have a bright red color, a natural shine, and fresh looking green caps. Keep the strawberries refrigerated and wash under cool water right before eating or preparing.

Choices/Exchanges 1 Fat

Calories 70
Calories from Fat 40
Total Fat 4.5 g
Saturated Fat 1.7 g
Trans Fat 0.0 g

Cholesterol 5 mg
Sodium 90 mg
Potassium 100 mg
Total Carbohydrate 4 g
Dietary Fiber 1 g

Sugars 2 g
Added Sugars 0 g
Protein 4 g
Phosphorus 65 mg

CURRIED CHICKEN SALAD LETTUCE CUPS

This punched-up chicken salad uses curry powder, a mixture of spices like turmeric, ginger, and coriander traditionally used in Indian cuisine. One of these spices, turmeric, gives curry powder its distinct yellow color and is well known for its phenols, potent antioxidants that can help prevent cell damage from free radicals.

TOTAL TIME 20 minutes
PREP TIME 20 minutes
COOK TIME 0 minutes

SERVES 7
SERVING SIZE 2 lettuce cups

- 1/4 cup light mayonnaise
- 3 tablespoons nonfat plain Greek yogurt
- 2 teaspoons freshly squeezed lemon juice
- 1/2 teaspoon curry powder
- 1/2 teaspoon zero-calorie stevia sweetener (such as Truvia or Splenda)
- 1/8 teaspoon salt
- 1/8 teaspoon ground black pepper
- 8 ounces leftover chicken breast or skinless rotisserie chicken, finely chopped
- 1 rib celery, finely chopped
- 1 scallion (green and white parts), finely chopped
- 1/4 cup unsalted raw or dry-roasted almonds, finely chopped
- 1 1/2 small heads Bibb lettuce (14 leaves)

1 In a medium bowl, whisk together the mayonnaise, yogurt, lemon juice, curry powder, sweetener, salt, and black pepper until well combined.

2 Add the chicken, celery, scallion, almonds, and 1/4 cup seedless yellow raisins (optional), and toss to evenly coat.

3 Spoon 2 tablespoons of the chicken mixture into each of 14 lettuce cups and serve immediately.

For a fun spin on this recipe, use zucchini boats instead of lettuce cups. To make a zucchini boat, slice a small zucchini lengthwise and, using a teaspoon, scoop out the zucchini flesh on each side. Fill the zucchini boats with the curried chicken salad.

Choices/Exchanges 1 Lean Protein, 1 Fat

Calories 100
Calories from Fat 45
Total Fat 5.0 g
Saturated Fat 0.7 g
Trans Fat 0.0 g

Cholesterol 30 mg
Sodium 140 mg
Potassium 190 mg
Total Carbohydrate 3 g
Dietary Fiber 1 g

Sugars 1 g
Added Sugars 0 g
Protein 12 g
Phosphorus 110 mg

TOTAL TIME 20 minutes
PREP TIME 20 minutes
COOK TIME 0 minutes

SERVES 6
SERVING SIZE 3 pieces

18 cherry tomatoes

1/4 plus 1/8 teaspoon sea salt, divided

1 avocado, halved and pit removed

1/4 cup nonfat plain Greek yogurt

Juice of 1 lime

1 tablespoon water

1 clove garlic, crushed

1/4 teaspoon ground coriander

1/4 teaspoon ground black pepper

1 tablespoon chopped fresh cilantro, as garnish

CHERRY TOMATOES STUFFED WITH AVOCADO CREAM

Avocados are certainly a healthy food high in heart-healthy monounsaturated fat. They also provide the antioxidant lutein, which can help keep eyes healthy, and the plant sterol beta-sitosterol, which may help lower blood cholesterol levels. While they are nutrient rich, avocados are also high in calories–there are about 250 calories in 1 medium-sized avocado. Because of the higher calorie and fat content, keep portions to about 1/5 of the fruit.

1 Slice the tops off the cherry tomatoes. Using a small melon baller or teaspoon, scoop the seeds and pulp from the inside of the tomatoes. Sprinkle the insides with 1/4 teaspoon of the sea salt. Place the tomato shells upside down on a paper towel for at least 30 minutes or up to 2 hours.

2 Place the avocado flesh, yogurt, lime juice, water, garlic, remaining 1/8 teaspoon sea salt, coriander, and black pepper in a blender and blend until smooth.

3 Add the avocado mixture to a resealable plastic bag and cut off a 1/4-inch piece at the bottom corner of the bag. Pipe the filling into the tomato shells and place on a serving platter. Sprinkle with 1 tablespoon of cilantro to garnish.

 Try using the avocado cream in this recipe as a filling for deviled eggs.

Choices/Exchanges 1 Fat

Calories 50
Calories from Fat 35
Total Fat 4.0 g
Saturated Fat 0.6 g
Trans Fat 0.0 g

Cholesterol 0 mg
Sodium 140 mg
Potassium 210 mg
Total Carbohydrate 4 g
Dietary Fiber 2 g

Sugars 1 g
Added Sugars 0 g
Protein 2 g
Phosphorus 35 mg

TOTAL TIME 30 minutes plus
10 minutes cooling time
PREP TIME 15 minutes
COOK TIME 15 minutes

SERVES 11
SERVING SIZE 2 pieces

Nonstick cooking spray

2 medium zucchini (about
1 pound)

1 (14-ounce) can artichokes,
drained and rinsed

1 clove garlic, minced

1 scallion (green and white
parts), chopped

6 ounces soft silken tofu

1/8 teaspoon ground black
pepper

5 1/2 teaspoons grated
Parmesan cheese, divided

ARTICHOKE ZUCCHINI BITES

Zucchini makes a nice base for appetizers as it's low in calories and low in carbohydrates. It also provides healthy doses of vitamins B-6, riboflavin, folate, vitamins C and K, potassium, and manganese.

1 Preheat the oven to 400°F. Coat 2 baking sheets with nonstick cooking spray.

2 Slice the zucchini into 22 (1/2-inch) rounds.

3 Roughly chop the artichokes and place in a blender or food processor. Add the garlic, scallion, tofu, and black pepper. Pulse until still slightly chunky, about 30 seconds.

4 Spread 1 tablespoon of the artichoke mixture over each of the zucchini slices. Top each with 1/4 teaspoon of Parmesan cheese. Place zucchini on the baking sheets in a single layer, and bake until the cheese has melted and zucchini is softened, about 12–15 minutes. Remove the baking sheets from the oven and set aside 10 minutes to slightly cool. Serve immediately.

 Use the artichoke mixture as a dip for your favorite vegetables.

Choices/Exchanges 1 Nonstarchy Vegetable

Calories 35
Calories from Fat 10
Total Fat 1.0 g
Saturated Fat 0.2 g
Trans Fat 0.0 g

Cholesterol 0 mg
Sodium 75 mg
Potassium 190 mg
Total Carbohydrate 4 g
Dietary Fiber 2 g

Sugars 1 g
Added Sugars 0 g
Protein 2 g
Phosphorus 45 mg

SPINACH AND FETA–STUFFED MUSHROOMS

It's easy to keep frozen vegetables like spinach on hand so you can use them anytime. When buying frozen vegetables, read the ingredients listed to make sure it only contains the vegetable. You can then add the flavor you want and have the most control over them. Avoid frozen vegetable varieties that contain sauces or butter.

TOTAL TIME 35 minutes plus 10 minutes cooling time
PREP TIME 15 minutes
COOK TIME 20 minutes

SERVES 15
SERVING SIZE 1 stuffed mushroom

Nonstick cooking spray

1/2 cup water

5 ounces frozen spinach (3/4 cup cooked spinach)

1/2 cup panko bread crumbs (preferably whole-wheat)

1/3 cup crumbled feta cheese

1/4 cup nonfat plain Greek yogurt

1 large egg, beaten

2 teaspoons dried parsley

1/4 teaspoon salt

1/8 teaspoon ground black pepper

15 large white mushrooms, washed and stems removed

1 Preheat the oven to 375°F. Coat a baking sheet with nonstick cooking spray and set it aside.

2 In a small saucepan, bring the water to a boil over high heat. Add the spinach and lower the heat to medium low. Using a wooden spoon, break up the pieces of spinach and cook until heated through, 5 minutes. Set aside to cool for at least 10 minutes. Drain the spinach of excess water.

3 In a medium bowl, stir together the cooled spinach, panko, feta, yogurt, egg, parsley, salt, and black pepper.

4 Arrange the mushrooms, stem side up, in an even layer on the prepared baking sheet. Stuff each mushroom with 1 tablespoon of the spinach mixture. Bake until the mushrooms are fragrant and slightly browned, about 15 minutes. Remove the baking sheet from the oven and set aside to cool for 10 minutes. Serve warm.

Toby Tip *Store prepackaged mushrooms in the refrigerator in their package. Fresh, loose mushrooms should be stored in a paper bag or in a damp cloth in the refrigerator so they can stay firm longer. Avoid storing mushrooms in a plastic bag, as they can spoil faster.*

Choices/Exchanges 1/2 Carbohydrate

Calories 30
Calories from Fat 10
Total Fat 1.0 g
Saturated Fat 0.5 g
Trans Fat 0.0 g

Cholesterol 15 mg
Sodium 85 mg
Potassium 115 mg
Total Carbohydrate 3 g
Dietary Fiber 1 g

Sugars 1 g
Added Sugars 0 g
Protein 3 g
Phosphorus 45 mg

TOTAL TIME 30 minutes plus 10 minutes cooling time
PREP TIME 15 minutes
COOK TIME 15 minutes

SERVES 4
SERVING SIZE About 5–6 pieces

Nonstick cooking spray

1 pound peeled and deveined raw jumbo shrimp (about 21–25 count)*

1/4 teaspoon salt

1/8 teaspoon ground black pepper

2 large eggs, beaten

1/2 teaspoon ground coriander

3/4 cup panko bread crumbs

1/2 cup 100%-whole-wheat flour

3 tablespoons unsweetened shredded coconut

If possible, use fresh, never frozen shrimp that are free of preservatives (for example, shrimp that have not been treated with salt or STPP [sodium tripolyphosphate]).

BAKED COCONUT SHRIMP

Coconut contains saturated fat, which you want to minimize, especially if you have diabetes. However, coconut does add a delicious flavor to many foods. The saturated fat content doesn't mean you need to avoid all coconut products–just compromise. In this coconut shrimp recipe, only 3 tablespoons of shredded coconut are used. A small amount of a big flavor really does go a long way!

1 Preheat the oven to 425°F. Coat a baking sheet with nonstick cooking spray.

2 Place the shrimp in a medium bowl and sprinkle with the salt and black pepper.

3 In a separate medium bowl, whisk together the eggs and coriander. In a separate medium dish or bowl, combine the bread crumbs, whole-wheat flour, and coconut. Stir to combine.

4 Dip both sides of the shrimp in the egg mixture, shaking to remove excess mixture. Next, dip both sides of the shrimp in the panko mixture. Lay the shrimp flat on the prepared baking sheet. Repeat with the remaining shrimp.

5 Bake until the coating is browned and the shrimp reach an internal temperature is 145°F, about 12–15 minutes. Remove the baking sheet from the oven and set aside to cool for 10 minutes before serving.

 Serve with Sriracha-Yogurt Dip (page 213).

Choices/Exchanges 1 Starch, 2 Lean Protein

Calories 150	**Cholesterol** 170 mg	**Sugars** 1 g
Calories from Fat 25	**Sodium** 200 mg	**Added Sugars** 0 g
Total Fat 3.0 g	**Potassium** 250 mg	**Protein** 19 g
Saturated Fat 1.5 g	**Total Carbohydrate** 12 g	**Phosphorus** 225 mg
Trans Fat 0.0 g	**Dietary Fiber** 2 g	

MOZZARELLA-STUFFED TURKEY MEATBALLS

Instead of using plain or flavored bread crumbs in meatballs, hamburgers, and meatloaf, blend whole-grain rolled oats and use them in the mix. It's an easy way to add more whole grains into dishes.

---

1 Place the oats in a blender and pulse until blended into a fine powder.

2 In a large bowl, combine the oats, ground turkey, onion, garlic, basil, egg, salt, and black pepper. Shape 2 tablespoons of the turkey mixture into a ball. Insert a clean thumb into the center and open into a disc. Insert one piece of mozzarella in the center and seal the meatball again. Repeat with the remaining turkey mixture and mozzarella to make 26 meatballs.

3 In a large skillet over medium heat, heat the olive oil. When the oil is shimmering, add the meatballs and cook, covered, for about 15 minutes, turning every few minutes to brown all sides. Cook until a thermometer inserted into a meatball reads 165°F.

 Serve with warmed low-sodium tomato sauce for dipping or Sriracha-Yogurt Dip (page 213).

TOTAL TIME 30 minutes
PREP TIME 15 minutes
COOK TIME 15 minutes

SERVES 13
SERVING SIZE 2 meatballs

1/2 cup rolled oats

1 pound lean ground turkey (at least 93% lean)

1 small yellow onion, finely chopped

1 clove garlic, minced

1 tablespoon dried basil

1 large egg, beaten

1/4 teaspoon salt

1/4 teaspoon ground black pepper

4 ounces part-skim mozzarella, cut into 26 pieces

2 tablespoons olive oil

Choices/Exchanges 1 Lean Protein, 1 1/2 Fat

Calories 120
Calories from Fat 60
Total Fat 7.0 g
Saturated Fat 2.1 g
Trans Fat 0.0 g

Cholesterol 45 mg
Sodium 130 mg
Potassium 120 mg
Total Carbohydrate 3 g
Dietary Fiber 1 g

Sugars 0 g
Added Sugars 0 g
Protein 10 g
Phosphorus 130 mg

TOTAL TIME 18 minutes plus at least 30 minutes marinating time
PREP TIME 15 minutes
COOK TIME 3 minutes

SERVES 12
SERVING SIZE 1 skewer

1 pound top round steak

12 wooden skewers

1/4 cup lower-sodium teriyaki sauce

1/2 teaspoon sriracha

Nonstick cooking spray

BEEF SATAY

With many appetizers providing carbohydrates, it's always nice to have a delicious, protein-filled choice on the table. This appetizer can be marinated and cooked in advance—or you can bring the marinated beef skewered and grill when you get to the party (with the host's permission, of course!).

1 Slice the steak into 6 even strips lengthwise, then cut each strip in half for a total of 12 pieces. Soak the wooden skewers in water for at least 10 minutes.

2 Place the steak pieces, teriyaki sauce, and sriracha in a resealable container or plastic bag. Shake to evenly coat. Place in the refrigerator to marinate for at least 30 minutes or up to 24 hours.

3 Thread the steak pieces onto the skewers, threading in and out. Shake off excess marinade and discard leftover marinade.

4 Preheat a grill pan or grill over medium-high heat. Coat the grill pan with nonstick cooking spray. (If using a grill, brush with 1 tablespoon of olive oil or use nonflammable cooking spray.) When the grill or grill pan is hot, cook the skewers for at least 2–3 minutes on each side or until a thermometer inserted into a skewer reads 145°F.

 Serve with Peanut Sauce (page 216).

Choices/Exchanges 1 Lean Protein

Calories 45
Calories from Fat 10
Total Fat 1.0 g
Saturated Fat 0.4 g
Trans Fat 0.0 g

Cholesterol 20 mg
Sodium 80 mg
Potassium 85 mg
Total Carbohydrate 1 g
Dietary Fiber 0 g

Sugars 0 g
Added Sugars 0 g
Protein 8 g
Phosphorus 50 mg

ZUCCHINI TOPPED WITH SAUTÉED SPINACH AND MUSHROOMS

Zucchini is used as a low-calorie and low-carb "cracker" to hold the delicious mixture of spinach and mushrooms in this recipe. Other vegetables that you can use instead include yellow summer squash or carrots.

TOTAL TIME 25 minutes
PREP TIME 15 minutes
COOK TIME 10 minutes

SERVES 7
SERVING SIZE 2 topped zucchini slices

2 medium zucchini

2 tablespoons olive oil, divided

2 cups crimini mushrooms, chopped

1 clove garlic, minced

2 cups baby spinach, rinsed and patted dry

1 tablespoon grated Parmesan cheese

1/8 teaspoon red pepper flakes

1/8 teaspoon ground black pepper

Nonstick cooking spray

1 Slice each zucchini into 7 rounds (for a total of 14 slices). Using 1 tablespoon of the olive oil, brush both sides of the zucchini rounds.

2 Heat the remaining 1 tablespoon of oil in a large sauté pan. Once the oil is shimmering, add the mushrooms and garlic and cook until the mushrooms begin to soften, 5 minutes. Add the spinach and continue to cook until the spinach is wilted, an additional 2–3 minutes. Spoon the vegetable mixture into a medium bowl and stir in the cheese, red pepper flakes, and black pepper. Wipe the inside of the sauté pan with a paper towel.

3 Coat the same large sauté pan with nonstick cooking spray and heat over medium heat. When the cooking spray is shimmering, add the zucchini rounds and cook on one side until slightly browned, about 3 minutes, then flip and cook the other side for an additional 2–3 minutes.

4 Place the zucchini slices on a serving plate and top each with 1 tablespoon of the mushroom mixture.

 Have extra mushrooms? Reduce the food waste in your home by using whatever type of mushroom you have. You can also swap the spinach for chopped kale.

Choices/Exchanges 1 Nonstarchy Vegetable, 1/2 Fat

Calories 50
Calories from Fat 35
Total Fat 4.0 g
Saturated Fat 0.6 g
Trans Fat 0.0 g

Cholesterol 0 mg
Sodium 15 mg
Potassium 290 mg
Total Carbohydrate 3 g
Dietary Fiber 1 g

Sugars 2 g
Added Sugars 0 g
Protein 2 g
Phosphorus 55 mg

TOTAL TIME 30 minutes
PREP TIME 20 minutes
COOK TIME 10 minutes

SERVES 4
SERVING SIZE 2 fritters and
2 tablespoons sauce

LEMON-YOGURT SAUCE

1/2 cup nonfat plain Greek
    yogurt

Juice of 1/2 lemon (1 tablespoon)

2 tablespoons chopped fresh
    dill

1 clove garlic, minced

1/8 teaspoon ground black
    pepper

FRITTERS

2 medium zucchini, shredded
    (3 cups)

1/2 cup whole-wheat pastry
    flour

2 tablespoons chopped fresh
    dill

1/4 teaspoon salt

1 large egg, beaten

1 large egg white, beaten

1 tablespoon olive oil

ZUCCHINI FRITTERS WITH LEMON-YOGURT SAUCE

This diabetes-friendly version of a fritter recipe uses only 1 tablespoon of olive oil to help keep the calories low, but the flavor and crunch will have you making them regularly for the holidays, for guests, or just as an everyday appetizer.

1 To make the yogurt sauce, whisk together the Lemon-Yogurt Sauce ingredients in a small bowl. Set aside.

2 To make the fritters, place the shredded zucchini in a colander and, using clean hands, squeeze out the excess water. Then place the zucchini in a large bowl.

3 Add the flour, dill, and salt to the zucchini and toss to combine. Add the beaten egg and egg white and mix thoroughly.

4 In a large sauté pan, heat the olive oil over medium heat. Scoop 1/4 cup of the zucchini batter and gently press with your hands to flatten into a fritter. When the oil is shimmering place the fritter in the pan; repeat with the remaining batter. Cook until the fritters are slightly browned, about 4 minutes on each side.

5 To serve, place 2 fritters on a plate and top with 2 tablespoons of the sauce.

 The skin of zucchini contains a nice amount of fiber, so when shredding the zucchini, leave the skin on.

Choices/Exchanges 1/2 Starch, 1 Nonstarchy Vegetable, 1 Lean Protein, 1/2 Fat

Calories 140	**Cholesterol** 50 mg	**Sugars** 4 g
Calories from Fat 45	**Sodium** 200 mg	**Added Sugars** 0 g
Total Fat 5.0 g	**Potassium** 400 mg	**Protein** 8 g
Saturated Fat 1.0 g	**Total Carbohydrate** 16 g	**Phosphorus** 155 mg
Trans Fat 0.0 g	**Dietary Fiber** 3 g	

TOTAL TIME 38 minutes
PREP TIME 15 minutes
COOK TIME 23 minutes

SERVES 8
SERVING SIZE 2 crostini

3/4 whole-wheat baguette
  (7.5 ounces)*

Nonstick cooking spray

2 cups sliced strawberries
  (3/4 pound)

1 tablespoon dried tarragon or
  4 sprigs of fresh tarragon

1 tablespoon olive oil

1 cup part-skim ricotta cheese

1/2 teaspoon lemon zest

2 tablespoons water

2 tablespoons balsamic vinegar

*Baguettes come in all sizes. Using
your food scale is the best way to
ensure you're using the correct
bread portions in this recipe.*

CROSTINI WITH PAN-ROASTED STRAWBERRIES AND RICOTTA

Crostini are small, toasted pieces of bread topped with deliciousness. These crostini are made with a combination of warmed strawberries and cool, creamy ricotta cheese. The variety of textures, flavors, and food groups (it has three!) makes it an ideal appetizer for those with or without diabetes.

1 Preheat the oven to 400°F.

2 Slice the baguette on an angle into 16 (1/2-inch) slices.

3 Coat a grill pan or a cast-iron pan with nonstick cooking spray and heat over medium-high heat. When the cooking spray is shimmering, reduce the heat to medium and place 8 slices of bread on the pan. Cook until the bread is browned on each side, about 3 minutes per side. Remove and set on a large plate to cool. Repeat with the remaining slices.

4 Add the strawberries and tarragon to a small bowl; stir to combine. Heat the olive oil in an ovenproof sauté pan over medium heat. When the oil is shimmering, add the strawberry mixture. Cook the strawberries until warmed, about 3 minutes, occasionally tossing gently. Place the pan into the oven and roast until the strawberries have softened, about 8 minutes. Using an oven mitt, carefully remove the pan from the oven and use a slotted spoon to scoop the strawberries into a medium bowl. Allow to cool for 10 minutes.

5 In a small bowl, mix together the ricotta and lemon zest. Set aside.

Choices/Exchanges 1 Starch, 1 Lean Protein, 1/2 Fat

Calories 140	**Cholesterol** 10 mg	**Sugars** 3 g
Calories from Fat 40	**Sodium** 140 mg	**Added Sugars** 0 g
Total Fat 4.5 g	**Potassium** 150 mg	**Protein** 6 g
Saturated Fat 1.8 g	**Total Carbohydrate** 18 g	**Phosphorus** 110 mg
Trans Fat 0.0 g	**Dietary Fiber** 2 g	

6 Return the sauté pan to the stove and heat over medium-low heat. Add the water and, using a wooden spoon, scrape the bits from the bottom of the pan. Add the balsamic vinegar and bring the mixture to a boil. Then lower the heat and simmer until the liquid is reduced by half, about 2–3 minutes. Using an oven mitt to grab the handle, set the pan aside to cool.

7 On each slice of toast, spread 1 tablespoon of the ricotta, then top with 1 teaspoon of the strawberry mixture and a drizzle of the balsamic syrup.

When buying strawberries, look for berries with a bright red color, natural shine, and fresh-looking green caps. Store in the refrigerator and rinse just before using or preparing. Rinse the strawberries with the green stems still intact under cool water and gently blot dry.

Chapter 7
Smoothies & Low-Calorie Beverages

How Beverages Fit on Your Plate

Whenever possible, choose zero-calorie beverages such as water, seltzer, unsweetened hot or cold tea, or unsweetened hot or cold coffee. More about zero-calorie beverages can be found on pages 9–10.

If you choose to drink calorie-containing beverages—like smoothies or the other beverage recipes in this chapter, for example—then they should be considered part of your plate. The smoothie recipes found in this chapter are made with a combination of foods including fruits, vegetables, protein, and/or dairy foods. Adding protein and fat, like tofu, nut butter, or avocado, into smoothies helps reduce the effect that any carbohydrate-containing ingredients have on your blood glucose.

TOTAL TIME 5 minutes
PREP TIME 5 minutes
COOK TIME 0 minutes

SERVES 1
SERVING SIZE 8 fluid ounces

3/4 cup fresh or frozen unsweetened blueberries

1/2 cup unsweetened soy milk

2 ounces soft silken tofu (1/4 cup)

1/4 teaspoon zero-calorie stevia sweetener (such as Truvia or Splenda)

BLUEBERRY SOY SMOOTHIE

The gorgeously hued blueberry provides 4 grams of fiber per cup. It's also a good source of vitamin K, which is beneficial for bone health, and the antioxidant vitamin C. Blueberries are also brimming with an antioxidant called anthocyanidins, which some research suggests may help protect against prostate cancer and glaucoma.

_____

1 Combine the blueberries, soy milk, tofu, and sweetener in a blender and blend until smooth. Pour into a glass and enjoy immediately.

Toby Tip *Pick up a bag of frozen wild blueberries, which are slightly smaller and sweeter than regular blueberries and are slightly lower in carbohydrates.*

Choices/Exchanges 1 Fruit, 1 Lean Protein, 1/2 Fat

Calories 140	**Cholesterol** 0 mg	**Sugars** 13 g
Calories from Fat 35	**Sodium** 30 mg	**Added Sugars** 0 g
Total Fat 4.0 g	**Potassium** 370 mg	**Protein** 8 g
Saturated Fat 0.6 g	**Total Carbohydrate** 18 g	**Phosphorus** 110 mg
Trans Fat 0.0 g	**Dietary Fiber** 3 g	

PINEAPPLE SPINACH SMOOTHIE

Pineapple is a sweet fruit, but getting the portions right in your recipe is important to keep your carbohydrates under control. One cup of pineapple chunks provides 82 calories, 22 grams of carbohydrate, and 2 grams of fiber. It also provides a whopping 131% of the daily recommended amount of the antioxidant vitamin C and 76% of the recommended amount of manganese, which is beneficial for bone heath. Pineapple also contains a phytochemical called bromelain, which may help fight inflammation.

_____

1 Combine the pineapple, spinach, yogurt, almond milk, lemon juice, and sweetener in a blender and blend until smooth. Pour into a glass and enjoy.

TOTAL TIME 5 minutes
PREP TIME 5 minutes
COOK TIME 0 minutes

SERVES 1
SERVING SIZE 10 fluid ounces

3/4 cup fresh or frozen unsweetened pineapple chunks

1 cup baby spinach, washed and patted dry

1/2 cup nonfat plain Greek yogurt

1/2 cup unsweetened almond milk

2 teaspoons freshly squeezed lemon juice

1/2 teaspoon zero-calorie stevia sweetener (such as Truvia or Splenda)

 Try swapping the spinach out for kale.

Choices/Exchanges 1 Fruit, 1/2 Fat-Free Milk, 1 Lean Protein

Calories 150
Calories from Fat 20
Total Fat 2.0 g
Saturated Fat 0.2 g
Trans Fat 0.0 g

Cholesterol 5 mg
Sodium 130 mg
Potassium 480 mg
Total Carbohydrate 23 g
Dietary Fiber 3 g

Sugars 16 g
Added Sugars 0 g
Protein 14 g
Phosphorus 190 mg

REFRESHING GREEN SMOOTHIE

Cucumbers are a perfect way to bulk up a smoothie without adding many carbohydrates. Cucumbers are primarily made from water, making them a great addition to this refreshing smoothie. They are also a source of vitamin C, magnesium, and potassium.

---

1 Combine the cucumber, honeydew, grapes, soy milk, lime juice, and sweetener and blend until smooth. Add the ice cubes and blend to incorporate. Divide evenly between 2 glasses and enjoy.

TOTAL TIME 5 minutes
PREP TIME 5 minutes
COOK TIME 0 minutes

SERVES 2
SERVING SIZE 10 fluid ounces

1/2 cup sliced hothouse cucumber (2 1/2 ounces)

2/3 cup cubed honeydew melon

2/3 cup green seedless grapes

1/2 cup unsweetened soy or almond milk

Juice of 1 lime (about 1 tablespoon)

1/4 teaspoon zero-calorie stevia sweetener (such as Truvia or Splenda)

3 ice cubes

 For smoothie recipes, choose cucumbers without seeds like Kirby, Persian, or hothouse cucumbers and leave the skin on for some added fiber!

Choices/Exchanges 1 Fruit, 1/2 Fat

Calories 80	**Cholesterol** 0 mg	**Sugars** 14 g
Calories from Fat 15	**Sodium** 25 mg	**Added Sugars** 0 g
Total Fat 1.5 g	**Potassium** 380 mg	**Protein** 3 g
Saturated Fat 0.3 g	**Total Carbohydrate** 17 g	**Phosphorus** 55 mg
Trans Fat 0.0 g	**Dietary Fiber** 1 g	

TOTAL TIME 5 minutes
PREP TIME 5 minutes
COOK TIME 0 minutes

SERVES 1
SERVING SIZE 12 fluid ounces

1 small apple, cored, skin removed, and cut into chunks

1/3 cup roughly chopped fresh cauliflower

1/2 cup unsweetened almond milk

2 teaspoons freshly squeezed lemon juice

1/8 teaspoon ground cinnamon

1/2 teaspoon zero-calorie stevia sweetener (such as Truvia or Splenda)

4 ice cubes

APPLE CINNAMON SMOOTHIE

When making smoothies, spices help bring out the flavor of the delicious blend. In this apple-cinnamon combination, all you need is a sprinkle of ground cinnamon to get a nice depth of flavor.

1 Combine the apple, cauliflower, almond milk, lemon juice, cinnamon, and sweetener and blend until smooth. Add the ice cubes and blend to incorporate. Pour into a glass and enjoy.

 A "small" apple is about 2 3/4 inches in diameter.

Choices/Exchanges 1 Fruit, 1/2 Carbohydrate

Calories 90	**Cholesterol** 0 mg	**Sugars** 14 g
Calories from Fat 15	**Sodium** 75 mg	**Added Sugars** 0 g
Total Fat 1.5 g	**Potassium** 250 mg	**Protein** 2 g
Saturated Fat 0.1 g	**Total Carbohydrate** 20 g	**Phosphorus** 45 mg
Trans Fat 0.0 g	**Dietary Fiber** 3 g	

PB&J SMOOTHIE

Love peanut butter and jelly sandwiches? Now you can sip them for breakfast or as a snack! The raspberries in this recipe add that jelly or jam flavor, the oats add fiber, and of course, what's a PB&J sandwich without the milk?!

_____

1 Combine the raspberries, oats, milk, peanut butter, and sweetener in a blender and blend until smooth. Add the ice cubes and blend to incorporate. Pour into a glass and enjoy.

TOTAL TIME 5 minutes
PREP TIME 5 minutes
COOK TIME 0 minutes

SERVES 1
SERVING SIZE 8 fluid ounces

3/4 cup frozen unsweetened raspberries

1 tablespoon dry quick-cooking oats

1/2 cup nonfat milk

2 teaspoons creamy peanut butter

1/4 teaspoon zero-calorie stevia sweetener (such as Truvia or Splenda)

4 ice cubes

Toby Tip

When purchasing frozen fruit, like raspberries, make sure the name of the fruit is the only ingredient listed. Avoid purchasing frozen fruit with sugar listed under the ingredients.

Choices/Exchanges 1 Fruit, 1/2 Fat-Free Milk, 1 Lean Protein, 1/2 Fat

Calories 180	**Cholesterol** 6 mg	**Sugars** 12 g
Calories from Fat 50	**Sodium** 100 mg	**Added Sugars** 0 g
Total Fat 6.0 g	**Potassium** 440 mg	**Protein** 9 g
Saturated Fat 1.2 g	**Total Carbohydrate** 24 g	**Phosphorus** 215 mg
Trans Fat 0.0 g	**Dietary Fiber** 3 g	

TOTAL TIME 5 minutes
PREP TIME 5 minutes
COOK TIME 0 minutes

SERVES 6
SERVING SIZE About 3/4 cup

2 cups ice cubes

2 1/2 cups seltzer

1 1/2 cups 100% cranberry juice

1/2 cup 100% orange juice

CRANBERRY ORANGE SPRITZER

Alcohol is tough when you have diabetes; that's why it's always nice to have a virgin drink on standby—especially if it takes only 5 minutes to whip up a pitcher. Place this simple combo of 100% fruit juices and seltzer on the table at any gathering and it's sure to be a hit with everyone.

1 Add ice cubes to a pitcher. Pour seltzer, cranberry juice, and orange juice into the pitcher and stir to combine. Garnish with orange slices, if desired.

 Swap the cranberry juice for 100% pomegranate juice, if desired.

Choices/Exchanges 1/2 Fruit

Calories 40
Calories from Fat 0
Total Fat 0.0 g
Saturated Fat 0.0 g
Trans Fat 0.0 g

Cholesterol 0 mg
Sodium 20 mg
Potassium 90 mg
Total Carbohydrate 10 g
Dietary Fiber 0 g

Sugars 9 g
Added Sugars 0 g
Protein 0 g
Phosphorus 10 mg

ICED MOJITO GREEN TEA

Green tea contains a high amount of polyphenols–powerful antioxidants that may help fight certain diseases. Other nutrients you'll find in green tea include vitamin C, numerous B vitamins, vitamin E, and fluoride (good for strong bones and teeth). Green tea also contains caffeine, so do limit your amount to 1 or 2 cups per day.

---

1 Place the green tea bags into a medium pot. Pour 3 cups of boiling water over the tea bags and steep for 3 minutes. Remove the tea bags and discard. Add the sweetener and stir until dissolved.

2 Add the lime slices and mint to a large pitcher. Pour the steeped tea into the pitcher and add 3 cups of cool water. Carefully add the ice cubes.

TOTAL TIME 13 minutes
PREP TIME 10 minutes
COOK TIME 3 minutes

SERVES 6
SERVING SIZE 1 cup

5 bags green tea

6 cups water, divided

1 1/2 teaspoons zero-calorie stevia sweetener (such as Truvia or Splenda)

4 limes, sliced

1 bunch fresh mint leaves, washed and patted dry

2 cups ice cubes

 To make a perfectly tasty green tea, time the steeping and remove the tea bags after exactly 3 minutes. The longer you let the tea steep, the more bitter it gets.

Choices/Exchanges 0

Calories 10
Calories from Fat 00
Total Fat 0.0 g
Saturated Fat 0.0 g
Trans Fat 0.0 g

Cholesterol 0 mg
Sodium 15 mg
Potassium 50 mg
Total Carbohydrate 3 g
Dietary Fiber 0 g

Sugars 0 g
Added Sugars 0 g
Protein 0 g
Phosphorus 5 mg

TOTAL TIME 8 minutes plus
30 minutes refrigeration time
PREP TIME 5 minutes
COOK TIME 3 minutes

SERVES 8
SERVING SIZE 1 1/4 cups
(12 ounces)

8 cups water, divided

2 teaspoons zero-calorie stevia
  sweetener (such as Truvia or
  Splenda)

2 cups sliced strawberries

1/2 cup freshly squeezed lemon
  juice (about 4 lemons)

STRAWBERRY LEMONADE

The secret to adding sweetness to a beverage without sugar: fruit! This lemonade uses fresh strawberries to add sweetness, which also helps cut the tartness of the fresh lemon juice. The combo is delicious, refreshing, and has less than 5 grams of carbohydrate per 1-cup serving. It's perfect for someone with diabetes.

1 In a small saucepan, bring 1 cup of the water and the sweetener to a boil. Lower the heat and simmer, stirring regularly, until the sweetener is dissolved, about 3 minutes. Set aside to cool.

2 Add the strawberries, lemon juice, cooled water with sweetener, and the remaining 7 cups of water to a large pitcher. Stir to combine. Refrigerate for 30 minutes to allow flavors to combine before serving.

Swap the strawberries with blueberries to make blueberry lemonade.

Choices/Exchanges 0

Calories 15
Calories from Fat 00
Total Fat 0.0 g
Saturated Fat 0.0 g
Trans Fat 0.0 g

Cholesterol 0 mg
Sodium 0 mg
Potassium 80 mg
Total Carbohydrate 4 g
Dietary Fiber 1 g

Sugars 2 g
Added Sugars 0 g
Protein 0 g
Phosphorus 10 mg

TOTAL TIME 10 minutes
PREP TIME 5 minutes
COOK TIME 5 minutes

SERVES 2
SERVING SIZE 1 cup

1 tablespoon unsweetened cocoa powder

1 tablespoon stevia brown sugar blend (such as Truvia)

1/2 cup boiling water

1 1/2 cups nonfat milk

1/8 teaspoon ground cinnamon

1 tablespoon shaved 60% dark chocolate (1/8 ounce)

CINNAMON HOT CHOCOLATE

While dark chocolate does have beneficial components, overindulging can quickly increase your calories, saturated fat, and sugar intake. So how do you make a sugar-controlled killer hot chocolate? Use unsweetened cocoa powder combined with milk and top it off with a pinch of cinnamon and dark chocolate shavings. You won't believe there's only 15 grams of carbohydrate in each serving!

1 In a medium saucepan, combine the cocoa power and brown sugar blend. Add the boiling water and stir until the dry ingredients are dissolved. Add the milk and heat over low heat, stirring regularly until the ingredients are combined. Sprinkle in the cinnamon and stir to incorporate.

2 Pour 1 cup of hot chocolate into each of 2 mugs. Top each with 1/2 tablespoon of the dark chocolate shavings. Serve warm.

A microplane is an inexpensive kitchen tool perfect for grating chocolate, zesting lemons and limes, and grating cheese. Pick one up to use to easily grate the chocolate for this recipe.

Choices/Exchanges 1 Fat-Free Milk

Calories 90	**Cholesterol** 1 mg	**Sugars** 13 g
Calories from Fat 10	**Sodium** 80 mg	**Added Sugars** 4 g
Total Fat 1.0 g	**Potassium** 340 mg	**Protein** 7 g
Saturated Fat 0.7 g	**Total Carbohydrate** 15 g	**Phosphorus** 210 mg
Trans Fat 0.0 g	**Dietary Fiber** 1 g	

SLOW-COOKER SPICED CIDER

Toss the apple cider, orange slices, and spices into your slow cooker in the morning and you'll have your entire house smelling cozy and warm all day long.

TOTAL TIME 4 hours 5 minutes
PREP TIME 5 minutes
COOK TIME 4 hours (on low)

SERVES 20
SERVING SIZE 1/2 cup

1 Place the apple cider, water, orange slices, brown sugar blend, cinnamon sticks, allspice, and cloves into a slow cooker and stir to combine. Seal the cover and cook on low until the flavors combine, at least 4 hours.

2 Place a large strainer over a large pot or heat-proof bowl. Pour the cider through the strainer and discard the spices and orange peels.

3 Serve the cider warm.

1/2 gallon apple cider

2 cups water

2 medium navel oranges, sliced

2 tablespoons stevia brown sugar blend (such as Truvia)

8 cinnamon sticks

1 teaspoon whole allspice

1 teaspoon whole cloves

Get creative by using different citrus fruits like Cara Cara oranges, blood oranges, Valencia oranges, tangerines, or clementines in this recipe.

Choices/Exchanges 1 Fruit

Calories 50
Calories from Fat 0
Total Fat 0.0 g
Saturated Fat 0.0 g
Trans Fat 0.0 g

Cholesterol 0 mg
Sodium 0 mg
Potassium 115 mg
Total Carbohydrate 13 g
Dietary Fiber 0 g

Sugars 11 g
Added Sugars 1 g
Protein 0 g
Phosphorus 10 mg

Chapter 8
Soups & Main Salads

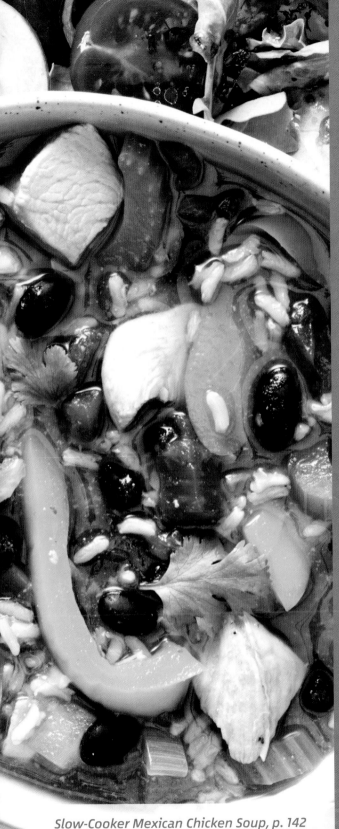

Slow-Cooker Mexican Chicken Soup, p. 142
Simple Side Salad with Balsamic Vinaigrette, p. 188

TOTAL TIME 33 minutes
PREP TIME 15 minutes
COOK TIME 18 minutes

SERVES 8
SERVING SIZE 1 cup

COMPLETE THE PLATE
This recipe: Nonstarchy Vegetable, Lean Protein, Carbohydrate Food
Pair with: A serving of Nonstarchy Vegetables and Lean Protein such as Baked Tilapia with Tomatoes and Onions (page 161), which provides both

1 tablespoon olive or canola oil

1 medium carrot, chopped

1 rib celery, chopped

1 small onion, chopped

1 clove garlic, minced

2 (15-ounce) cans brown lentils, drained and rinsed

1 (32-ounce) carton low-sodium vegetable broth

3 cups water

1 (14-ounce) can no-added-salt diced tomatoes, with the liquid

1/4 cup apple cider vinegar

3 bay leaves

4 cups packed baby spinach

1 teaspoon ground parsley

1 teaspoon ground cumin

1/8 teaspoon ground black pepper

LENTIL-SPINACH SOUP

Lentils—along with beans and peas—are a type of food called a pulse. Pulses provide both healthy protein and complex carbohydrates and are brimming with fiber to help keep you feeling satisfied. The soluble fiber found in pulses has also been shown to help lower cholesterol.

---

1 Heat the olive oil in a large pot over medium heat. When the oil is shimmering, add the carrot, celery, onion, and garlic, and cook until the onion is translucent and the garlic is fragrant, about 3 minutes.

2 Add the lentils and stir to combine. Add the vegetable broth, water, diced tomatoes, apple cider vinegar, and bay leaves. Turn the heat to high and bring to a boil. Then reduce the heat, cover the pot, and simmer over medium-low heat until the lentils are tender, about 15 minutes.

3 Remove and discard the bay leaves. Stir in the spinach, parsley, cumin, and black pepper and cook until the spinach is wilted, about 1 minute. Remove the pot from the heat and allow to cool slightly before serving.

 Swap the baby spinach out for the same amount of chopped kale or Swiss chard. Stir into the soup and allow it to continue cooking for 5–10 minutes or until wilted.

Choices/Exchanges 1 Starch, 1 Nonstarchy Vegetable, 1 Lean Protein

Calories 130
Calories from Fat 20
Total Fat 2.0 g
Saturated Fat 0.3 g
Trans Fat 0.0 g

Cholesterol 0 mg
Sodium 160 mg
Potassium 610 mg
Total Carbohydrate 21 g
Dietary Fiber 8 g

Sugars 5 g
Added Sugars 0 g
Protein 8 g
Phosphorus 200 mg

MUSHROOM SOUP

Mushrooms contain a powerful antioxidant called L-ergothioneine, which has been shown to help protect your kidneys and liver. Shiitake, oyster, and king oyster mushrooms have the highest amounts of this antioxidant, while button, cremini, and portobello mushrooms have lesser amounts but are still considered good sources.

TOTAL TIME 35 minutes plus 10 minutes cooling time
PREP TIME 15 minutes
COOK TIME 20 minutes

SERVES 6
SERVING SIZE 1 cup

COMPLETE THE PLATE
This recipe: Nonstarchy Vegetable
Pair with: A serving of Lean Protein and Carbohydrate Foods such as Slow-Cooker Salmon with Avocado-Grapefruit Salsa (page 166), which provides both

1 In a large saucepan, heat the olive oil over medium heat. Add the onion and cook until the onion is soft and translucent, 3 minutes. Add the garlic and thyme and stir to combine. Add the mushrooms and cook until browned and liquid is released, about 5 minutes. Sprinkle in the flour and toss with the onion mixture for 1 minute. Add the broth, salt, and black pepper, stirring constantly, until combined, then add the tofu and bay leaves.

2 Raise the heat to high and bring the mixture to a boil, then lower the heat to medium low and simmer until the flavors combine, 10 minutes. Remove the pot from the heat and allow to cool for 10 minutes. Remove the bay leaves and discard.

3 Using an immersion blender or tabletop blender, purée the soup until smooth.

1 tablespoon olive oil

1 medium onion, chopped

2 cloves garlic, minced

2 teaspoons dried thyme

1 (10-ounce) container whole white button mushrooms, thinly sliced

3 tablespoons unbleached all-purpose flour

4 cups low-sodium vegetable broth

1/4 teaspoon salt

1/4 teaspoon ground black pepper

12 ounces soft silken tofu, sliced into small chunks

2 bay leaves

Toby Tip

Leftover tofu can be refrigerated for up to 1 week. Cover the tofu with cool water and store it in a resealable container or the tub it came in with plastic wrap. Change the water daily to keep the tofu fresh and moist.

Choices/Exchanges 2 Nonstarchy Vegetable, 1 Fat

Calories 100
Calories from Fat 35
Total Fat 4.0 g
Saturated Fat 0.6 g
Trans Fat 0.0 g

Cholesterol 0 mg
Sodium 190 mg
Potassium 390 mg
Total Carbohydrate 10 g
Dietary Fiber 2 g

Sugars 4 g
Added Sugars 0 g
Protein 5 g
Phosphorus 140 mg

TOTAL TIME 5 hours 15 minutes
PREP TIME 15 minutes
COOK TIME 5 hours (on high)

SERVES 8
SERVING SIZE 1 1/2 cups

COMPLETE THE PLATE
This recipe: Nonstarchy Vegetable, Lean Protein, Carbohydrate Food
Pair with: A serving of Nonstarchy Vegetables such as Charred Cabbage with Cilantro-Lime Sauce (page 199)

1 pound skinless, boneless chicken breasts, cut into 1-inch cubes

2 ribs celery, chopped

1 medium onion, chopped

1 yellow or red bell pepper, sliced into thin strips

2 (14.5-ounce) cans no-added-salt diced tomatoes, with the liquid

1 (32-ounce) container low-sodium chicken broth

1 (15-ounce) can low-sodium black beans, drained and rinsed

1 (4-ounce) can diced green chilies

1 cup water

1 cup brown rice

1 teaspoon garlic powder

1 teaspoon ground cumin

1 teaspoon ground coriander

1/2 teaspoon salt

1/4 teaspoon ground black pepper

2 teaspoons fresh lime juice

SLOW-COOKER MEXICAN CHICKEN SOUP

This warming meal made with a combination of rice, beans, chicken, vegetables, and Mexican-inspired spices is perfect to make ahead of time and freeze. Let your slow cooker run on Sunday and then freeze half the soup for later and enjoy the other half during the week.

---

1 Place the chicken cubes, celery, onion, bell peppers, diced tomatoes, chicken broth, black beans, chilies, water, rice, garlic powder, cumin, coriander, salt, and black pepper in a slow cooker. Stir to combine all the ingredients. Place the lid on the slow cooker and seal. Cook on high for 5 hours or low for 8 hours.

2 Carefully remove the lid of the slow cooker and stir in the lime juice before serving. Serve warm.

 Top this soup with nonfat plain Greek yogurt or salsa.

Choices/Exchanges 1 1/2 Starch, 2 Nonstarchy Vegetable, 2 Lean Protein

Calories 240	**Cholesterol** 35 mg	**Sugars** 5 g
Calories from Fat 20	**Sodium** 360 mg	**Added Sugars** 0 g
Total Fat 2.0 g	**Potassium** 770 mg	**Protein** 22 g
Saturated Fat 0.4 g	**Total Carbohydrate** 35 g	**Phosphorus** 305 mg
Trans Fat 0.0 g	**Dietary Fiber** 5 g	

TOMATO, SHRIMP, AND ORZO SOUP

Orzo, which translates to "barley" in Italian, is a versatile rice-shaped pasta that is used in both Italy and the U.S. for main courses and side salads. It is also perfect for soups. Orzo is made from semolina and takes 9-10 minutes to cook.

1 Heat the olive oil in a large pot over medium heat. When the oil is shimmering, add the celery, garlic, onion, and carrots and cook until the onion is translucent, about 4 minutes. Add the vegetable broth, crushed tomatoes, and orzo and bring the mixture to a boil. Lower the heat to medium low and simmer, covered, until the orzo softens, about 5 minutes.

2 Add the shrimp and bring the mixture back to a boil. Lower the heat to medium low and simmer, covered, until the shrimp is cooked through, about 5-7 minutes. Add the salt, black pepper, and basil and stir to combine.

Swap out the orzo for the same amount of ditalini pasta or pastina. You can also choose to swap out the orzo for about 1 cup of cooked brown rice, farro, buckwheat, or barley.

TOTAL TIME 30 minutes
PREP TIME 15 minutes
COOK TIME 15 minutes

SERVES 8
SERVING SIZE 1 1/3 cups

COMPLETE THE PLATE
This recipe: Nonstarchy Vegetable, Lean Protein, Carbohydrate Food
Pair with: A serving of Carbohydrate Foods such as a small piece of crusty, whole-grain bread

2 tablespoons olive oil

2 ribs celery, chopped

2 cloves garlic, minced

1 medium onion, chopped

1 medium carrot, chopped

6 cups low-sodium vegetable broth

1 (28-ounce) can crushed tomatoes

4 ounces orzo

1 1/2 pounds peeled and deveined raw large shrimp (47–53 count), tails cut off*

1/4 teaspoon salt

1/8 teaspoon ground black pepper

1/4 cup fresh basil, cut into ribbons

*If possible, use fresh, never frozen shrimp that are free of preservatives (for example, shrimp that have not been treated with salt or STPP [sodium tripolyphosphate]).

Choices/Exchanges 1/2 Starch, 3 Nonstarchy Vegetable, 1 Lean Protein, 1/2 Fat

Calories 190
Calories from Fat 35
Total Fat 4.0 g
Saturated Fat 0.6 g
Trans Fat 0.0 g

Cholesterol 100 mg
Sodium 380 mg
Potassium 660 mg
Total Carbohydrate 23 g
Dietary Fiber 4 g

Sugars 8 g
Added Sugars 0 g
Protein 17 g
Phosphorus 260 mg

TOTAL TIME 1 hour 30 minutes
PREP TIME 15 minutes
COOK TIME 1 hour 15 minutes

SERVES 6
SERVING SIZE 2 cups

COMPLETE THE PLATE

This recipe: Nonstarchy Vegetable, Lean Protein, Carbohydrate Food
Pair with: This recipe is a complete meal

3 tablespoons olive oil, divided

1 1/2 pounds beef chuck roast, trimmed of fat and cut into 2-inch cubes

1 large onion, chopped

1 clove garlic, minced

2 ribs celery, chopped

1 medium carrot, chopped

1 (32-ounce) container low-sodium beef broth

2 cups water

1 (14.5-ounce) can no-added-salt diced tomatoes

3/4 cup barley

1 medium sweet potato, cut into 1/2-inch chunks

2 bay leaves

1/2 teaspoon salt

1/2 teaspoon ground black pepper

BEEF BARLEY SOUP WITH SWEET POTATOES

This soup pairs hearty beef and barley with sweet potatoes. This starchy vegetable is brimming with fiber and vitamin A, which is important for vision health. Sweet potatoes are a good substitute for traditional potatoes because they are a lower-glycemic food.

1 Heat 2 tablespoons of the olive oil in a large pot over medium heat. When the oil is shimmering, add the beef cubes and cook until browned on all sides, about 8 minutes. Using a slotted spoon, remove the beef and place it on a clean plate.

2 Heat the remaining 1 tablespoon of olive oil over medium heat. Add the onion, garlic, celery, and carrots and cook until the onion is soft and translucent, about 4 minutes. Add the beef broth, water, diced tomatoes, barley, sweet potatoes, bay leaves, and cooked beef and bring the mixture to a boil. Reduce the heat to medium low and simmer, covered, until the barley is cooked and the flavors have combined, 1 hour. Add the salt and black pepper and stir to combine. Remove the bay leaves and discard before serving.

 Substitute barley with the same amount of farro, freekeh, or brown rice.

Choices/Exchanges 2 Starch, 2 Nonstarchy Vegetable, 3 Lean Protein, 1 Fat

Calories 380
Calories from Fat 110
Total Fat 12.0 g
Saturated Fat 3.0 g
Trans Fat 0.2 g

Cholesterol 60 mg
Sodium 400 mg
Potassium 910 mg
Total Carbohydrate 38 g
Dietary Fiber 8 g

Sugars 9 g
Added Sugars 0 g
Protein 29 g
Phosphorus 325 mg

TURKEY VEGETABLE SOUP WITH QUINOA

Turkey isn't just for Thanksgiving! A 3-ounce serving of skinless, boneless turkey breast provides 26 grams of protein, 1 gram of fat, and 0 grams of saturated fat. Try using turkey breast in place of chicken breast in poultry dishes.

TOTAL TIME 47 minutes
PREP TIME 15 minutes
COOK TIME 32 minutes

SERVES 6
SERVING SIZE 1 2/3 cups

COMPLETE THE PLATE
This recipe: Nonstarchy Vegetable, Lean Protein, Carbohydrate Food
Pair with: This recipe is a complete meal

1 In a large pot, heat 2 tablespoons of the olive oil over medium heat. Add the cubed turkey or chicken and brown on all sides, about 8 minutes. Using a slotted spoon, remove the turkey cubes and place them on a plate.

2 Heat the remaining 2 tablespoons of olive oil in the same pot over medium heat. Add the onion, garlic, celery, and carrots and cook until the onion is soft and translucent, about 4 minutes. Add the broth, water, parsnips, turnips, quinoa, cooked turkey, parsley, thyme, salt, and black pepper and bring the mixture to a boil. Lower the heat to medium low and simmer, covered, until the quinoa is cooked and the flavor combine, 20 minutes.

1/4 cup olive oil, divided

1 pound skinless, boneless turkey or chicken breasts, cut into 1-inch cubes

1 medium onion, chopped

1 clove garlic, minced

3 ribs celery, diced

3 medium carrots, diced

1 (32-ounce) container low-sodium chicken or vegetable broth

4 cups water

2 medium parsnips, diced

1 medium turnip, diced

1 cup quinoa

1 teaspoon dried parsley

1 teaspoon dried thyme

1/2 teaspoon salt

1/4 teaspoon ground black pepper

Ask your butcher to cut the exact amount of turkey breast you need for a recipe like this one. If a larger portion is all that is available, slice it into 1-pound portions and freeze the portions in individual resealable bags for later.

Choices/Exchanges 1 1/2 Starch, 2 Nonstarchy Vegetable, 3 Lean Protein, 1 Fat

Calories 350	**Cholesterol** 50 mg	**Sugars** 7 g
Calories from Fat 110	**Sodium** 410 mg	**Added Sugars** 0 g
Total Fat 12.0 g	**Potassium** 810 mg	**Protein** 27 g
Saturated Fat 1.9 g	**Total Carbohydrate** 32 g	**Phosphorus** 370 mg
Trans Fat 0.0 g	**Dietary Fiber** 5 g	

TOTAL TIME 1 hour 15 minutes
PREP TIME 15 minutes
COOK TIME 1 hour

SERVES 4
SERVING SIZE 2 cups

COMPLETE THE PLATE
This recipe: Nonstarchy Vegetable, Lean Protein, Carbohydrate Food
Pair with: This recipe is a complete meal

1/2 cup barley

1 3/4 cups low-sodium chicken broth

3 tablespoons olive oil, divided

2 cloves garlic, minced

1 pound skinless, boneless chicken tenders, tendons removed

2 teaspoons dried rosemary

1/4 teaspoon salt

1 (8-ounce) container shiitake mushrooms, thinly sliced

1 (8-ounce) container cremini mushrooms, thinly sliced

1 cup Brussels sprouts, trimmed and halved (4 ounces)

3 tablespoons water, divided

2 tablespoons balsamic vinegar

2 cups spring mix greens

BARLEY SALAD WITH WARMED CHICKEN, MUSHROOMS, AND BRUSSELS SPROUTS

Fun fact: Egyptians buried mummies with necklaces made of barley. Barley is one of the oldest cultivated grains. It's a highly adaptable crop that can be grown north of the Arctic Circle and as far south as Ethiopia. Barley has a tough hull, which is difficult to remove without losing some of the nutrients of the barley. To make sure you're getting the most nutrients when purchasing barley, look for whole barley, hulled barley, or hull-less barley.

1 In a medium saucepan, bring the barley and chicken broth to a boil. Lower the heat to medium low and simmer, covered, until the barley is tender and most of the liquid has been absorbed, 40 minutes. Set aside to cool.

2 Heat 2 tablespoons of the olive oil in a large sauce pan over medium heat. When the oil is shimmering, add the garlic and cook until it is fragrant, 30 seconds to 1 minute. Add the chicken and sprinkle with the rosemary and salt. Cook the chicken for 4 minutes on each side, until the chicken reaches an internal temperature of 165°F. Remove the chicken to a clean mixing bowl.

3 In the same pan, heat the remaining 1 tablespoon of olive oil over medium heat. Add the mushrooms and cook until browned, about 5 minutes. Using a slotted spoon, remove the mushrooms and place with the chicken in the mixing bowl.

Choices/Exchanges 1 Starch, 2 Nonstarchy Vegetable, 4 Lean Protein, 1 1/2 Fat

Calories 370	**Cholesterol** 65 mg	**Sugars** 4 g
Calories from Fat 130	**Sodium** 290 mg	**Added Sugars** 0 g
Total Fat 14.0 g	**Potassium** 960 mg	**Protein** 33 g
Saturated Fat 2.4 g	**Total Carbohydrate** 28 g	**Phosphorus** 420 mg
Trans Fat 0.0 g	**Dietary Fiber** 7 g	

Cremini mushrooms are sometimes also called baby bella or baby portobello mushrooms.

4 Add the Brussels sprouts into the hot pan and toss in the juices for 1 minute. Add 2 tablespoons of the water and cover the pan. Cook the Brussels sprouts until softened, about 5 minutes, then remove the lid. Add the balsamic vinegar and the remaining 1 tablespoon of water to the pan and toss to combine. Add the mushrooms and chicken to the pan and toss. Remove the pan from the heat.

5 Place the mixed greens in a large salad bowl, top with the barley, and spoon over the chicken and mushroom mixture.

TOTAL TIME 33 minutes
PREP TIME 15 minutes
COOK TIME 18 minutes

SERVES 4
SERVING SIZE 2 3/4 cups

COMPLETE THE PLATE
This recipe: Nonstarchy Vegetable, Lean Protein, Carbohydrate Food
Pair with: A serving of Nonstarchy Vegetables such as Grilled Eggplant (page 193)

1 1/2 cups low-sodium chicken broth

1/2 cup whole-wheat couscous

1 pound skinless, boneless chicken tenders

1/8 teaspoon salt

1/8 teaspoon ground black pepper

2 tablespoons olive oil

5 cups baby arugula

1 medium gala apple, quartered and thinly sliced

2 ribs celery, thinly sliced

1/2 cup red onion, thinly sliced

ARUGULA, COUSCOUS, AND APPLE SALAD TOPPED WITH CHICKEN

Couscous is a combination of semolina wheat and water and tastes like pasta. Small Moroccan couscous is about three times the size of cornmeal. Whole-wheat couscous is more nutritious than the regular variety and contains about 5-6 grams of fiber per serving—so it may help you meet the recommended daily intake for fiber.

1 In a medium saucepan, bring the chicken broth to a boil. Add the couscous into the boiling broth, cover the saucepan, and let the saucepan stand off the heat for 5-10 minutes. Once the broth has been absorbed, fluff the couscous with a fork and set it aside to cool.

2 Sprinkle the chicken with salt and black pepper. Heat the olive oil in a medium skillet over medium heat. When the oil is shimmering, add the chicken and cook for 4 minutes on each side, until the chicken reaches an internal temperature of 165°F. Remove the chicken from the skillet and set aside to cool.

3 Add the arugula, apple, celery, and onion to a large mixing bowl and top with the couscous and chicken.

 Try topping this salad with my Pesto Sauce (page 217) or store-bought pesto. You can also toss the cooked chicken in pesto before placing over the salad.

Choices/Exchanges 1 Starch, 1/2 Fruit, 1 Nonstarchy Vegetable, 4 Lean Protein

Calories 310
Calories from Fat 90
Total Fat 10.0 g
Saturated Fat 1.8 g
Trans Fat 0.0 g

Cholesterol 65 mg
Sodium 210 mg
Potassium 530 mg
Total Carbohydrate 25 g
Dietary Fiber 4 g

Sugars 6 g
Added Sugars 0 g
Protein 30 g
Phosphorus 265 mg

SALMON AND WHITE BEAN SALAD WITH FENNEL AND ORANGE

Fennel is a member of the parsley family. It has an oddly shaped layered bulb with multiple bright green stalks and feathery leaves called fronds. This vegetable tastes like anise, or black licorice, especially when raw. To help balance the anise flavor of this salad, sweet mandarin oranges are tossed into the mix.

TOTAL TIME 17 minutes
PREP TIME 15 minutes
COOK TIME 2 minutes

SERVES 4
SERVING SIZE 2 cups

COMPLETE THE PLATE
This recipe: Nonstarchy Vegetable, Lean Protein, Carbohydrate Food
Pair with: A serving of Nonstarchy Vegetables such as Sautéed Mushroom Medley (page 198)

1 1/2 teaspoons fennel seeds

3 black peppercorns

1 pound salmon fillets

2 cups baby spinach, washed and patted dry

1 (15-ounce) can low-sodium cannellini beans, drained and rinsed

1 fennel bulb, washed, trimmed, and thinly sliced

1/2 red onion, thinly sliced

1 (15-ounce) can mandarin oranges packed in water, drained

1 In a medium saucepan or high-sided skillet, bring 8 cups of water to a boil over high heat. Add the fennel seeds and peppercorns. Add the salmon, making sure it's completely covered by the water, and bring the water back to a boil. Cook the salmon for 2 minutes, then turn off the heat and cover the pan. Let the salmon poach for 20 minutes. Carefully remove the fish from the pan and let it cool. Discard the liquid.

2 Add the spinach, beans, fennel, and red onion to a large bowl and toss to combine. Gently fold in the mandarin oranges.

3 Slice the salmon into pieces and remove the skin. Top the salad with the pieces of salmon.

Serve this salad with Lighter Italian Dressing (page 222).

Choices/Exchanges 1 Starch, 1/2 Fruit, 1 Nonstarchy Vegetable, 4 Lean Protein

Calories 310
Calories from Fat 60
Total Fat 7.0 g
Saturated Fat 1.5 g
Trans Fat 0.0 g

Cholesterol 50 mg
Sodium 85 mg
Potassium 1080 mg
Total Carbohydrate 30 g
Dietary Fiber 8 g

Sugars 10 g
Added Sugars 0 g
Protein 32 g
Phosphorus 410 mg

TURKEY, WALNUT, AND POMEGRANATE SALAD

How do you get your hands on a thick chunk of low-sodium turkey breast? You'll notice at the grocery store that turkey breast is sold in slices, not chunks. But it's fun to cut your turkey in chunks, especially for salads or hors d'oeuvres. So, head over to your deli counter and ask them to cut a 10-ounce chunk of turkey breast for you (or whatever size your recipe calls for). The ladies and gentlemen behind the counter are always happy to accommodate the request.

_____

1 Heat the walnuts in a small skillet over medium-low heat until fragrant and browned, about 3 minutes. Remove the walnuts from the skillet and place on a clean plate or bowl; set aside to cool.

2 Add the spinach, cubed turkey, red onion, pears, pomegranate arils, and toasted walnuts to a large bowl. Top with the goat cheese.

TOTAL TIME 15 minutes
PREP TIME 12 minutes
COOK TIME 3 minutes

SERVES 4
SERVING SIZE 2 cups

COMPLETE THE PLATE
This recipe: Lean Protein, Carbohydrate Food
Pair with: A serving of Nonstarchy Vegetables such as Grilled Eggplant (page 193)

1/2 cup raw walnuts, roughly chopped

2 cups baby spinach, rinsed and patted dry

10 ounces lower-sodium deli turkey breast, cut into 1/2-inch cubes

1/2 red onion, thinly sliced

2 medium pears, quartered and thinly sliced

1/2 cup pomegranate arils

2 ounces crumbled goat cheese (1/2 cup)

Serve this salad with Pomegranate Vinaigrette (page 223).

Choices/Exchanges 1 Fruit, 1/2 Carbohydrate, 3 Lean Protein, 1 1/2 Fat

Calories 290
Calories from Fat 130
Total Fat 14.0 g
Saturated Fat 3.3 g
Trans Fat 0.0 g

Cholesterol 45 mg
Sodium 440 mg
Potassium 530 mg
Total Carbohydrate 22 g
Dietary Fiber 5 g

Sugars 13 g
Added Sugars 0 g
Protein 21 g
Phosphorus 275 mg

TOTAL TIME 45 minutes
PREP TIME 15 minutes
COOK TIME 30 minutes

SERVES 4
SERVING SIZE 2 cups

COMPLETE THE PLATE
This recipe: Nonstarchy
Vegetable, Lean Protein,
Carbohydrate Food
Pair with: A serving of
Nonstarchy Vegetables such
as Roasted Beets with Lemon
and Dill (page 201) and
Carbohydrate Foods such
as a whole-wheat pita

1 1/3 cups low-sodium
vegetable broth

1/2 cup farro

2 cups chopped romaine
lettuce

1 cucumber, halved lengthwise
and thinly sliced

2 plum tomatoes, halved
lengthwise and thinly sliced

1 red bell pepper, cut into
1/2-inch strips

12 ounces canned chunk light
tuna packed in water, drained

1 ounce crumbled feta cheese
(1/4 cup)

GREEK-STYLE SALAD WITH TUNA AND FARRO

Farro is an Italian-born grain that dates back to ancient Rome. It has a similar taste to brown rice, but is slightly nuttier with a pleasant, chewy texture. Farro, like other grains, is cooked in water or broth and is ready in about 30 minutes. If you aren't ready to give farro a try, you can use brown rice in this recipe instead.

1 In a medium saucepan, bring the broth and farro to a boil. Reduce the heat to medium low, cover, and cook until the farro is tender, about 30 minutes. Set aside to cool.

2 Add the lettuce, cucumber, tomatoes, and bell pepper to a large bowl. Top with the cooled farro, tuna, and crumbled feta cheese.

Serve this salad with Lemon-Parsley Vinaigrette (page 224) or Lite Balsamic Vinaigrette (page 221).

Choices/Exchanges 1 Starch, 2 Nonstarchy Vegetable, 2 Lean Protein

Calories 210	**Cholesterol** 30 mg	**Sugars** 5 g
Calories from Fat 40	**Sodium** 360 mg	**Added Sugars** 0 g
Total Fat 4.5 g	**Potassium** 580 mg	**Protein** 19 g
Saturated Fat 1.2 g	**Total Carbohydrate** 26 g	**Phosphorus** 310 mg
Trans Fat 0.1 g	**Dietary Fiber** 6 g	

CAPRESE QUINOA SALAD WITH STEAK

Technically a seed, quinoa has such similar characteristics and preparation methods to a grain that it is grouped as such. It has a mild, nutty flavor and a pleasing chewy texture. Although the dry quinoa beads look rather tiny, they expand to four times their size when cooked!

1 In a medium pot, bring the quinoa and vegetable broth to a boil over high heat. Reduce the heat to medium low, cover the pot, and simmer until the broth has been absorbed and the quinoa is soft and fluffy, about 15 minutes. Remove the pot from the heat and use a fork to fluff the quinoa. Set aside to cool.

2 In a medium bowl, whisk together the extra-virgin olive oil, garlic, thyme, salt, and black pepper. Add the steak and toss to evenly coat. Preheat a grill pan or grill over high heat. Coat the grill pan with nonstick cooking spray. (If using a grill, brush with 1 tablespoon of olive oil or use nonflammable cooking spray.) When the spray or oil is shimmering, place the steak on the grill and discard the excess rub. Grill until the steak reaches an internal temperature of 145°F, 3–5 minutes on each side. Transfer the steak to a plate and let rest for 10 minutes before slicing into 1-inch strips.

3 Add the cooled quinoa, tomatoes, scallions, and mozzarella to a large bowl and toss to combine. Top with the steak strips.

> (Toby Tip) *Serve this salad with Red Wine Vinaigrette (page 225) or Lite Balsamic Vinaigrette (page 221).*

TOTAL TIME 40 minutes
PREP TIME 15 minutes
COOK TIME 25 minutes

SERVES 4
SERVING SIZE 1 3/4 cups

COMPLETE THE PLATE
This recipe: Nonstarchy Vegetable, Lean Protein, Carbohydrate Food
Pair with: A serving of Nonstarchy Vegetables such as Charred Cabbage with Cilantro-Lime Sauce (page 199)

3/4 cup quinoa

1 1/2 cups low-sodium vegetable broth

2 tablespoons olive oil

2 cloves garlic, minced

1 tablespoon fresh thyme

1/8 teaspoon salt

1/8 teaspoon ground black pepper

1 pound beef loin or strip steak, trimmed of fat

Nonstick cooking spray

3 cups grape tomatoes, halved

3 scallions (green and white parts), thinly sliced

1 1/2 ounces part-skim mozzarella cheese, cut into 1-inch cubes

Choices/Exchanges 1 1/2 Starch, 1 Nonstarchy Vegetable, 4 Lean Protein, 1 Fat

Calories 360
Calories from Fat 120
Total Fat 13.0 g
Saturated Fat 3.6 g
Trans Fat 0.2 g

Cholesterol 50 mg
Sodium 220 mg
Potassium 830 mg
Total Carbohydrate 29 g
Dietary Fiber 4 g

Sugars 6 g
Added Sugars 0 g
Protein 31 g
Phosphorus 435 mg

Chapter 9
Main Dishes

*Grilled Chicken and
Vegetable Skewers, p. 174*
Kale Apple Slaw, p. 192

TOTAL TIME 27 minutes
PREP TIME 15 minutes
COOK TIME 12 minutes

SERVES 4
SERVING SIZE 1 1/4 cups

COMPLETE THE PLATE
This recipe: Nonstarchy Vegetable, Medium-Fat Protein, Carbohydrate Food
Pair with: A serving of Nonstarchy Vegetables such as Weeknight Vegetable Stir-Fry (page 202) and Carbohydrate Foods such as Brown Rice with Scallions (page 206)

3 tablespoons olive oil, divided

2 tablespoons reduced-sodium soy sauce

1 tablespoon freshly squeezed lemon juice

2 cloves garlic, minced

1 teaspoon dried thyme

1/2 teaspoon stevia brown sugar blend (such as Truvia)

1/8 teaspoon red pepper flakes

1 tablespoon cornstarch

1 yellow bell pepper, cut into 1-inch strips

5 cups chopped Napa cabbage (about 1/2 cabbage)

12 ounces extra-firm tofu, diced into 1-inch chunks

SKILLET TOFU AND CABBAGE

Cabbage, a cruciferous vegetable in the same family as broccoli, cauliflower, and mustard greens, contains isothiocyanates, powerful plant chemicals with potential cancer-fighting benefits. A 1-cup serving of this delicious vegetable has more than 50% of the recommended daily intake of vitamin C and more than 80% of the recommended daily intake of vitamin K.

---

1 In a medium bowl, whisk together 2 tablespoons of the olive oil, the soy sauce, lemon juice, garlic, thyme, brown sugar blend, and red pepper flakes. Add the cornstarch and whisk until incorporated. Set aside.

2 Heat the remaining 1 tablespoon of olive oil in a medium skillet over medium heat. When the oil is shimmering, add the bell pepper and cabbage and cook until slightly softened, 5 minutes. Add the tofu and cook until warmed through, an additional 4 minutes. Add the sauce and cook until the sauce slightly thickens, about 2 minutes.

 Swap out the cabbage for other low-carbohydrate vegetables like kale, spinach, broccoli, or cauliflower.

Choices/Exchanges 1/2 Carbohydrate, 1 Nonstarchy Vegetable, 1 Medium-Fat Protein, 1 1/2 Fat

Calories 210	**Cholesterol** 0 mg	**Sugars** 4 g
Calories from Fat 140	**Sodium** 290 mg	**Added Sugars** 0 g
Total Fat 15.0 g	**Potassium** 660 mg	**Protein** 11 g
Saturated Fat 1.9 g	**Total Carbohydrate** 11 g	**Phosphorus** 165 mg
Trans Fat 0.0 g	**Dietary Fiber** 2 g	

SLOW-COOKER RATATOUILLE WITH WHITE BEANS

Ratatouille is a Disney movie, but it's also a well-known vegetable stew that originated in Provence, a region in France known for its bounty of fresh vegetables. This diabetes-friendly version of the classic dish incorporates white beans to up the protein. While you may find that it's traditionally cooked on a stovetop, this modern-day version allows you to use a slow cooker–so you can press a button and go about your day.

1 Brush the inside of the slow cooker with the olive oil. Add the remaining ingredients to the slow cooker; stir to combine.

2 Cover and cook on low for 6 hours, until the vegetables and beans soften. Remove and discard the bay leaves before serving.

Many carbohydrate foods pair nicely with this ratatouille, including brown rice, quinoa, farro, or a small whole-wheat roll.

TOTAL TIME 6 hours 15 minutes
PREP TIME 15 minutes
COOK TIME 6 hours (on low)

SERVES 6
SERVING SIZE 1 1/2 cups

COMPLETE THE PLATE
This recipe: Nonstarchy Vegetable, Lean Protein, Carbohydrate Food
Pair with: A serving of Lean Protein such as a hard-boiled egg and Carbohydrate Foods such as a small piece of crusty, whole-grain bread

1 tablespoon olive oil

2 (15-ounce) cans low-sodium great northern or cannellini beans, drained and rinsed

1 (14.5-ounce) can no-added-salt fire-roasted diced tomatoes

1 cup low-sodium tomato sauce

1 1/2 cups low-sodium vegetable broth

1/2 medium eggplant, diced with peel on

2 cups shredded green cabbage

1 red bell pepper, sliced into 1-inch strips

3 cloves garlic, minced

2 tablespoons apple cider vinegar

1 teaspoon dried oregano

3 bay leaves

1/4 plus 1/8 teaspoon salt

1/4 teaspoon ground black pepper

Choices/Exchanges 1 Starch, 3 Nonstarchy Vegetable, 1 Lean Protein

Calories 180
Calories from Fat 30
Total Fat 3.5 g
Saturated Fat 0.5 g
Trans Fat 0.0 g

Cholesterol 0 mg
Sodium 230 mg
Potassium 970 mg
Total Carbohydrate 30 g
Dietary Fiber 10 g

Sugars 8 g
Added Sugars 0 g
Protein 10 g
Phosphorus 225 mg

TOTAL TIME 15 minutes plus 10 minutes cooling time
PREP TIME 3 minutes
COOK TIME 12 minutes

SERVES 4
SERVING SIZE 1 (5-ounce) piece salmon and 2 tablespoons sauce

COMPLETE THE PLATE
This recipe: Lean Protein
Pair with: A serving of Nonstarchy Vegetables such as Chopped Romaine Salad (page 190) and Carbohydrate Foods such as Red Beans and Rice (page 205)

Nonstick cooking spray

4 (5-ounce) salmon fillets

1/2 cup Chimichurri Sauce (page 219)

ROASTED SALMON WITH CHIMICHURRI SAUCE

Roasted salmon is a quick, delicious dish you can make on any busy weeknight. Make the chimichurri sauce the night before—it only takes 5 minutes!

1 Preheat the oven to 400°F.

2 Coat a medium ovenproof pan with nonstick cooking spray and heat over medium heat. When the pan is hot, add the salmon and cook for 1 minute, then turn and cook the other side for an additional minute.

3 Using an oven mitt, carefully place the pan into the oven and continue cooking the salmon until a thermometer inserted into the thickest part of a fillet reads 145°F, 10 minutes.

4 Carefully remove the hot pan and place on the stove to cool for about 10 minutes. Serve each piece of salmon with 2 tablespoons of the Chimichurri Sauce.

 If you don't see salmon fillets in the seafood section of the grocery store, ask your fishmonger to make some for you. They'll take the skin off beautifully and slice the salmon into fillets of whatever size you choose.

Choices/Exchanges 4 Lean Protein, 2 Fat

Calories 280	**Cholesterol** 75 mg	**Sugars** 0 g
Calories from Fat 150	**Sodium** 240 mg	**Added Sugars** 0 g
Total Fat 17.0 g	**Potassium** 580 mg	**Protein** 28 g
Saturated Fat 3.3 g	**Total Carbohydrate** 2 g	**Phosphorus** 375 mg
Trans Fat 0.0 g	**Dietary Fiber** 1 g	

BOILED SHRIMP WITH GREEN GODDESS SAUCE

Shrimp is one of the lowest-calorie protein sources around. Three ounces of cooked shrimp contains about 83 calories, 1 gram of fat, and 18 grams of protein. It's an excellent source of selenium and a source of vitamins B-12 and D. Shrimp also provides a healthy dose of omega-3 fatty acids. Many of my clients have voiced concern about the cholesterol found in shrimp; however, research has shown that saturated fat has a greater impact on raising your "bad" (LDL) cholesterol. In the U.S. Department of Agriculture's 2015-2020 Dietary Guidelines for Americans, the guidelines for cholesterol were removed for good.

1 Fill a large saucepan three-quarters full with water. Add the sliced lemon, bay leaf, peppercorns, and salt and bring to a boil. Add the shrimp and bring the water back to a boil. Immediately turn off the heat, cover the saucepan, and move the pot off the burner. Allow the shrimp to sit for 10 minutes until they are pink and cooked through.

2 Drain the shrimp and discard the lemon slices, bay leaf, and peppercorns.

3 Spoon 2 tablespoons of Green Goddess Sauce on each of 4 plates and top with 4 ounces of cooked shrimp.

Toby Tip *Fresh shrimp can last in your refrigerator for 1-2 days, so be mindful of the timing when you buy shrimp and when you'll cook it.*

TOTAL TIME 6 minutes
PREP TIME 5 minutes
COOK TIME 1 minute

SERVES 4
SERVING SIZE 4 ounces shrimp (about 7) and 2 tablespoons sauce

COMPLETE THE PLATE
This recipe: Lean Protein
Pair with: A serving of Nonstarchy Vegetables such as Collard Greens and Yellow Squash (page 194) and Carbohydrate Foods such as Brown Rice with Scallions (page 206)

1 lemon, sliced

1 bay leaf

4 black peppercorns

1/2 teaspoon salt

1 pound raw extra-large shrimp (26-30 count), peeled, deveined, and tails cut off*

1/2 cup Green Goddess Sauce (page 220)

*If possible, use fresh, never frozen shrimp that are free of preservatives (for example, shrimp that have not been treated with salt or STPP [sodium tripolyphosphate]).

Choices/Exchanges 3 Lean Protein

Calories 120
Calories from Fat 30
Total Fat 3.5 g
Saturated Fat 0.4 g
Trans Fat 0.0 g

Cholesterol 140 mg
Sodium 240 mg
Potassium 250 mg
Total Carbohydrate 4 g
Dietary Fiber 0 g

Sugars 1 g
Added Sugars 0 g
Protein 19 g
Phosphorus 200 mg

TOTAL TIME 25 minutes
PREP TIME 10 minutes
COOK TIME 15 minutes

SERVES 4
SERVING SIZE 1 piece cod and
1 tablespoon relish

COMPLETE THE PLATE
This recipe: Lean Protein
Pair with: A serving of
Nonstarchy Vegetables
such as Simple Side Salad
with Balsamic Vinaigrette
(page 188) and Carbohydrate
Foods such as Red Beans
and Rice (page 205)

Nonstick cooking spray

2 tablespoons light
   mayonnaise

4 (5-ounce) cod fillets

1 1/2 cups fresh parsley,
   finely chopped

1 clove garlic, minced

Juice of 1 lime

1 tablespoon olive oil

1/2 teaspoon kosher salt

COD WITH PARSLEY-LIME RELISH

Besides being an excellent source of protein, cod provides an array of nutrients including vitamins B-6 and B-12, selenium, potassium, and phosphorus. It's an easy-to-cook, light-tasting fish that goes with many sauces found in this cookbook.

---

1 Preheat the oven to 400°F. Coat a baking sheet with nonstick cooking spray.

2 Brush the mayonnaise over the top of the fish fillets and place on the baking sheet. Bake in the oven until a thermometer inserted into the fish reads 145°F, about 13–15 minutes.

3 Add the parsley, garlic, lime juice, olive oil, and salt to a small bowl; stir to combine.

4 Place 1 piece of cod onto each of 4 dinner plates. Top with 1 tablespoon of the relish. Serve immediately.

You can also serve the Parsley-Lime Relish with the Roasted Salmon (page 158) or the Boiled Shrimp (page 159).

Choices/Exchanges 4 Lean Protein

Calories 170
Calories from Fat 50
Total Fat 6.0 g
Saturated Fat 0.8 g
Trans Fat 0.0 g

Cholesterol 60 mg
Sodium 400 mg
Potassium 410 mg
Total Carbohydrate 3 g
Dietary Fiber 1 g

Sugars 1 g
Added Sugars 0 g
Protein 26 g
Phosphorus 170 mg

BAKED TILAPIA WITH TOMATOES AND ONIONS

This sheet pan dinner can be whipped up in about 30 minutes—perfect for a busy weeknight! Prep the vegetables in the morning before you head to work or the night before and you can shave off 10 minutes of the prep time.

1 Preheat the oven to 400°F. Coat a baking sheet with nonstick cooking spray.

2 Place the tomatoes and onions in a single layer toward the end of the baking sheet and cook in the oven for 5 minutes.

3 Remove the baking sheet from the oven and place the lemon slices in a single layer on the empty area on the baking sheet. Lay the fish over the lemon slices and sprinkle the entire pan, fish and vegetables, with basil, salt, and black pepper.

4 Return the baking sheet to the oven and cook until the fish is opaque and a thermometer inserted into the fish reads 145°F, 13 minutes. Remove the baking sheet from the pan and set aside for 10 minutes to cool.

5 Toss the vegetables with the juices on the sheet pan and serve over the fish.

TOTAL TIME 33 minutes plus 10 minutes cooling time
PREP TIME 15 minutes
COOK TIME 18 minutes

SERVES 4
SERVING SIZE 5 ounces fish and 1/3 cup vegetables

COMPLETE THE PLATE
This recipe: Nonstarchy Vegetable, Lean Protein
Pair with: A serving of Carbohydrate Foods such as Mashed Red Potatoes (page 203)

Nonstick cooking spray

8 ounces Campari tomatoes, quartered

2 medium red onions, sliced lengthwise into 1/4-inch strips

2 lemons, cut into 1/4-inch slices

1 1/4 pounds tilapia fillets

1 teaspoon dried basil

1/2 teaspoon kosher salt

1/4 teaspoon ground black pepper

Campari tomatoes are round tomatoes that are larger than cherry tomatoes but smaller then plum tomatoes. You can substitute the Campari tomatoes with the same weight of cherry or plum tomatoes, if needed.

Choices/Exchanges 2 Nonstarchy Vegetable, 3 Lean Protein

Calories 180
Calories from Fat 25
Total Fat 3.0 g
Saturated Fat 1.0 g
Trans Fat 0.0 g

Cholesterol 60 mg
Sodium 310 mg
Potassium 680 mg
Total Carbohydrate 11 g
Dietary Fiber 2 g

Sugars 5 g
Added Sugars 0 g
Protein 29 g
Phosphorus 255 mg

TOTAL TIME 27 minutes plus
20 minutes to 1 hour
refrigeration time and
10 minutes cooling time
PREP TIME 15 minutes
COOK TIME 12 minutes

SERVES 4
SERVING SIZE 1 piece tuna and
6 spears asparagus

COMPLETE THE PLATE
This recipe: Nonstarchy
Vegetable, Lean Protein
Pair with: A serving of
Nonstarchy Vegetables and
Carbohydrate Foods such as
Tabbouleh with Cucumber,
Strawberries, and Mint (page
204), which provides both

Nonstick cooking spray

3 tablespoons olive oil, divided

Juice and zest of 1 lemon
   (2 tablespoons juice and
   1 tablespoon zest)

2 cloves garlic, minced, divided

1 teaspoon ground oregano

1/2 teaspoon ground thyme

1/2 teaspoon kosher salt,
   divided

1/4 teaspoon ground black
   pepper, divided

4 (5-ounce) tuna steaks

1 bunch asparagus (3/4 pound),
   washed and trimmed

SHEET PAN TUNA WITH ASPARAGUS

Tuna is sold as steaks, but often the steaks may be bigger than you want. Your best bet is to visit your local fishmonger, or head to the fish counter at your local market, and request tuna steaks in the exact size you want. You'll be surprised how willing many fishmongers are to get you exactly what you need!

_____

1 Preheat oven to 400°F. Coat a baking sheet with nonstick cooking spray.

2 In a medium bowl, whisk together 1 tablespoon of the olive oil, the lemon juice and zest, 1 minced garlic clove, oregano, thyme, 1/4 teaspoon of the kosher salt, and 1/8 teaspoon of the black pepper. Add the tuna steaks and toss to evenly coat. Cover and place in the refrigerator for at least 20 minutes (but no longer than 1 hour).

3 In a separate medium bowl, whisk together the remaining 2 tablespoons of oil, the remaining garlic, the remaining 1/4 teaspoon of kosher salt, and remaining 1/8 teaspoon of black pepper. Add the asparagus and toss to evenly coat.

4 Remove the tuna steaks from the refrigerator and place in the center of the baking sheet. Arrange the asparagus around the tuna in a single layer. Place the sheet pan in the oven and bake for 12 minutes or until a thermometer inserted into the tuna reads 145°F, flipping the tuna steaks halfway through the cooking time.

5 Remove the sheet pan from the oven and allow to cool for 10 minutes before serving.

Choices/Exchanges 1 Nonstarchy Vegetable, 5 Lean Protein, 1 1/2 Fat

Calories 320	**Cholesterol** 55 mg	**Sugars** 1 g
Calories from Fat 160	**Sodium** 310 mg	**Added Sugars** 0 g
Total Fat 18.0 g	**Potassium** 560 mg	**Protein** 36 g
Saturated Fat 3.3 g	**Total Carbohydrate** 5 g	**Phosphorus** 420 mg
Trans Fat 0.0 g	**Dietary Fiber** 2 g	

When buying asparagus, make sure that the spears are the same thickness so they cook evenly.

TOTAL TIME 13 minutes
PREP TIME 10 minutes
COOK TIME 3 minutes

SERVES 4
SERVING SIZE 4 scallops and 2 tablespoons sauce

COMPLETE THE PLATE
This recipe: Lean Protein, Carbohydrate Food
Pair with: A serving of Nonstarchy Vegetables such as Weeknight Vegetable Stir-Fry (page 202) and Carbohydrate Foods such as Brown Rice with Scallions (page 206)

3/4 pound sea scallops (about 16)*

1/4 teaspoon ground black pepper

2 tablespoons olive oil

1 tablespoon unsalted butter

1/2 cup Pesto Sauce (page 217)

If possible, use fresh, never frozen scallops that are free of preservatives (for example, scallops that have not been treated with salt or STPP [sodium tripolyphosphate]).

SEARED SCALLOPS WITH PESTO SAUCE

Sea scallops are quite simple to cook and have a mild, delicious ocean flavor. Top these scallops with your favorite sauce. They're great with my Pesto Sauce, but you can swap out the pesto for Chimichurri Sauce (page 219) or even a simple squeeze of lemon.

1 Dry the scallops with a paper towel and sprinkle with the black pepper.

2 Heat the olive oil and butter in a large saucepan over medium-high heat. Add the scallops and cook until browned, 1 1/2–2 minutes per side. Using tongs, remove the scallops and place them on a clean plate to cool.

3 Spoon 2 tablespoons of the Pesto Sauce onto each of 4 plates and place the warm scallops over top.

Sea scallops are up to three times larger than bay scallops. Swapping out the types of scallops used in a recipe may not give you the best results, as the cooking time can vary based on the scallop size. The smaller bay scallops take a shorter time to cook.

Choices/Exchanges 1/2 Carbohydrate, 2 Lean Protein, 3 Fat

Calories 250
Calories from Fat 180
Total Fat 20.0 g
Saturated Fat 4.3 g
Trans Fat 0.1 g

Cholesterol 30 mg
Sodium 220 mg
Potassium 300 mg
Total Carbohydrate 5 g
Dietary Fiber 1 g

Sugars 1 g
Added Sugars 0 g
Protein 13 g
Phosphorus 265 mg

EASY BROCCOLI AND SHRIMP STIR-FRY

There's nothing more satisfying then whipping up a healthy, tasty dinner is less than 30 minutes. If you're looking to reduce food waste, you can use 3 cups of any leftover, low-carbohydrate vegetables you have on hand (like cauliflower, zucchini, or cabbage) instead of the broccoli.

TOTAL TIME 25 minutes
PREP TIME 15 minutes
COOK TIME 10 minutes

SERVES 4
SERVING SIZE 1 1/4 cups

COMPLETE THE PLATE
This recipe: Nonstarchy Vegetable, Lean Protein, Carbohydrate Food
Pair with: A serving of Nonstarchy Vegetables such as Simple Side Salad with Balsamic Vinaigrette (page 188) and Carbohydrate Foods such as Brown Rice with Scallions (page 206)

1 In a small bowl, whisk together the vegetable broth, rice vinegar, soy sauce, cornstarch, ginger, sriracha, and brown sugar blend.

2 Heat 2 tablespoons of the olive oil in a large wok or skillet. When the oil is shimmering, add the garlic and cook until fragrant, 30 seconds. Add the shrimp and cook until opaque, 4 minutes. Using a slotted spoon, remove the shrimp and place on a clean plate.

3 Heat the remaining 1 tablespoon of olive oil in the same large wok or skillet. Add the broccoli florets and cook until tender, 4 minutes.

4 Add the cooked shrimp back into the skillet and toss to combine with the broccoli. Pour the broth mixture over the shrimp and broccoli and toss to coat. Continue cooking until the broth mixture slightly thickens, about 1 additional minute.

1/4 cup low-sodium vegetable broth

2 tablespoons unseasoned rice vinegar

1 1/2 tablespoons reduced-sodium soy sauce

1 tablespoon cornstarch

1 teaspoon ground ginger

1/2 teaspoon sriracha

1/2 teaspoon stevia brown sugar blend (such as Truvia)

3 tablespoons olive oil, divided

1 clove garlic, minced

1 1/4 pounds raw medium shrimp (52–63 count), peeled, deveined, and tails cut off*

3 cups broccoli florets (about 1 pound)

*If possible, use fresh, never frozen shrimp that are free of preservatives (for example, shrimp that have not been treated with salt or STPP [sodium tripolyphosphate]).

This dish works beautifully with skinless, boneless chicken breast. Cut the chicken into 2-inch cubes and cook for a total of 8 minutes, until browned on all sides.

Choices/Exchanges 1/2 Carbohydrate, 1 Nonstarchy Vegetable, 4 Lean Protein, 1/2 Fat

Calories 270
Calories from Fat 100
Total Fat 11.0 g
Saturated Fat 1.5 g
Trans Fat 0.0 g

Cholesterol 235 mg
Sodium 400 mg
Potassium 890 mg
Total Carbohydrate 10 g
Dietary Fiber 3 g

Sugars 3 g
Added Sugars 0 g
Protein 34 g
Phosphorus 385 mg

TOTAL TIME 2 hours 55 minutes
PREP TIME 25 minutes
COOK TIME 2 hours 30 minutes
(on low)

SERVES 4
SERVING SIZE 5 ounces fish and
1/3 cup of salsa

COMPLETE THE PLATE
This recipe: Lean Protein,
Carbohydrate Food
Pair with: A serving of
Nonstarchy Vegetables such
as Chopped Romaine Salad
(page 190) and Carbohydrate
Foods such as a small piece of
crusty, whole-grain bread

1 1/4 pounds skin-on salmon

1/4 teaspoon salt

1/8 teaspoon ground black
  pepper

1 1/2 cups low-sodium
  vegetable broth

AVOCADO-GRAPEFRUIT SALSA

1 medium grapefruit

1 avocado, diced

1/2 jalapeño pepper, seeded
  and finely diced

1/4 small onion, finely diced

1/4 cup fresh cilantro, chopped

Juice of 1 lime

1/4 teaspoon kosher salt

1/8 teaspoon ground black
  pepper

SLOW-COOKER SALMON WITH AVOCADO-GRAPEFRUIT SALSA

The slow cooker is an amazing kitchen tool. You can pick up a standard slow cooker for around $30 at your local kitchen store (possibly less if you have a coupon!). Besides chili, soup, and stews, you can also cook a moist, delicious salmon dish in there!

1 Cut a large piece of aluminum foil or parchment paper and line the bottom of a slow cooker.

2 Sprinkle the flesh side of the salmon with the salt and black pepper. Place the salmon skin-side down in the bottom of the slow cooker and pour in the vegetable broth. Cook on low for 2 hours to 2 hours 30 minutes.

3 Lift the foil or parchment paper, and gently slide the salmon onto a serving plate. Discard the cooking liquid.

4 Prepare the Avocado-Grapefruit Salsa. Remove the peel and the white pith from around the grapefruit. Using a paring knife, cut in between the membranes to release the grapefruit segments, and slice them into thirds. Place the grapefruit pieces into a medium bowl. Add the remaining Avocado-Grapefruit Salsa ingredients and gently toss to combine.

5 To plate, place 5 ounces of salmon on each of 4 dinner plates and spoon 1/3 cup of salsa on the side or over each serving of salmon.

 When choosing a grapefruit, look for brightly colored skin that is firm, yet springs back to the touch. The heavier the fruit, the juicier it will be. Store whole grapefruit in the refrigerator for up to 2 weeks.

Choices/Exchanges 1 Fruit, 4 Lean Protein, 1 Fat

Calories 300	**Cholesterol** 75 mg	**Sugars** 7 g
Calories from Fat 130	**Sodium** 300 mg	**Added Sugars** 0 g
Total Fat 14.0 g	**Potassium** 850 mg	**Protein** 32 g
Saturated Fat 2.5 g	**Total Carbohydrate** 12 g	**Phosphorus** 415 mg
Trans Fat 0.0 g	**Dietary Fiber** 4 g	

TURKEY AND BLACK BEAN SLOPPY JOES

This warming weeknight meal may take 40 minutes to prepare from start to finish, but to save time, you can make a double batch of the recipe over the weekend and freeze half for a busy week. That way, you'll have a delicious meal any time you need one.

1 Heat the olive oil in a large skillet over medium heat. When the oil is shimmering, add the onion, bell pepper, and garlic and cook until the onions are translucent, about 4 minutes.

2 Add the turkey and cook, breaking up the meat with a wooden spoon, until the meat is no longer pink, about 6 minutes. Add the black beans, diced tomatoes, tomato paste, vinegar, sriracha, and brown sugar blend and stir to combine.

3 Raise the heat to high and bring the mixture to a boil. Lower the heat to medium low and simmer, covered, until the flavors combine, 15 minutes.

Toby Tip *Serve on whole-wheat buns or over whole-wheat pasta or quinoa.*

TOTAL TIME 40 minutes
PREP TIME 15 minutes
COOK TIME 25 minutes

SERVES 4
SERVING SIZE 1 1/4 cups

COMPLETE THE PLATE
This recipe: Nonstarchy Vegetable, Lean Protein, Carbohydrate Food
Pair with: This recipe is a complete meal

2 tablespoons olive oil

1 medium onion, chopped

1 medium green bell pepper, chopped

2 cloves garlic, minced

1 pound lean ground turkey (at least 93% lean)

1 (15.5-ounce) can low-sodium black beans, drained and rinsed

1 (14.5-ounce) can no-added-salt diced tomatoes

1/4 cup no-added-salt tomato paste

2 teaspoons apple cider vinegar

1 teaspoon sriracha

1/2 teaspoon stevia brown sugar blend (such as Truvia)

Choices/Exchanges 1 Starch, 3 Nonstarchy Vegetable, 3 Lean Protein, 2 Fat

Calories 380
Calories from Fat 140
Total Fat 16.0 g
Saturated Fat 3.5 g
Trans Fat 0.1 g

Cholesterol 85 mg
Sodium 170 mg
Potassium 1040 mg
Total Carbohydrate 30 g
Dietary Fiber 7 g

Sugars 9 g
Added Sugars 0 g
Protein 30 g
Phosphorus 370 mg

SOUTHWEST-STYLE TURKEY MEATLOAF

A nice way to add whole grains into protein dishes—such as meatloaf, hamburgers, and meatballs—is to use quick-cooking oats instead of regular bread crumbs. The fiber in the oats has been shown to help lower cholesterol.

1 Preheat the oven to 350°F. Coat a 9 × 5-inch loaf pan with nonstick cooking spray.

2 Add all of the remaining ingredients to a large bowl. Gently mix the ingredients until well combined.

3 Spoon the mixture into the prepared loaf pan, using the back of the spoon or a spatula to even out the top. Place the loaf pan in the oven and bake until a thermometer inserted into the center of the meatloaf reads 165°F, 1 hour.

Toby Tip

If you don't have a loaf pan or want to try something new, make a "free-form" meatloaf on a sheet pan. Place the mixture on the sheet pan and, using clean hands, shape it into the form of a meatloaf. Bake it for the same amount of time.

TOTAL TIME 1 hour 15 minutes
PREP TIME 15 minutes
COOK TIME 1 hour

SERVES 8
SERVING SIZE 1-inch slice

COMPLETE THE PLATE
This recipe: Nonstarchy Vegetable, Lean Protein, Carbohydrate Food
Pair with: A serving of Nonstarchy Vegetables such as sautéed spinach and Carbohydrate Foods such as Mashed Red Potatoes (page 203)

Nonstick cooking spray

1 1/2 pounds lean ground turkey (at least 93% lean)

1 cup quick-cooking oats

1 large yellow onion, finely chopped

2 large eggs, beaten

1 medium green bell pepper, finely diced

1/2 cup ketchup

3 cloves garlic, minced

1 tablespoon chili powder

2 teaspoons ground cumin

1 teaspoon dried oregano

1/2 teaspoon salt

1/4 teaspoon ground black pepper

Choices/Exchanges 1/2 Starch, 1 Nonstarchy Vegetable, 3 Lean Protein, 1/2 Fat

Calories 220
Calories from Fat 70
Total Fat 8.0 g
Saturated Fat 2.4 g
Trans Fat 0.1 g

Cholesterol 110 mg
Sodium 400 mg
Potassium 410 mg
Total Carbohydrate 15 g
Dietary Fiber 2 g

Sugars 5 g
Added Sugars 0 g
Protein 20 g
Phosphorus 250 mg

TOTAL TIME 1 hour plus 10 minutes cooling time
PREP TIME 15 minutes
COOK TIME 45 minutes

SERVES 4
SERVING SIZE 2 drumsticks and 1 cup vegetables

COMPLETE THE PLATE
This recipe: Nonstarchy Vegetable, Lean Protein
Pair with: A serving of Carbohydrate Foods such as roasted baby potatoes

2 small red onions, peeled and quartered (with ends still attached so the quarters stay intact)

1 (9-ounce) package frozen artichoke hearts, thawed

1 tablespoon canola oil

8 drumsticks, skin removed (about 2 pounds total)

2 cloves garlic, minced

1/4 teaspoon salt

8 fresh basil leaves

2 lemons, thinly sliced

SHEET PAN CHICKEN WITH ARTICHOKES AND ONIONS

The slightly higher fat content of dark meat chicken imparts a lot of flavor and helps the chicken stay moist when cooked in the oven. The fat found in the dark meat (without the skin) is mostly heart-healthy monounsaturated and polyunsaturated fat. Plus, dark meat is more plentiful in iron and zinc than white meat chicken.

1 Preheat the oven to 375°F.

2 Add the red onion and artichoke hearts to a medium bowl. Add the canola oil and toss to coat. Place the vegetables in a single layer on a sheet pan.

3 Add the drumsticks to the empty medium bowl. Add the garlic and salt and toss to evenly coat the chicken. Place the drumsticks in the center of the vegetables on the sheet pan. Top each drumstick with a basil leaf and place the lemon slices on top and on the sides of the chicken.

4 Bake until a thermometer inserted into a drumstick reads 165°F, 45 minutes. Remove the sheet pan from the oven and allow to cool for 10 minutes before serving.

 Swap out the artichokes for a hearty, low-carbohydrate vegetable like carrots or Brussels sprouts.

Choices/Exchanges 2 Nonstarchy Vegetable, 4 Lean Protein, 1 Fat

Calories 270
Calories from Fat 90
Total Fat 10.0 g
Saturated Fat 1.9 g
Trans Fat 0.0 g

Cholesterol 95 mg
Sodium 290 mg
Potassium 530 mg
Total Carbohydrate 13 g
Dietary Fiber 5 g

Sugars 4 g
Added Sugars 0 g
Protein 32 g
Phosphorus 250 mg

MEDITERRANEAN CHICKEN AND VEGETABLE BAKE

The simple sauce in this recipe is made with olive oil, garlic, onion powder, and an Italian spice blend with marjoram, thyme, rosemary, savory, sage, oregano, and basil. These ingredients allow the flavors of the tomatoes, broccoli, cauliflower, and artichokes to really shine through in this easy-to-assemble Mediterranean-inspired dish.

_____

1 Preheat the oven to 350°F. Coat an 8 × 11 1/2-inch casserole dish with nonstick cooking spray.

2 In a medium bowl, toss together the chicken breasts, artichoke hearts, tomatoes, broccoli, cauliflower, and bell pepper.

3 In a small bowl, whisk together the olive oil, garlic, Italian seasoning, onion powder, salt, and black pepper. Add the olive oil mixture to the bowl with the chicken and vegetables and toss to combine.

4 Pour the chicken and vegetables into the prepared casserole dish, spreading out the vegetables and chicken so they are evenly distributed in the dish. Sprinkle the mozzarella cheese over the top. Cover the casserole dish with aluminum foil and bake until the cheese is bubbling and a thermometer inserted into the center of the dish reads 165°F, 50 minutes.

5 Remove the aluminum foil and continue cooking for an additional 15 minutes. Remove the casserole dish from the oven and allow to cool for 10 minutes before serving.

 Make sure to cover the casserole dish with aluminum foil before baking. Leaving it uncovered for too long in the oven can dry out the chicken.

TOTAL TIME 1 hour 10 minutes plus 10 minutes cooling time
PREP TIME 20 minutes
COOK TIME 50 minutes

SERVES 8
SERVING SIZE 1 1/4 cups

COMPLETE THE PLATE
This recipe: Nonstarchy Vegetable, Lean Protein
Pair with: A serving of Carbohydrate Foods such as a whole-wheat dinner roll

Nonstick cooking spray

2 pounds skinless, boneless chicken breasts, cut into 1-inch chunks

1 (15-ounce) can artichoke hearts, drained and rinsed

2 cups cherry tomatoes, halved

2 cups broccoli florets

2 cups cauliflower florets

1 yellow bell pepper, sliced into 1-inch strips

1/4 cup olive oil

3 cloves garlic, minced

1 tablespoon Italian seasoning

1 teaspoon onion powder

1/2 teaspoon salt

1/4 teaspoon ground black pepper

1 cup shredded part-skim mozzarella cheese

Choices/Exchanges 2 Nonstarchy Vegetable, 4 Lean Protein, 1 Fat

Calories 270
Calories from Fat 110
Total Fat 12.0 g
Saturated Fat 3.2 g
Trans Fat 0.0 g

Cholesterol 75 mg
Sodium 400 mg
Potassium 590 mg
Total Carbohydrate 10 g
Dietary Fiber 4 g

Sugars 3 g
Added Sugars 0 g
Protein 30 g
Phosphorus 305 mg

TOTAL TIME 28 minutes
PREP TIME 15 minutes
COOK TIME 13 minutes

SERVES 4
SERVING SIZE 5 ounces chicken
tenders

COMPLETE THE PLATE
This recipe: Lean Protein
Pair with: A serving of
Nonstarchy Vegetables such
as Side Greek Salad with Red
Wine Vinaigrette (page 189)
and Carbohydrate Foods such
as a baked sweet potato

Juice and zest of 1 lemon
  (2 tablespoons juice and
  1 tablespoon zest), divided

2 tablespoons white wine

2 teaspoons cornstarch

1 1/4 pounds skinless,
  boneless chicken tenders

1/4 teaspoon kosher salt

1/8 teaspoon ground black
  pepper

2 tablespoons olive or
  canola oil

2 tablespoons fresh rosemary,
  chopped

2 cloves garlic, minced

LEMON CHICKEN WITH ROSEMARY AND GARLIC

Cooking chicken on the stovetop can be tricky, and if the breasts are too thick, they may not cook through. Your best bet is to use quick-cooking chicken tenders, or you can use a mallet to pound the same amount of chicken breasts to an even 1-inch thickness.

1 In a small bowl, whisk together the lemon juice, wine, and cornstarch. Set aside.

2 Sprinkle both sides of the chicken with the salt, black pepper, and lemon zest.

3 Heat the olive oil in a medium skillet over medium heat. Add the rosemary and garlic and cook until fragrant, 30 seconds. Add the chicken and cook until a thermometer inserted into a chicken tender reaches 165°F, 5 minutes on each side. Add the lemon juice mixture and toss to coat. Continue cooking for 3 minutes; the liquid will slightly thicken. Serve warm.

 Choose fresh rosemary that has a bright color. To store, wrap in a damp paper towel and place in a plastic bag in the refrigerator for up to 5 days.

Choices/Exchanges 4 Lean Protein, 1 Fat

Calories 230	**Cholesterol** 80 mg	**Sugars** 0 g
Calories from Fat 90	**Sodium** 190 mg	**Added Sugars** 0 g
Total Fat 10.0 g	**Potassium** 270 mg	**Protein** 30 g
Saturated Fat 1.9 g	**Total Carbohydrate** 3 g	**Phosphorus** 220 mg
Trans Fat 0.0 g	**Dietary Fiber** 0 g	

CHICKEN AND MUSHROOM SKILLET

Mushrooms add an umami flavor to dishes. This 5th flavor of "umami" was discovered by Dr. Kikunae Ikeda in 1908. He discovered the flavor in a Japanese dish called kombu dashi, a soup stock made of kelp, and realized that the taste component came from glutamate.

1 In a small bowl, whisk together the chicken broth, wine, lemon juice and zest, parsley, 1/4 teaspoon of the salt, and 1/8 teaspoon of the black pepper. Set aside.

2 Heat 2 tablespoons of the olive oil in a large skillet over medium heat. When the oil is shimmering, add the onion and garlic and cook until the onion softens and the garlic is fragrant, 3 minutes.

3 Season the chicken with the remaining 1/4 teaspoon of the salt and 1/8 teaspoon of the black pepper. Add the chicken to the skillet and cook for 8 minutes, flipping once, until cooked through. Remove the chicken from the skillet and place on a clean plate.

4 Add the remaining 1 tablespoon of olive oil into the skillet and heat over medium heat. Add the mushrooms and cook until softened, 8 minutes. Add the chicken back into the skillet and toss to combine. Add the broth mixture and bring to a boil. Then reduce the heat and simmer, covered, until the flavors combine and a thermometer inserted into the chicken reads 165°F, about 10 minutes.

 To take the best reading with your thermometer, insert the bottom 1–2 inches into the thickest part of the food. If you can't go straight down, then insert the thermometer into the food at a diagonal angle.

TOTAL TIME 46 minutes
PREP TIME 15 minutes
COOK TIME 31 minutes

SERVES 4
SERVING SIZE 5 ounces chicken and 1/3 cup mushroom sauce

COMPLETE THE PLATE
This recipe: Nonstarchy Vegetable, Lean Protein
Pair with: A serving of Nonstarchy Vegetables such as Steamed Green Beans with Cashews (page 197) and Carbohydrate Foods such as Brown Rice with Scallions (page 206)

1/3 cup low-sodium chicken broth

2 tablespoons cooking wine

Juice and zest of 1 lemon (2 tablespoons juice and 1 tablespoon zest)

2 teaspoons dried parsley

1/2 teaspoon salt, divided

1/4 teaspoon ground black pepper, divided

3 tablespoons olive oil, divided

1 medium onion, chopped

1 clove garlic, minced

1 1/4 pounds skinless, boneless chicken tenders

1 (8-ounce) container baby bella or cremini mushrooms, sliced

Choices/Exchanges 1 Nonstarchy Vegetable, 4 Lean Protein, 1 1/2 Fat

Calories 290
Calories from Fat 130
Total Fat 14.0 g
Saturated Fat 2.4 g
Trans Fat 0.0 g
Cholesterol 80 mg
Sodium 380 mg
Potassium 600 mg
Total Carbohydrate 7 g
Dietary Fiber 1 g
Sugars 3 g
Added Sugars 0 g
Protein 32 g
Phosphorus 305 mg

TOTAL TIME 36 minutes
plus 20–30 minutes
refrigeration time
PREP TIME 20 minutes
COOK TIME 16 minutes

SERVES 4
SERVING SIZE 2 skewers

COMPLETE THE PLATE
This recipe: Nonstarchy
Vegetable, Lean Protein
Pair with: A serving of
Carbohydrate Foods such
as grilled corn

1 1/4 pounds skinless,
   boneless chicken breast,
   cut into 24 (2-inch) cubes

16 cherry tomatoes

2 medium zucchini, each cut
   into 8 slices

1 medium yellow bell
   pepper, cut into 16 pieces

1/2 cup Lite Balsamic
   Vinaigrette (page 221) or
   bottled light balsamic
   vinaigrette

Nonstick cooking spray

8 wooden or metal skewers

GRILLED CHICKEN AND VEGETABLE SKEWERS

*You don't have to wait for warm weather to grill. A grill
pan can get the job done just as easily, so you can enjoy
grilled food any time of the year!*

_____

1 Add the chicken cubes, tomatoes, zucchini, and bell peppers
to a medium bowl. Add the balsamic vinaigrette and toss
to combine. Cover the bowl and place in the refrigerator to
marinate for 20–30 minutes.

2 Coat a grill pan with nonstick cooking spray. Preheat the
grill pan or a grill to medium heat. If using wooden skewers,
soak for at least 10 minutes.

3 To assemble the skewers, thread a piece of the chicken
followed by a tomato, slice of zucchini, and slice of pepper.
Repeat once more on the same skewer and finish with a third
piece of chicken. Prepare the remaining 7 skewers the same
way. Discard the marinade.

4 Grill the skewers until the chicken is cooked through, about
4 minutes on each side. Serve warm.

 *Look for nonflammable cooking spray to
use on your grill. If that's not available,
brush olive oil on the grill grates to prevent
the chicken and vegetables from sticking.*

Choices/Exchanges 2 Nonstarchy Vegetable, 4 Lean Protein, 1/2 Fat

Calories 260	**Cholesterol** 80 mg	**Sugars** 7 g
Calories from Fat 90	**Sodium** 140 mg	**Added Sugars** 0 g
Total Fat 10.0 g	**Potassium** 730 mg	**Protein** 32 g
Saturated Fat 1.9 g	**Total Carbohydrate** 10 g	**Phosphorus** 280 mg
Trans Fat 0.0 g	**Dietary Fiber** 2 g	

SLOW-COOKER CHICKEN, SWEET POTATO, AND BLACK BEAN STEW

"Low and slow" does the trick with this stew. Give yourself 15 minutes in the morning in order to toss the ingredients into the slow cooker, close the lid, and set it on low. Then the only thing you need to do is wait for your timer to go off in 6 hours—and dinner is ready to be served.

TOTAL TIME 6 hours 15 minutes
PREP TIME 15 minutes
COOK TIME 6 hours (on low)

SERVES 8
SERVING SIZE 1 1/4 cups

COMPLETE THE PLATE
This recipe: Nonstarchy Vegetable, Lean Protein, Carbohydrate Food
Pair with: A serving of Nonstarchy Vegetables such as Simple Side Salad with Balsamic Vinaigrette (page 188)

1 Add all the ingredients into a slow cooker. Stir to combine. Cover the slow cooker and cook on low for 6 hours.

- 1 pound skinless, boneless chicken thighs
- 2 sweet potatoes, washed, peeled, sliced lengthwise, and then cut into 1-inch-thick slices
- 1 (15.5-ounce) can low-sodium black beans, drained and rinsed
- 1 (14.5-ounce) can no-added-salt diced tomatoes
- 1 1/2 cups low-sodium chicken broth
- 1 1/2 cups water
- 1 cup frozen sweet corn kernels
- 3 cloves garlic, minced
- 1 (6-ounce) can no-added-salt tomato paste
- 2 teaspoons ground parsley
- 1 1/2 teaspoons paprika
- 1/2 teaspoon salt
- 1/4 teaspoon ground black pepper

If you don't like dark meat or don't have chicken thighs handy, you can swap out the chicken thighs for 1 pound of skinless, boneless chicken breasts, cut into 2-inch cubes.

Choices/Exchanges 1 1/2 Starch, 1 Nonstarchy Vegetable, 2 Lean Protein

Calories 220
Calories from Fat 35
Total Fat 4.0 g
Saturated Fat 1.0 g
Trans Fat 0.0 g

Cholesterol 45 mg
Sodium 290 mg
Potassium 800 mg
Total Carbohydrate 31 g
Dietary Fiber 6 g

Sugars 9 g
Added Sugars 0 g
Protein 18 g
Phosphorus 200 mg

 Browning the pork chops before baking in the oven gives them a deeper flavor without adding more calories or fat. Try this technique when cooking chicken, lamb, or beef.

PORK CHOPS WITH FENNEL AND SHALLOTS

Pork loin chops are a lean cut of meat, so pair them with a robust flavor! Fennel seed, which has a slightly black licorice flavor, has few calories and no fat, and helps punch up the flavor of this dish.

---

1 Preheat the oven to 450°F.

2 Heat a large ovenproof sauté pan over medium-low heat. Add the fennel seeds and toast until fragrant, 2 minutes. Carefully remove the seeds from the pan and place into a medium bowl. Set aside to cool for 10 minutes.

3 Into the bowl with the cool fennel seeds, add 2 tablespoons of the olive or canola oil, the garlic, salt, and black pepper and whisk into a paste. Dip both sides of each pork chop into the fennel paste, pushing gently to allow the paste to adhere to the chop.

4 Heat the remaining 1 tablespoon of olive or canola oil in the same ovenproof sauté pan. When the oil is shimmering, add the shallots and cook until softened, 2 minutes. Using a wooden spoon, push the shallots to the side of the pan and add the pork chops. Brown the pork for 1 minute on each side.

5 Using oven mitts, carefully move the pan into the oven. Cook until a thermometer inserted into a pork chop reaches 145°F, 10 minutes. Using oven mitts, carefully remove the pan from the oven and place on the stovetop to cool.

6 Using a spatula or slotted spoon, place the pork chops on a serving plate, leaving the shallots and juices in the pan. Add the parsley and vinegar to the pan and toss with the shallots to combine. Pour the mixture over the pork chops. Serve warm.

TOTAL TIME 31 minutes plus 10 minutes cooling time
PREP TIME 15 minutes
COOK TIME 16 minutes

SERVES 4
SERVING SIZE 1 pork chop and 1/4 cup sauce

COMPLETE THE PLATE
This recipe: Lean Protein
Pair with: A serving of Nonstarchy Vegetables such as Simple Side Salad with Balsamic Vinaigrette (page 188) and Carbohydrate Foods such as Mashed Red Potatoes (page 203)

1 1/2 tablespoons fennel seeds

3 tablespoons olive or canola oil, divided

2 cloves garlic, minced

1/2 teaspoon salt

1/8 teaspoon ground black pepper

4 boneless pork loin chops (1 pound), trimmed of fat

2 large shallots, sliced lengthwise into 1/8-inch slices

1/2 cup fresh parsley, chopped

1 tablespoon red wine vinegar

Choices/Exchanges 1 Nonstarchy Vegetable, 3 Lean Protein, 2 1/2 Fat

Calories 270
Calories from Fat 160
Total Fat 18.0 g
Saturated Fat 4.0 g
Trans Fat 0.0 g

Cholesterol 60 mg
Sodium 350 mg
Potassium 430 mg
Total Carbohydrate 5 g
Dietary Fiber 2 g

Sugars 1 g
Added Sugars 0 g
Protein 22 g
Phosphorus 200 mg

TOTAL TIME 50 minutes plus
10 minutes resting time
PREP TIME 10 minutes
COOK TIME 40 minutes

SERVES 4
SERVING SIZE 4 ounces

COMPLETE THE PLATE
This recipe: Lean Protein
Pair with: A serving of
Nonstarchy Vegetables
such as Collard Greens and
Yellow Squash (page 194)
and Carbohydrate Foods such
as a baked sweet potato

Nonstick cooking spray

2 tablespoons olive oil

1 tablespoon Dijon mustard

3 cloves garlic, minced

1 teaspoon dried basil

1 teaspoon dried thyme

1 teaspoon dried rosemary

1/2 teaspoon salt, divided

1/4 teaspoon ground black
    pepper, divided

1 pound pork tenderloin

MUSTARD-HERB
ROASTED PORK TENDERLOIN

*One of the simplest ways to cook pork tenderloin is in
the oven. Brush the seasonings onto the tenderloin and
within 40 minutes you have a perfectly cooked, delicious,
lean protein.*

1 Preheat the oven to 400°F. Coat a baking sheet with nonstick
cooking spray.

2 In a small bowl, whisk together the olive oil, Dijon mustard,
garlic, basil, thyme, rosemary, 1/4 teaspoon of the salt, and
1/8 teaspoon of the black pepper.

3 Sprinkle the pork tenderloin with the remaining 1/4 teaspoon
of salt and 1/8 teaspoon of black pepper. Using a brush, spread
the mustard mixture over all sides of the pork tenderloin.
Discard any unused mustard mixture. Place the pork tenderloin
on the prepared baking sheet and cook until a thermometer
inserted into the thickest part of the tenderloin reads 145°F,
about 40 minutes. Let the pork rest for 10 minutes before slicing.

 *Cut any leftover pork tenderloin into cubes and serve
over a green salad with a small whole-wheat roll.*

Choices/Exchanges 3 Lean Protein, 1 Fat

Calories 190	**Cholesterol** 60 mg	**Sugars** 0 g
Calories from Fat 90	**Sodium** 420 mg	**Added Sugars** 0 g
Total Fat 10.0 g	**Potassium** 380 mg	**Protein** 22 g
Saturated Fat 2.0 g	**Total Carbohydrate** 2 g	**Phosphorus** 205 mg
Trans Fat 0.0 g	**Dietary Fiber** 0 g	

PORK STIR-FRY WITH ORANGE SAUCE

The tenderloin is one of the most tender and leanest cuts of pork. The best way to use it is to either slice it into medallions, as in this recipe, or use a rub, marinade, or flavorful sauce over the entire tenderloin and then grill or roast it, as in my Mustard-Herb Roasted Pork Tenderloin recipe (page 178).

1 Zest 2 of the oranges and juice all 3 (to yield about 3/4 cup juice). Set the zest aside and place the juice in a medium bowl. Add the white wine vinegar, agave nectar, ground mustard, garlic, salt, and ginger to the bowl and whisk to combine. Add the cornstarch and continue whisking until it is incorporated.

2 In a large wok or cast-iron pan, warm the olive or canola oil over medium-high heat. When the oil is shimmering, add the broccoli, cauliflower, and carrots to the pan and cook until crisp, 2 minutes. Add the water and cover the wok or pan until the vegetables slightly soften, an additional 2 minutes. Add the pork slices and cook until browned on all sides, 3 minutes per side.

3 Add the orange juice mixture to the pan and bring to a boil, then reduce the heat to medium. Stir the sauce into the mixture and toss until well combined. Continue cooking until the sauce thickens, 2–3 minutes. Add the orange zest and toss to combine. Serve warm.

(Toby Tip) *Swap out the pork for skinless, boneless chicken breast cut into 2-inch cubes. Cook for a total of 8 minutes, until browned on all sides.*

TOTAL TIME 30 minutes
PREP TIME 15 minutes
COOK TIME 15 minutes

SERVES 4
SERVING SIZE 1 1/4 cups

COMPLETE THE PLATE
This recipe: Nonstarchy Vegetable, Lean Protein, Carbohydrate Food
Pair with: A serving of Nonstarchy Vegetables such as Chopped Romaine Salad (page 190) and Carbohydrate Foods such as Brown Rice with Scallions (page 206)

3 oranges

2 tablespoons white wine vinegar

2 teaspoons agave nectar

2 teaspoons ground mustard

2 cloves garlic, minced

1/2 teaspoon salt

1/4 teaspoon ground ginger

2 tablespoons cornstarch

1 tablespoon olive or canola oil

2 cups broccoli florets

1 cup cauliflower florets

1 medium carrot, thinly cut into matchsticks

2 tablespoons water

1 pound pork tenderloin, sliced into 1/4-inch slices

Choices/Exchanges 1 Carbohydrate, 1 Nonstarchy Vegetable, 3 Lean Protein

Calories 230
Calories from Fat 60
Total Fat 7.0 g
Saturated Fat 1.5 g
Trans Fat 0.0 g

Cholesterol 60 mg
Sodium 360 mg
Potassium 720 mg
Total Carbohydrate 17 g
Dietary Fiber 3 g

Sugars 8 g
Added Sugars 2 g
Protein 24 g
Phosphorus 260 mg

TOTAL TIME 30 minutes
PREP TIME 15 minutes
COOK TIME 15 minutes

SERVES 8
SERVING SIZE 3 meatballs

COMPLETE THE PLATE
This recipe: Lean Protein, Carbohydrate Food
Pair with: A serving of Nonstarchy Vegetables such as Steamed Green Beans with Cashews (page 197) and Carbohydrate Foods such as whole-wheat pasta

1 pound lean ground beef (at least 95% lean)

1 portobello mushroom cap (4 ounces), chopped

1 small onion, chopped

2/3 cup quick-cooking oats

1/2 cup parsley, chopped

2 cloves garlic, minced

2 tablespoons Worcestershire sauce

2 tablespoons no-added-salt tomato paste

1/4 teaspoon salt

1/8 teaspoon ground black pepper

3 tablespoons olive or canola oil

BLENDED BEEF AND MUSHROOM MEATBALLS

Adding mushrooms to meatballs has numerous benefits. First, it can help bulk up the meatballs without adding saturated fat. Second, mushrooms add a delicious umami flavor. Lastly, it's another way to take in more nonstarchy vegetables!

1 Add all ingredients except the oil to a medium bowl. Using clean hands, mix the beef mixture until well combined.

2 Scoop about 1 tablespoon of the beef mixture into clean hands, roll into a ball, and place on a large plate. Repeat with the remaining mixture to make 24 meatballs.

3 Heat the olive or canola oil in a saucepan over medium heat. When the oil is shimmering, add the meatballs, cover, and cook for about 15 minutes, browning all sides, until a thermometer inserted into a meatball reads 155°F. Serve warm.

Choices/Exchanges 1/2 Starch, 2 Lean Protein, 1 Fat

Calories 160	**Cholesterol** 35 mg	**Sugars** 2 g
Calories from Fat 70	**Sodium** 160 mg	**Added Sugars** 0 g
Total Fat 8.0 g	**Potassium** 380 mg	**Protein** 13 g
Saturated Fat 2.1 g	**Total Carbohydrate** 9 g	**Phosphorus** 160 mg
Trans Fat 0.1 g	**Dietary Fiber** 1 g	

You can use the same amount of cremini or button mushrooms instead of the portobello mushrooms or use a combination of your favorite mushrooms.

TOTAL TIME 20 minutes plus at least 20 minutes marinating time
PREP TIME 10 minutes
COOK TIME 10 minutes

SERVES 4
SERVING SIZE 1 steak

COMPLETE THE PLATE
This recipe: Lean Protein
Pair with: A serving of Nonstarchy Vegetables such as Sautéed Mushroom Medley (page 198) and Carbohydrate Foods such as a baked potato

Nonstick cooking spray

2 tablespoons white wine vinegar

1 tablespoon olive oil

2 cloves garlic, minced

1 teaspoon onion powder

1/4 teaspoon kosher salt

1/8 teaspoon ground black pepper

1 1/4 pounds top sirloin steaks, cut into 4 steaks

Nonstick cooking spray

SIMPLE GRILLED STEAKS

Due to increased trimming practices over the past few decades, there are now more than 30 cuts of beef that qualify as lean. Lean beef is loaded with 10 essential nutrients and contains less than 10 grams of total fat and 4.5 grams or less of saturated fat per 3-ounce cooked portion.

———————————

1 In a medium bowl, whisk together the white wine vinegar, olive oil, garlic, onion powder, salt, and black pepper. Place the steaks in the bowl and toss to evenly coat with the marinade. Cover and marinate in the refrigerator for at least 20 minutes or up to 24 hours.

2 Preheat the grill or grill pan on medium heat. Coat the grill pan with nonstick cooking spray (or brush the grill with 1 tablespoon of olive oil).

3 Place the steaks on the grill pan and discard any excess marinade. Cook until a thermometer inserted into the thickest part of the steak reads 145°F, 5 minutes per side.

 A marinade contains an acidic ingredient, like vinegar, to help soften the meat and add flavor. The longer you can marinade these steaks, the better they will taste! Prepare the marinade the night before and allow the steak to soak in the flavors until the next day.

Choices/Exchanges 4 Lean Protein

Calories 190
Calories from Fat 70
Total Fat 8.0 g
Saturated Fat 2.4 g
Trans Fat 0.2 g

Cholesterol 55 mg
Sodium 150 mg
Potassium 370 mg
Total Carbohydrate 1 g
Dietary Fiber 0 g

Sugars 0 g
Added Sugars 0 g
Protein 28 g
Phosphorus 225 mg

LAMB AND CHICKPEA CURRY

Curry powder is made from a blend of spices such as coriander, cumin, turmeric, ginger, fenugreek, nutmeg, red pepper, and onion. The spice blend can vary slightly in homemade curry recipes and between food manufacturers.

---

1 Heat the olive or canola oil in a medium sauté pan over medium heat. Add the onion and garlic and cook until onion is translucent and garlic is fragrant, 4 minutes. Add the curry powder, ginger, turmeric, cumin, and red pepper flakes and toss with the onion mixture. Cook for an additional 1 minute to allow the flavors to combine.

2 Add the lamb pieces and brown on all sides, 4 minutes. Add the chickpeas, tomatoes, water, bay leaves, and salt and stir to combine. Raise the heat and bring the mixture to a boil, then reduce the heat to low and cover. Simmer, stirring occasionally, until the lamb cooks through, about 20–25 minutes, or until a thermometer inserted into 1 or 2 lamb pieces reaches 145°F. Remove and discard the bay leaves before serving.

When cooking on the stovetop, use an oil with a high smoke point like olive or canola oil. Save your delicious extra-virgin olive oil for recipes where there is no cooking, like dressings.

TOTAL TIME 53 minutes
PREP TIME 15 minutes
COOK TIME 38 minutes

SERVES 4
SERVING SIZE 1 cup

COMPLETE THE PLATE
This recipe: Nonstarchy Vegetable, Lean Protein, Carbohydrate Food
Pair with: This recipe is a complete meal

1 tablespoon olive or canola oil

1 medium onion, thinly sliced

3 cloves garlic, minced

2 tablespoons curry powder

1 teaspoon ground ginger

1/2 teaspoon turmeric

1/2 teaspoon ground cumin

1/8 teaspoon red pepper flakes

1 pound lamb shoulder, cut into 1/2-inch pieces

1 (14.5-ounce) can low-sodium chickpeas (garbanzo beans), drained and rinsed

2 (14.5-ounce) cans no-added-salt crushed tomatoes

1/2 cup water

2 bay leaves

1/4 plus 1/8 teaspoon salt

Choices/Exchanges 1 1/2 Starch, 3 Nonstarchy Vegetable, 3 Lean Protein, 1 1/2 Fat

Calories 390
Calories from Fat 110
Total Fat 12.0 g
Saturated Fat 3.0 g
Trans Fat 0.0 g

Cholesterol 75 mg
Sodium 300 mg
Potassium 1170 mg
Total Carbohydrate 35 g
Dietary Fiber 10 g

Sugars 12 g
Added Sugars 0 g
Protein 33 g
Phosphorus 390 mg

TOTAL TIME 1 hour plus 10 minutes cooling time
PREP TIME 15 minutes
COOK TIME 45 minutes

SERVES 8
SERVING SIZE 1 cup

COMPLETE THE PLATE
This recipe: Nonstarchy Vegetable, Lean Protein, Carbohydrate Food
Pair with: A serving of Nonstarchy Vegetables such as Chopped Romaine Salad (page 190)

2 tablespoons olive or canola oil

1 medium onion, chopped

2 cloves garlic, minced

1 jalapeño, seeds removed

1 pound lean ground beef (at least 92% lean)

1 (15.5-ounce) can low-sodium kidney beans, drained and rinsed

1 (15-ounce) can low-sodium cannellini or great northern beans, drained and rinsed

1 (15.5-ounce) can low-sodium black beans, drained and rinsed

1 (14.5-ounce) can no-added-salt fire-roasted diced tomatoes

1 (6-ounce) can low-sodium tomato paste

1 cup low-sodium beef broth

2 tablespoons chili powder

2 teaspoons ground oregano

1 teaspoon ground cumin

1/2 teaspoon stevia brown sugar blend (such as Truvia)

1/4 teaspoon salt

1/4 teaspoon cayenne pepper

EASY BEEF CHILI

This diabetes-friendly dish is filled with lean beef–which provides 10 essential nutrients, including protein and iron–and beans, which provide fiber and more protein. It's a warming, nutritious meal you can feel good about serving to your entire family.

1 Heat the olive or canola oil in a medium pot over medium heat. When the oil is shimmering, add the onion, garlic, and jalapeño and cook until the onion is translucent and the garlic is fragrant, 3 minutes.

2 Add the ground beef and cook until browned, 8 minutes, breaking up the pieces using the back of a wooden spoon while cooking.

3 Add the remaining ingredients to the pot and stir to combine. Raise the heat to high and bring the mixture to a boil. Then lower the heat to medium low and simmer, covered, until the beef is cooked through and the flavors combine, 30 minutes. Stir occasionally during cooking time.

4 Remove the chili from the heat and allow to cool for 10 minutes before serving.

Choices/Exchanges 1 1/2 Starch, 2 Nonstarchy Vegetable, 2 Lean Protein, 1 Fat

Calories 290	**Cholesterol** 35 mg	**Sugars** 7 g
Calories from Fat 70	**Sodium** 180 mg	**Added Sugars** 0 g
Total Fat 8.0 g	**Potassium** 1120 mg	**Protein** 22 g
Saturated Fat 2.3 g	**Total Carbohydrate** 34 g	**Phosphorus** 300 mg
Trans Fat 0.2 g	**Dietary Fiber** 9 g	

Toby
Tip

Top this chili with salsa and/or nonfat plain Greek yogurt.

Chapter 10
Side Dishes

Zucchini with Basil, Mint, and Pine Nuts, p. 196
Tabbouleh with Cucumber, Strawberries, and Mint, p. 204
Chopped Romaine Salad, p. 190

TOTAL TIME 15 minutes
PREP TIME 15 minutes
COOK TIME 0 minutes

SERVES 4
SERVING SIZE 1 1/2 cups

COMPLETE THE PLATE
This recipe: Nonstarchy
Vegetable
Pair with: A serving of Lean
Protein and Carbohydrate
Foods such as Slow-Cooker
Salmon with Avocado-
Grapefruit Salsa (page 166),
which provides both

3 cups mixed greens

1 medium cucumber, thinly
sliced using a mandolin

1 cup cherry tomatoes, halved

1/4 cup Lite Balsamic Vinaigrette
(page 221) or store-bought
light balsamic vinaigrette

SIMPLE SIDE SALAD WITH BALSAMIC VINAIGRETTE

It's always good to have a go-to side salad with the right vegetable portions and a salad dressing to pour over it. It takes out the guesswork out of meal prep when you're in a rush, so you can sit back, relax, and enjoy your meal.

---

1 Add the mixed greens, cucumbers, and tomatoes to a large bowl. Toss to combine. Drizzle with the Lite Balsamic Vinaigrette and toss again to evenly coat the vegetables.

You can substitute the mixed greens with baby spinach, chopped kale, romaine lettuce, or red leaf lettuce.

Choices/Exchanges 1 Nonstarchy Vegetable, 1 Fat

Calories 70	**Cholesterol** 0 mg	**Sugars** 4 g
Calories from Fat 35	**Sodium** 50 mg	**Added Sugars** 0 g
Total Fat 4.0 g	**Potassium** 280 mg	**Protein** 1 g
Saturated Fat 0.6 g	**Total Carbohydrate** 7 g	**Phosphorus** 40 mg
Trans Fat 0.0 g	**Dietary Fiber** 1 g	

SIDE GREEK SALAD WITH RED WINE VINAIGRETTE

This side salad goes with almost any of the main dishes in Chapter 9. Whip up a double batch and save some for another meal. Store with the dressing on the side so it can last up to 3 days in your refrigerator.

1 Add the lettuce, onion, cucumber, tomato, and olives to a large bowl. Toss to combine. Drizzle with the Red Wine Vinaigrette and toss again to evenly coat the vegetables.

You can substitute the Red Wine Vinaigrette with the same amount of Lite Balsamic Vinaigrette (page 221) or Lemon-Parsley Vinaigrette (page 224).

TOTAL TIME 15 minutes
PREP TIME 15 minutes
COOK TIME 0 minutes

SERVES 4
SERVING SIZE 1 cup

COMPLETE THE PLATE
This recipe: Nonstarchy Vegetable
Pair with: A serving of Lean Protein such as Lemon Chicken with Rosemary and Garlic (page 172) and Carbohydrate Foods such as Red Quinoa and Farro (page 207)

3 cups shredded romaine lettuce

1/4 medium red onion, thinly sliced

1 medium cucumber, cut in half lengthwise and then into half-moons

1 medium tomato, halved then thinly sliced

3/4 ounce pitted Kalamata olives (about 8)

1/4 cup Red Wine Vinaigrette (page 225) or store-bought red wine vinaigrette

Choices/Exchanges 1 Nonstarchy Vegetable, 2 Fat

Calories 120
Calories from Fat 100
Total Fat 11.0 g
Saturated Fat 1.3 g
Trans Fat 0.0 g

Cholesterol 0 mg
Sodium 170 mg
Potassium 300 mg
Total Carbohydrate 7 g
Dietary Fiber 2 g

Sugars 3 g
Added Sugars 0 g
Protein 1 g
Phosphorus 40 mg

TOTAL TIME 15 minutes
PREP TIME 15 minutes
COOK TIME 0 minutes

SERVES 8
SERVING SIZE 1 cup

COMPLETE THE PLATE
This recipe: Nonstarchy Vegetable
Pair with: A serving of Lean Protein such as Simple Grilled Steaks (page 182) and Carbohydrate Foods such as Mashed Red Potatoes (page 203)

3 cups shredded romaine lettuce

2 medium plum tomatoes, chopped

4 Kirby or Persian cucumbers, chopped

1 red bell pepper, chopped

1 tablespoon olive oil

Juice of 1 lemon (2 tablespoons)

1 teaspoon dried parsley

1/4 teaspoon kosher salt

1/8 teaspoon ground black pepper

CHOPPED ROMAINE SALAD

When I was a girl, my grandfather made me this chopped salad for lunch and dinner. He used to cut the vegetables into very small pieces and would start preparing the salad 30 minutes before the meal was served. These days I use a vegetable chopper (also marketed as an onion chopper), and it only takes me about 10 minutes to chop everything I need.

1 Add the lettuce, tomatoes, cucumbers, and bell peppers to a large bowl. Toss to combine.

2 In a separate small bowl, whisk together the olive oil, lemon juice, parsley, kosher salt, and black pepper. Drizzle the olive oil dressing over the salad and toss to evenly coat the vegetables.

Instead of dried parsley, add 1/4 cup of fresh parsley (or more) if you'd like.

Choices/Exchanges 1 Nonstarchy Vegetable, 1/2 Fat

Calories 35
Calories from Fat 20
Total Fat 2.0 g
Saturated Fat 0.3 g
Trans Fat 0.0 g

Cholesterol 0 mg
Sodium 65 mg
Potassium 170 mg
Total Carbohydrate 4 g
Dietary Fiber 1 g

Sugars 2 g
Added Sugars 0 g
Protein 1 g
Phosphorus 20 mg

GREEN SALAD WITH ORANGE, AVOCADO, AND ONION

Get creative with your oranges! Try navel, Valencia, Cara Cara, or blood oranges when you see them at your local market. They each have a slightly different delicious flavor but all of them are filled with vitamin C, fiber, and other good-for-you nutrients.

1 In a small bowl, whisk together the lime juice, olive oil, red wine vinegar, sweetener, kosher salt, and black pepper.

2 Remove the peel and the white pith from around the oranges. Using a paring knife, cut in between the membranes to release the orange segments, and slice them into thirds. Place the orange pieces into a medium bowl.

3 Add the mixed greens, avocado cubes, and red onion to the bowl and drizzle with the lime juice mixture. Toss to combine. Sprinkle with the cilantro and serve.

Toby Tip *You can use my Red Wine Vinaigrette recipe (page 225) or a light store-bought version instead of the dressing made in step 1.*

TOTAL TIME 15 minutes
PREP TIME 15 minutes
COOK TIME 0 minutes

SERVES 4
SERVING SIZE 1 1/2 cups

COMPLETE THE PLATE

This recipe: Nonstarchy Vegetable, Carbohydrate Food
Pair with: A serving of Lean Protein such as grilled chicken and Carbohydrate Foods such as Brown Rice with Scallions (page 206)

1 tablespoon fresh lime juice

1 tablespoon olive oil

1 teaspoon red wine vinegar

1/8 teaspoon zero-calorie stevia sweetener (such as Truvia or Splenda)

1/4 teaspoon kosher salt

1/8 teaspoon ground black pepper

2 medium oranges

4 cups mixed greens

1 avocado, pitted and flesh cubed

1/4 small red onion, chopped

2 tablespoons chopped cilantro

Choices/Exchanges 1/2 Fruit, 1 Nonstarchy Vegetable, 2 Fat

Calories 140
Calories from Fat 80
Total Fat 9.0 g
Saturated Fat 1.3 g
Trans Fat 0.0 g

Cholesterol 0 mg
Sodium 135 mg
Potassium 440 mg
Total Carbohydrate 14 g
Dietary Fiber 5 g

Sugars 8 g
Added Sugars 0 g
Protein 2 g
Phosphorus 45 mg

TOTAL TIME 15 minutes plus
30 minutes refrigeration time
PREP TIME 15 minutes
COOK TIME 0 minutes

SERVES 4
SERVING SIZE 1 1/4 cups

COMPLETE THE PLATE
This recipe: Nonstarchy
Vegetable, Carbohydrate
Food
Pair with: A serving of Lean
Protein such as Mustard-Herb
Roasted Pork Tenderloin
(page 178) and Carbohydrate
Foods such as a whole-wheat
dinner roll

1/2 cup nonfat plain Greek
   yogurt

1 clove garlic, minced

1 teaspoon Dijon mustard

1 tablespoon extra-virgin
   olive oil

3 tablespoons freshly
   squeezed lemon juice

3 tablespoons water

1/4 teaspoon salt

1/8 teaspoon ground black
   pepper

2 cups chopped kale

3 cups shredded red cabbage

1 Fuji apple, shredded (with
   the skin)

KALE APPLE SLAW

Kale is part of the cabbage family along with cauliflower, broccoli, and mustard greens. Vegetables in the cabbage family may help protect against cancer. Kale also provides the natural plant compound lutein, which has been linked to healthy eyes.

1 In a large bowl, whisk together the yogurt, garlic, mustard, olive oil, lemon juice, water, salt, and black pepper.

2 Add the kale, cabbage, and apple to the bowl and toss to evenly coat. Cover and place in the refrigerator for 30 minutes before serving for the flavors to combine.

You can switch up the vegetables in this slaw by using chopped spinach, green cabbage, and shredded carrots.

Choices/Exchanges 1/2 Fruit, 1 Nonstarchy Vegetable, 1 Fat

Calories 100	**Cholesterol** 0 mg	**Sugars** 8 g
Calories from Fat 35	**Sodium** 210 mg	**Added Sugars** 0 g
Total Fat 4.0 g	**Potassium** 300 mg	**Protein** 5 g
Saturated Fat 0.5 g	**Total Carbohydrate** 13 g	**Phosphorus** 75 mg
Trans Fat 0.0 g	**Dietary Fiber** 3 g	

GRILLED EGGPLANT

Eggplants are a member of the nightshade family. They were originally named after European eggplants that looked like a white egg hanging from a tree. Today you can find eggplant in purple, white, or striped varieties. These firm, shiny fruits are delicious and packed with nutrients–1 cup of cubed eggplant provides 20 calories, 3 grams of fiber, and small amounts of potassium and folate. They're also brimming with natural plant compounds called chlorogenic acid and caffeic acid, which may help protect cells from damage.

1 Preheat a grill pan or grill over medium heat. Coat the grill pan with nonstick cooking spray. (If using a grill, brush with 1 tablespoon of olive oil or use nonflammable cooking spray.)

2 Lay the eggplant slices on a flat surface and coat both side with nonstick cooking spray.

3 In a small bowl, mix together the garlic powder, onion powder, cumin, kosher salt, and cayenne. Sprinkle the spice mixture over both sides of the eggplant.

4 Grill the eggplant until browned on one side, 5–6 minutes, and then flip and cook until the other side is slightly browned, an additional 2–3 minutes. Serve warm.

TOTAL TIME 15 minutes
PREP TIME 5 minutes
COOK TIME 10 minutes

SERVES 4
SERVING SIZE 3/4 cup

COMPLETE THE PLATE
This recipe: Nonstarchy Vegetable
Pair with: A serving of Lean Protein such as Cod with Parsley-Lime Relish (page 160) and Carbohydrate Foods such as Red Quinoa and Farro (page 207)

Nonstick cooking spray

1 medium eggplant (1 pound), sliced into 1/2-inch rounds

1/2 teaspoon garlic powder

1/2 teaspoon onion powder

1/2 teaspoon ground cumin

1/4 teaspoon kosher salt

1/8 teaspoon cayenne

Toby Tip

Choose eggplants that are firm, shiny, and heavy for their size. The flesh should spring back to the touch and stems should be green. Avoid those that are dull in color, have wrinkled skin, or have soft spots. Store fresh eggplant in a cool, dry place for up to 2 days. Or for longer storage, store in a plastic bag in the refrigerator.

Choices/Exchanges 2 Nonstarchy Vegetable

Calories 45
Calories from Fat 10
Total Fat 1.0 g
Saturated Fat 0.1 g
Trans Fat 0.0 g

Cholesterol 0 mg
Sodium 120 mg
Potassium 135 mg
Total Carbohydrate 10 g
Dietary Fiber 3 g

Sugars 3 g
Added Sugars 0 g
Protein 1 g
Phosphorus 20 mg

TOTAL TIME 35 minutes
PREP TIME 10 minutes
COOK TIME 25 minutes

SERVES 4
SERVING SIZE 3/4 cup

COMPLETE THE PLATE
This recipe: Nonstarchy Vegetable
Pair with: A serving of Lean Protein such as Pork Chops with Fennel and Shallots (page 177) and Carbohydrate Foods such as Red Beans and Rice (page 205)

1 bunch collard greens, washed and dried (8 ounces)

2 tablespoons olive oil, divided

2 slices turkey bacon (I like Applegate)

2 cloves garlic, minced

1 medium yellow squash, halved lengthwise and then cut into 1/2-inch half-moons

1 cup low-sodium vegetable broth

1/8 teaspoon ground black pepper

COLLARD GREENS AND YELLOW SQUASH

Collard greens are a member of the cruciferous vegetable (or cabbage) family. One cup of fresh chopped collard greens provides 11 calories, over 200% of the daily recommended intake of vitamin K, and over 20% of the recommended daily intake of the antioxidants vitamins A and C. It also has a healthy dose of folate. In Southern cuisine, collards are traditionally made with large amounts of pork fat and salt, but this version has all the flavor without the saturated fat and sodium.

1 Remove the woody stems that run down the center of the collard leaves. Neatly pile several leaves and tightly roll them up, then slice into ribbons. Repeat for the remaining collard greens.

2 Heat 1 tablespoon of the olive oil in a medium sauté pan over medium heat. When the oil is shimmering, add the turkey bacon and cook until golden brown, 3 minutes on each side. Remove the bacon and set aside to slightly cool. Dice the bacon once cool.

3 Heat the remaining 1 tablespoon of olive oil in the same sauté pan over medium heat. When the oil is shimmering, add the garlic and cook until fragrant, 30 seconds. Add the collard greens and squash and cook until the collards have wilted and the squash begins to soften, about 5 minutes. Add the vegetable broth and bring the mixture to a boil. Lower the heat and simmer, covered, until the vegetables are cooked through, 10 minutes.

4 Add 1/8 teaspoon salt (optional),* the black pepper, and cooked turkey bacon and toss to combine.

*Optional salt not included in nutrition analysis; 1/8 teaspoon salt adds 75 mg of sodium per serving.

Choices/Exchanges 1 Nonstarchy Vegetable, 1 1/2 Fat

Calories 100	**Cholesterol** 8 mg	**Sugars** 2 g
Calories from Fat 70	**Sodium** 130 mg	**Added Sugars** 0 g
Total Fat 8.0 g	**Potassium** 260 mg	**Protein** 3 g
Saturated Fat 1.3 g	**Total Carbohydrate** 5 g	**Phosphorus** 65 mg
Trans Fat 0.0 g	**Dietary Fiber** 2 g	

You can swap out the collard greens for another hearty green like kale or chard.

TOTAL TIME 19 minutes
PREP TIME 15 minutes
COOK TIME 4 minutes

SERVES 4
SERVING SIZE 3/4 cup

COMPLETE THE PLATE
This recipe: Nonstarchy Vegetable
Pair with: A serving of Lean Protein such as a grilled chicken breast and Carbohydrate Foods such as Red Quinoa and Farro (page 207)

1 tablespoon olive oil

2 tablespoons pine nuts

1 clove garlic, minced

2 medium zucchini, cut into 2-inch-long matchsticks

1/4 teaspoon salt

1 tablespoon freshly squeezed lemon juice

1/2 cup fresh basil leaves, chopped

1/2 cup fresh mint leaves, chopped

ZUCCHINI WITH BASIL, MINT, AND PINE NUTS

Pine nuts are a delicious and nutritious way to add crunch to salads, rice dishes, and cooked vegetable dishes. One-quarter cup of pine nuts provides 227 calories, 4 grams of carbohydrate, 1.25 grams of fiber, and 4.5 grams of protein. They are also brimming with vitamins and minerals like vitamins E and K, iron, magnesium, phosphorus, zinc, copper, and manganese.

1 Heat the olive oil in a large sauté pan over medium heat. Add the pine nuts and toast until fragrant, 1 minute. Add the garlic and cook until fragrant, an additional 30 seconds. Add the zucchini and salt and cook until the zucchini is heated through, 2 minutes.

2 Spoon the zucchini mixture into a serving bowl. Top with the lemon juice, basil, and mint and gently toss to combine. Serve warm.

Pine nuts may also be labeled as "pignoli nuts." They should be wrapped in plastic and can be stored in the refrigerator for up to 3 months or frozen for up to 9 months.

Choices/Exchanges 1 Nonstarchy Vegetable, 1 Fat

Calories 80	**Cholesterol** 0 mg	**Sugars** 3 g
Calories from Fat 60	**Sodium** 160 mg	**Added Sugars** 0 g
Total Fat 7.0 g	**Potassium** 350 mg	**Protein** 2 g
Saturated Fat 0.8 g	**Total Carbohydrate** 5 g	**Phosphorus** 70 mg
Trans Fat 0.0 g	**Dietary Fiber** 2 g	

STEAMED GREEN BEANS WITH CASHEWS

Green beans are an easy, everyday side dish that you can whip up quickly. This is a recipe that you can cook at the beginning of the week and keep on hand for several days during a busy work week. You can also shave off about 10 minutes of prep time by purchasing pre-trimmed green beans at your local grocery store.

1 In a medium sauté pan, toast the cashews until fragrant, 2 minutes. Remove the cashews and place in a small bowl. Set aside.

2 Pour the water into a medium pot fitted with a steamer basket and bring to a boil over high heat. Add the green beans, cover, and reduce the heat to medium. Cook until tender, 5 minutes. Remove the green beans from the steamer.

3 Heat the olive oil in the same sauté pan used for the cashews over medium heat. Add the garlic and cook until fragrant, 30 seconds. Add the green beans and toss to heat through. Add the salt, black pepper, and toasted cashews and toss to combine.

 In a rush? Just steam the green beans (step 2) and sprinkle with the salt and black pepper for a quick and easy side.

TOTAL TIME 25 minutes
PREP TIME 15 minutes
COOK TIME 10 minutes

SERVES 6
SERVING SIZE 1 cup

COMPLETE THE PLATE
This recipe: Nonstarchy Vegetable
Pair with: A serving of Lean Protein such as Roasted Salmon with Chimichurri Sauce (page 158) and Carbohydrate Foods such as Red Beans and Rice (page 205)

1/4 cup raw cashews, roughly chopped

1 1/2 pounds green beans, washed and trimmed

1 tablespoon olive oil

2 cloves garlic, minced

1/4 teaspoon salt

1/8 teaspoon ground black pepper

Choices/Exchanges 1 Nonstarchy Vegetable, 1 Fat

Calories 90
Calories from Fat 45
Total Fat 5.0 g
Saturated Fat 0.9 g
Trans Fat 0.0 g

Cholesterol 0 mg
Sodium 105 mg
Potassium 260 mg
Total Carbohydrate 9 g
Dietary Fiber 3 g

Sugars 4 g
Added Sugars 0 g
Protein 3 g
Phosphorus 75 mg

TOTAL TIME 30 minutes
PREP TIME 15 minutes
COOK TIME 15 minutes

SERVES 4
SERVING SIZE 2/3 cup

COMPLETE THE PLATE
This recipe: Nonstarchy Vegetable
Pair with: A serving of Lean Protein such as Mustard-Herb Roasted Pork Tenderloin (page 178) and Carbohydrate Foods such as Brown Rice with Scallions (page 206)

1 tablespoon olive oil

1 shallot, chopped

2 cloves garlic, minced

1 (8-ounce) container cremini mushrooms, sliced

2 (3.5-ounce) containers sliced shiitake mushrooms

1/2 tablespoon unsalted butter

2 tablespoons dry white wine

1/2 teaspoon dried thyme

1/4 teaspoon salt

1/8 teaspoon ground black pepper

SAUTÉED MUSHROOM MEDLEY

Mushrooms are a powerhouse of nutrition, especially considering how few calories they provide. One cup of sliced mushrooms contains about 20 calories and is brimming with many vitamins and minerals like folate, thiamin, vitamin B-6, iron, and zinc.

1 Heat the olive oil in a medium saucepan over medium heat. When the oil is shimmering, add the shallot and garlic and cook until the shallot is translucent and the garlic is fragrant, 2 minutes.

2 Add the mushrooms and cook until softened, 8 minutes, stirring occasionally.

3 Add the butter and stir until melted. Add the wine, thyme, salt, and black pepper and toss to combine. Continue cooking until the flavors are incorporated, 2 minutes. Serve warm.

 For a simpler spin on this recipe, omit the white wine, butter, and thyme, and just flavor with salt and black pepper.

Choices/Exchanges 2 Nonstarchy Vegetable, 1 Fat

Calories 80	**Cholesterol** 5 mg	**Sugars** 2 g
Calories from Fat 45	**Sodium** 150 mg	**Added Sugars** 0 g
Total Fat 5.0 g	**Potassium** 440 mg	**Protein** 3 g
Saturated Fat 1.4 g	**Total Carbohydrate** 8 g	**Phosphorus** 130 mg
Trans Fat 0.0 g	**Dietary Fiber** 2 g	

CHARRED CABBAGE WITH CILANTRO-LIME SAUCE

Cilantro is a delicious herb from the coriander plant that is known for its bright citrus flavor. One-quarter cup of fresh cilantro leaves has only 1 calorie and provides small amounts of folate and vitamins A, C, and K. While herbs tend to be eaten in small amounts, adding herbs regularly to your diet will allow the small amounts of nutrients to add up.

1 Slice the cabbage in half. Cut each half into 3 wedges while keeping the stem intact.

2 Heat a grill pan coated with nonstick cooking spray over medium-high heat. When the cooking spray is shimmering, add the cabbage and grill for 3 minutes. Turn the cabbage and continue grilling until browned, for an additional 2 minutes on each side. Place the cabbage on a serving plate. Sprinkle with the mint.

3 To make the sauce, add the lime juice, olive oil, capers, garlic, cilantro, and sweetener to a blender and blend until smooth. Serve the sauce with the cabbage.

You can substitute 1 tablespoon of chopped green olives for the capers.

TOTAL TIME 20 minutes
PREP TIME 15 minutes
COOK TIME 5 minutes

SERVES 6
SERVING SIZE 1 piece cabbage and 1 1/4 tablespoons sauce

COMPLETE THE PLATE
This recipe: Nonstarchy Vegetable
Pair with: A serving of Lean Protein such as grilled tuna steaks and Carbohydrate Foods such as grilled corn

1 small head of Napa cabbage

Nonstick cooking spray

1/4 cup fresh mint leaves, chopped

1/4 cup fresh lime juice

2 tablespoons olive oil

1 tablespoon capers, drained

1 clove garlic, sliced

1 cup fresh cilantro

1/4 teaspoon zero-calorie stevia sweetener (such as Truvia or Splenda)

Choices/Exchanges 1 Nonstarchy Vegetable, 1 Fat

Calories 60
Calories from Fat 45
Total Fat 5.0 g
Saturated Fat 0.7 g
Trans Fat 0.0 g

Cholesterol 0 mg
Sodium 50 mg
Potassium 310 mg
Total Carbohydrate 5 g
Dietary Fiber 2 g

Sugars 2 g
Added Sugars 0 g
Protein 2 g
Phosphorus 40 mg

Toby Tip *If you don't use gloves to prepare beets, you may find your fingers and hands stained with the red beet juices. You can use lemon juice to help get the beet stains off your fingers. Just soak your fingers or hands in lemon juice for a few minutes.*

ROASTED BEETS WITH LEMON AND DILL

Beets may be a little messy to prepare, but they're well worth it. These veggies may show promise to help protect against certain forms of cancer, heart disease, and type 2 diabetes. They also help fight inflammation in your body and are rich in antioxidants, which can help protect your cells from damage.

1 Preheat the oven to 450°F. Coat a baking dish with nonstick cooking spray.

2 Wash the beets, then pierce several times with a fork and place in the prepared baking dish. Cover with aluminum foil and bake until a fork can pierce the beets with ease, 1 hour. Remove the baking dish from the oven and allow the beets to cool for 15 minutes. Remove the skin and cut the beets into 1/4-inch slices.

3 Zest the lemon (setting zest aside), then use a paring knife to remove the remaining skin and pith (white part) of the lemon. Cut in between the membranes to release the lemon segments, and then chop.

4 In a medium bowl, combine the canola oil and cumin. Add the beets, red onion, lemon zest and chopped lemon, dill, salt, and black pepper and gently toss together. Transfer to a serving dish and serve warm.

TOTAL TIME 1 hour 15 minutes plus 15 minutes cooling time
PREP TIME 15 minutes
COOK TIME 1 hour

SERVES 8
SERVING SIZE 2/3 cup

COMPLETE THE PLATE

This recipe: Nonstarchy Vegetable
Pair with: A serving of Lean Protein such as Cod with Parsley-Lime Relish (page 160) and Carbohydrate Foods such as Red Quinoa and Farro (page 207)

Nonstick cooking spray

2 pounds beets

1 lemon

1 tablespoon canola oil

1 teaspoon ground cumin

1/2 medium red onion, finely chopped

1/2 cup fresh dill, chopped

1/4 teaspoon salt

1/8 teaspoon ground black pepper

Choices/Exchanges 2 Nonstarchy Vegetable, 1/2 Fat

Calories 70
Calories from Fat 20
Total Fat 2.0 g
Saturated Fat 0.2 g
Trans Fat 0.0 g

Cholesterol 0 mg
Sodium 150 mg
Potassium 340 mg
Total Carbohydrate 12 g
Dietary Fiber 2 g

Sugars 9 g
Added Sugars 0 g
Protein 2 g
Phosphorus 45 mg

WEEKNIGHT VEGETABLE STIR-FRY

TOTAL TIME 25 minutes
PREP TIME 15 minutes
COOK TIME 10 minutes

SERVES 4
SERVING SIZE 3/4 cup

COMPLETE THE PLATE
This recipe: Nonstarchy Vegetable
Pair with: A serving of Lean Protein such as a grilled chicken breast and Carbohydrate Foods such as Brown Rice with Scallions (page 206)

5 tablespoons low-sodium vegetable broth

2 1/2 teaspoons reduced-sodium soy sauce

2 teaspoons unseasoned rice vinegar

2 teaspoons cornstarch

1/2 teaspoon stevia brown sugar blend (such as Truvia)

1 tablespoon olive oil

2 cups baby spinach

2 medium carrots, cut into 1/4-inch rounds

1 red bell pepper, thinly sliced

1 (8-ounce) container white mushrooms, thinly sliced

Stir-frys are a perfect way to help reduce food waste in your home. If you have leftover low-carbohydrate vegetables, use them! Kale, cabbage, zucchini, broccoli, and cauliflower can be substituted for any of the vegetables listed below.

1 In a small bowl, whisk together the vegetable broth, soy sauce, rice vinegar, cornstarch, and brown sugar blend. Set aside.

2 Heat the olive oil in a wok or sauté pan over medium heat. When the oil is shimmering, add the spinach and carrots and cook until the spinach is wilted, 3 minutes. Add the bell pepper and mushrooms, and cook until slightly softened, an additional 5 minutes.

3 Add the broth mixture, raise the heat to high, and bring to a boil. Then lower the heat to medium and cook until the sauce is slightly thickened, 1 minute. Toss to evenly coat the vegetables with the sauce.

 Save time on a busy weeknight by slicing the vegetables for this recipe ahead of time, like in the morning before work or the night before.

Choices/Exchanges 2 Nonstarchy Vegetable, 1 Fat

Calories 80
Calories from Fat 35
Total Fat 4.0 g
Saturated Fat 0.5 g
Trans Fat 0.0 g

Cholesterol 0 mg
Sodium 150 mg
Potassium 560 mg
Total Carbohydrate 10 g
Dietary Fiber 3 g

Sugars 5 g
Added Sugars 0 g
Protein 3 g
Phosphorus 85 mg

MASHED RED POTATOES

There are over 200 varieties of potatoes sold throughout the U.S. Red potatoes are one of my favorites because they're so versatile. They have a waxy texture, which allows them to stay firm when cooked. Plus, their gorgeous red skin adds eye appeal and texture to mashed potatoes, side dishes, and salads.

TOTAL TIME 55 minutes
PREP TIME 20 minutes
COOK TIME 35 minutes

SERVES 8
SERVING SIZE 1/2 cup

COMPLETE THE PLATE
This recipe: Carbohydrate Food
Pair with: A serving of Nonstarchy Vegetables such as Collard Greens and Yellow Squash (page 194) and Lean Protein such as Simple Grilled Steaks (page 182)

2 pounds red potatoes, washed and cut into 1-inch cubes (leaving skin on)

1/2 cup low-fat (1%) milk

1 tablespoon unsalted butter

1/4 teaspoon salt

1/8 teaspoon ground black pepper

1 Pour 1/4 cup of water into a medium pot fitted with a steamer basket and bring to a boil over high heat. Add the red potatoes, cover, and reduce the heat to medium. Cook until the potatoes are tender, 25–30 minutes. Set aside to cool.

2 In a small saucepan, heat the milk and butter over medium heat until the butter melts, 2 minutes. Remove the saucepan from the heat and set aside to slightly cool.

3 Add the potatoes to a large bowl and, using a potato masher, mash until almost smooth. Add the milk mixture, salt, and black pepper and mix until well combined.

 Leave the skin on when making mashed potatoes to increase the fiber.

Choices/Exchanges 1 Starch, 1/2 Fat

Calories 100
Calories from Fat 15
Total Fat 1.5 g
Saturated Fat 1.0 g
Trans Fat 0.0 g

Cholesterol 2 mg
Sodium 100 mg
Potassium 540 mg
Total Carbohydrate 19 g
Dietary Fiber 2 g

Sugars 2 g
Added Sugars 0 g
Protein 3 g
Phosphorus 85 mg

TOTAL TIME 50 minutes plus 10 minutes cooling time
PREP TIME 20 minutes
COOK TIME 30 minutes

SERVES 5
SERVING SIZE 1 cup

COMPLETE THE PLATE
This recipe: Nonstarchy Vegetable, Carbohydrate Food
Pair with: A serving of Nonstarchy Vegetables and Lean Protein such as Grilled Chicken and Vegetable Skewers (page 174), which provides both

2 1/2 cups water

2/3 cup bulgur

Juice of 2 lemons (1/4 cup)

Zest of 1 lemon (1 tablespoon)

1/4 cup walnuts, chopped (3/4 ounce)

2 1/2 cups strawberries, diced

1 hothouse cucumber, diced (about 2 cups)

1/2 cup chopped parsley leaves

1/2 cup chopped mint leaves

1/2 small red onion, finely chopped

1/4 teaspoon salt

1/8 teaspoon ground black pepper

TABBOULEH WITH CUCUMBER, STRAWBERRIES, AND MINT

Bulgur, the grain used to make tabbouleh, is a form of whole wheat that cooks rather quickly. This ancient grain has been around for thousands of years and originated in the Mediterranean region. It has a chewy texture and nutty flavor and is prepared with the same cooking method as rice using hot water or broth. Just check the package directions for the exact grain-to-liquid ratio and cooking time.

1 In a medium saucepan, bring 2 cups of the water to a boil. Stir in the bulgur, cover the pot, and remove it from the heat. Allow the bulgur to sit until almost all the liquid is absorbed, 30 minutes. Uncover the pot and drain any excess liquid (if any). Fluff the bulgur with a fork and allow to cool for 10 minutes.

2 Add the lemon juice and zest, walnuts, strawberries, cucumber, parsley, mint, and red onion to a large bowl. Toss together gently until combined. Add the bulgur, salt, and black pepper and toss until the bulgur is well incorporated.

 Swap out the strawberries for tomato to get a serving of vegetables.

Choices/Exchanges 1 Starch, 1/2 Fruit, 1 Nonstarchy Vegetable, 1/2 Fat

Calories 150	**Cholesterol** 0 mg	**Sugars** 6 g
Calories from Fat 30	**Sodium** 130 mg	**Added Sugars** 0 g
Total Fat 3.5 g	**Potassium** 380 mg	**Protein** 5 g
Saturated Fat 0.4 g	**Total Carbohydrate** 28 g	**Phosphorus** 95 mg
Trans Fat 0.0 g	**Dietary Fiber** 7 g	

RED BEANS AND RICE

Canned foods, including beans, are a real time saver in the kitchen–plus they are inexpensive and nutritious. According to a recent study, kids and adults who use 6 or more canned foods per week are more likely to have diets higher in 18 essential nutrients, including potassium, calcium, and fiber. When buying canned foods, like beans and vegetables, look for no-added-salt or low-sodium varieties. You can also rinse them to remove up to 40% of the sodium.

TOTAL TIME 55 minutes
PREP TIME 10 minutes
COOK TIME 45 minutes

SERVES 8
SERVING SIZE 1/2 cup

COMPLETE THE PLATE
This recipe: Carbohydrate Food
Pair with: A serving of Nonstarchy Vegetables and Lean Protein such as Sheet Pan Tuna with Asparagus (page 162), which provides both

1 cup brown basmati rice

2 cups low-sodium vegetable broth

1 tablespoon olive oil

1 small yellow onion, chopped

1 clove garlic, minced

1 (15.5-ounce) can low-sodium kidney beans, drained and rinsed

1/2 teaspoon chili powder

1/2 teaspoon ground cumin

1/4 teaspoon salt

1/4 teaspoon smoked paprika

1 In a medium saucepan over high heat, bring the rice and broth to a boil. Reduce the heat to medium low and simmer for about 40 minutes, or until the rice is tender. (Alternatively, you can use a rice cooker to cook the rice.)

2 While the rice is cooking, heat the olive oil in a separate medium saucepan over medium heat. When the oil is shimmering, add the onion and garlic and cook until the onion is translucent and the garlic is fragrant, 3 minutes. Add the beans, chili powder, cumin, salt, and paprika and toss to combine. Cook the bean mixture until heated through, 2 minutes. Set aside to slightly cool.

3 Add the cooked rice and the bean mixture to a large bowl and toss to combine. Spoon into a serving dish and serve warm.

Swap in your favorite type of beans, like black or pinto beans, for the kidney beans.

Choices/Exchanges 2 Starch

Calories 150
Calories from Fat 20
Total Fat 2.5 g
Saturated Fat 0.4 g
Trans Fat 0.0 g

Cholesterol 0 mg
Sodium 110 mg
Potassium 250 mg
Total Carbohydrate 27 g
Dietary Fiber 4 g

Sugars 2 g
Added Sugars 0 g
Protein 5 g
Phosphorus 150 mg

TOTAL TIME 55 minutes
PREP TIME 15 minutes
COOK TIME 40 minutes

SERVES 6
SERVING SIZE 1/2 cup

COMPLETE THE PLATE
This recipe: Carbohydrate Food
Pair with: A serving of
Nonstarchy Vegetables such
as Steamed Green Beans with
Cashews (page 197) and Lean
Protein such as Boiled Shrimp
with Green Goddess Sauce
(page 159)

1 cup brown basmati rice

2 cups low-sodium vegetable
broth

2 tablespoons reduced-sodium
soy sauce

1 tablespoon olive oil

1 tablespoon unseasoned rice
vinegar

1/4 teaspoon ground ginger

5 scallions (green and white
parts), thinly sliced

BROWN RICE WITH SCALLIONS

*Basmati rice is a long-grain rice that comes out fluffy
and drier than other rice varieties like short-grain rice
(used to make risotto). If you can't find basmati at your
local store, use regular brown rice instead.*

---

1 In a saucepan over high heat, bring the rice and broth to a
boil. Reduce the heat to medium low and simmer until the rice
is tender, about 40 minutes. (Alternatively, you can use a rice
cooker to cook the rice.) Fluff the rice with a fork and place in a
large bowl.

2 In a small bowl, whisk together the soy sauce, olive oil,
rice vinegar, and ginger. Drizzle the soy sauce mixture onto
the rice and toss to evenly coat. Add the scallions and toss to
incorporate.

 *Swap out the scallions for 1/4 cup of
chopped cilantro or parsley.*

Choices/Exchanges 1 1/2 Starch, 1/2 Fat

Calories 140	**Cholesterol** 0 mg	**Sugars** 2 g
Calories from Fat 30	**Sodium** 230 mg	**Added Sugars** 0 g
Total Fat 3.5 g	**Potassium** 310 mg	**Protein** 3 g
Saturated Fat 0.5 g	**Total Carbohydrate** 25 g	**Phosphorus** 140 mg
Trans Fat 0.0 g	**Dietary Fiber** 2 g	

RED QUINOA AND FARRO

Quinoa comes in various colors including white, red, and black, or tri-colored (when they're all mixed together). White is the most popular variety, but you can find red or tri-colored quinoa at local specialty stores or online. All varieties of quinoa cook up the same way and have a similar nutrient content, so choose whatever is most convenient for you.

TOTAL TIME 55 minutes plus 20 minutes cooling time
PREP TIME 15 minutes
COOK TIME 40 minutes

SERVES 4
SERVING SIZE 1/3 cup

COMPLETE THE PLATE
This recipe: Carbohydrate Food
Pair with: A serving of Nonstarchy Vegetables such as Simple Side Salad with Balsamic Vinaigrette (page 188) and Lean Protein such as Pork Chops with Fennel and Shallots (page 177)

1 In a medium saucepan over high heat, bring the farro and 1 1/2 cups of the broth to a boil. Reduce the heat to medium low and simmer for about 25 minutes, or until the farro is tender. Place the farro into a large bowl and allow to cool for 10 minutes.

2 In the same medium saucepan over high heat, add the quinoa and the remaining 1/2 cup of broth and bring to a boil. Reduce the heat to medium low and simmer for about 15 minutes, or until the quinoa is tender. Fluff with a fork and allow to cool for 10 minutes before adding it to the large bowl with the farro.

3 In a small bowl, whisk together the olive oil, lime juice, vinegar, oregano, garlic powder, brown sugar blend, salt, pepper, and red pepper flakes.

4 Toss the farro and quinoa in the large bowl to combine. Drizzle the olive oil mixture over the grains and toss again to combine.

1/2 cup farro

2 cups low-sodium vegetable broth, divided

1/4 cup red quinoa

1 tablespoon olive oil

1 tablespoon fresh lime juice

1 teaspoon white wine vinegar

1 teaspoon dried oregano

1/2 teaspoon garlic powder

1/4 teaspoon stevia brown sugar blend (such as Truvia)

1/4 teaspoon salt

1/8 teaspoon ground black pepper

1/8 teaspoon red pepper flakes

 Swap out the farro for 2/3 cup of brown basmati rice cooked with 1 1/3 cups vegetable broth to make a brown rice-quinoa blend.

Choices/Exchanges 2 Starch, 1/2 Fat

Calories 180
Calories from Fat 45
Total Fat 5.0 g
Saturated Fat 0.7 g
Trans Fat 0.0 g

Cholesterol 0 mg
Sodium 220 mg
Potassium 240 mg
Total Carbohydrate 28 g
Dietary Fiber 5 g

Sugars 2 g
Added Sugars 0 g
Protein 5 g
Phosphorus 195 mg

Chapter 11
*Dips,
Condiments &
Salad Dressings*

TOTAL TIME 10 minutes
PREP TIME 10 minutes
COOK TIME 0 minutes

SERVES 12
SERVING SIZE 2 tablespoons

1 (15.5-ounce) can low-sodium chickpeas (garbanzo beans), drained and rinsed

2 tablespoons tahini

Juice of 2 lemons (1/4 cup)

Zest of 1 lemon (1 tablespoon)

1 clove garlic, minced

1/2 teaspoon salt

1/4 teaspoon ground black pepper

1/4 cup extra-virgin olive oil

LEMON HUMMUS

Hummus is made by blending chickpeas (also called garbanzo beans). It provides healthy unsaturated fat, along with protein and fiber. Whip up a batch to snack on or try it as a condiment for turkey, chicken, eggs, or even a grilled vegetable sandwich.

1 Place the chickpeas, tahini, lemon juice and zest, garlic, salt, and black pepper in a food processor and blend until smooth, about 30 seconds. With the machine still running, gradually add the extra-virgin olive oil and blend until well incorporated.

 Change up your hummus by adding 1/2 cup of your favorite herb, like parsley or dill.

Choices/Exchanges 1/2 Starch, 1 Fat

Calories 100
Calories from Fat 50
Total Fat 6.0 g
Saturated Fat 0.9 g
Trans Fat 0.0 g

Cholesterol 0 mg
Sodium 105 mg
Potassium 90 mg
Total Carbohydrate 8 g
Dietary Fiber 2 g

Sugars 1 g
Added Sugars 0 g
Protein 3 g
Phosphorus 60 mg

CREAMY AVOCADO DIP

This tasty guacamole-style dip takes just 10 minutes to whip up in the blender—and it's perfect for a gathering with friends. Serve with low-carbohydrate vegetables like cauliflower florets or sliced zucchini.

---

1 Remove the flesh of the avocados and place in a blender. Add the remaining ingredients. Blend until smooth.

When handling chile peppers like jalapeños, the oils and capsaicin from the peppers can get onto your hands. Your best bet is to wear gloves when handling peppers like jalapeños or wash your hands thoroughly after handling and to avoid touching your face, especially your eyes.

TOTAL TIME 10 minutes
PREP TIME 10 minutes
COOK TIME 0 minutes

SERVES 12
SERVING SIZE 2 tablespoons

2 Haas avocados

Juice of 1 lime

1/2 jalapeño pepper, seeded and roughly chopped

1 clove garlic, minced

1/4 medium red onion, roughly chopped

1/2 medium red bell pepper, roughly chopped

1/4 cup fresh cilantro

1/4 teaspoon kosher salt

1/8 teaspoon ground black pepper

Choices/Exchanges 1 Fat

Calories 40
Calories from Fat 25
Total Fat 3.0 g
Saturated Fat 0.5 g
Trans Fat 0.0 g

Cholesterol 0 mg
Sodium 45 mg
Potassium 135 mg
Total Carbohydrate 3 g
Dietary Fiber 2 g

Sugars 1 g
Added Sugars 0 g
Protein 1 g
Phosphorus 15 mg

TOTAL TIME 10 minutes plus
1 hour refrigeration time
PREP TIME 10 minutes
COOK TIME 0 minutes

SERVES 12
SERVING SIZE 2 tablespoons

8 ounces soft silken tofu

4 ounces neufchatel cheese

1 medium scallion (green
   and white parts), roughly
   chopped

1/4 cup fresh parsley, chopped

1/4 cup fresh basil, chopped

1 small clove garlic, roughly
   chopped

3 tablespoons freshly
   squeezed lemon juice

1/4 teaspoon salt

HERB DIP

*Silken tofu adds protein, unsaturated fat, and minerals
like potassium, magnesium, and phosphorus to a dish.
It works beautifully in dips and smoothies, any dish
where you want a creamy, smooth texture. Tofu picks
up the flavor of whatever it's mixed with—for example,
in this dip it tastes like delicious herbs.*

1 Place the tofu and cheese in a food processor and blend until
smooth. Add the scallion, parsley, basil, garlic, lemon juice, and
salt. Continue blending until smooth, about 30 seconds.

2 Spoon the herb dip into a resealable container or bowl.
Cover and place in the refrigerator to allow flavors to combine,
at least 1 hour. Store in the refrigerator for up to 5 days.

 *Minimize food waste by using whatever fresh
herbs you have laying around, such as cilantro,
mint, or rosemary, in this recipe.*

Choices/Exchanges 1 Fat

Calories 35	**Cholesterol** 5 mg	**Sugars** 1 g
Calories from Fat 20	**Sodium** 90 mg	**Added Sugars** 0 g
Total Fat 2.5 g	**Potassium** 70 mg	**Protein** 2 g
Saturated Fat 1.3 g	**Total Carbohydrate** 1 g	**Phosphorus** 25 mg
Trans Fat 0.0 g	**Dietary Fiber** 0 g	

SRIRACHA-YOGURT DIP

Sriracha is an American-born chile sauce developed in Los Angeles, California, in the early 1980s. This chile sauce adds big flavor for only a few calories. Chile peppers also provide a natural plant compound called capsacin, which may help fight inflammation.

---

1 In a medium bowl, whisk all the ingredients together until combined.

TOTAL TIME 5 minutes
PREP TIME 5 minutes
COOK TIME 0 minutes

SERVES 8
SERVING SIZE 2 tablespoons

1 cup nonfat plain Greek yogurt

1 tablespoon sriracha

Juice of 1 lime (about 1 tablespoon)

1 clove garlic, minced

1/4 teaspoon salt

 Serve with Baked Coconut Shrimp (page 116) or Mozzarella-Stuffed Turkey Meatballs (page 117).

Choices/Exchanges 0

Calories 20
Calories from Fat 0
Total Fat 0.0 g
Saturated Fat 0.0 g
Trans Fat 0.0 g

Cholesterol 0 mg
Sodium 120 mg
Potassium 45 mg
Total Carbohydrate 2 g
Dietary Fiber 0 g

Sugars 1 g
Added Sugars 0 g
Protein 3 g
Phosphorus 40 mg

TOTAL TIME 16 minutes plus 10 minutes cooling time
PREP TIME 10 minutes
COOK TIME 6 minutes

SERVES 10
SERVING SIZE 2 tablespoons

1 (10-ounce) package frozen spinach, thawed

1 tablespoon olive or canola oil

1 clove garlic, minced

3 tablespoons grated Parmesan cheese

1/8 teaspoon salt

1/8 teaspoon ground black pepper

1/2 cup fresh basil leaves

1/4 cup whipped cream cheese

1/4 cup nonfat plain Greek yogurt

SPINACH-PARMESAN DIP

Many spinach dips are made with heavy cream and gobs of other fat-heavy ingredients. This version gets its flavor from the sautéed garlic and fresh basil, and its creaminess from a small amount of whipped cream cheese and Greek yogurt. Make this your go-to spinach dip. It can easily be whipped up in about 15 minutes!

1 Drain the water from the spinach through a colander. Using clean hands or a clean towel, press or squeeze the extra liquid through the colander.

2 Heat the olive or canola oil in a medium skillet over medium heat. When the oil is shimmering, add the garlic and cook until it is fragrant, 30 seconds. Add the spinach and cook until warmed through, 5 minutes. Add the Parmesan cheese, salt, and black pepper; toss to combine. Set the spinach mixture aside to slightly cool for 10 minutes.

3 Add the cooled spinach mixture, basil, cream cheese, and Greek yogurt to a blender and blend until smooth.

4 Place dip into a serving bowl and serve immediately.

 You can store whole garlic bulbs, without breaking them apart, at room temperature in a cool, dry place for up to a few months. Once you break the bulb apart, individual cloves will keep for up to 10 days.

Choices/Exchanges 1 Fat

Calories 40
Calories from Fat 25
Total Fat 3.0 g
Saturated Fat 1.0 g
Trans Fat 0.0 g

Cholesterol 5 mg
Sodium 90 mg
Potassium 120 mg
Total Carbohydrate 2 g
Dietary Fiber 1 g

Sugars 1 g
Added Sugars 0 g
Protein 2 g
Phosphorus 35 mg

ALMOST SMOOTH SALSA

Are you a smooth or chunky salsa lover? If you like your salsa smooth, then blend until smooth. If you like your salsa chunky, then skip the blending altogether.

1 Add the tomatoes, bell pepper, onion, jalapeño, and cilantro to a medium bowl. Add the lime juice, olive oil, salt, and black pepper. Toss to evenly coat.

2 Using an immersion blender, blend until almost smooth, leaving some chunks in the salsa.

 For dishes where the tomato will be finely chopped or diced, use plum tomatoes. These oblong-shaped tomatoes do not have many seeds and won't make your dish as watery. If you only have regular tomatoes on hand, then I recommend scooping out the seeds and pulp before chopping.

TOTAL TIME 15 minutes
PREP TIME 15 minutes
COOK TIME 0 minutes

SERVES 12
SERVING SIZE 2 tablespoons

2 medium plum tomatoes (1/2 pound)

1/4 green bell pepper, chopped

1/4 red onion, chopped (about 1/4 cup)

1/2 jalapeño, seeded, veins removed, and chopped

3 tablespoons chopped cilantro

Juice of 1/2 lime (1 tablespoon)

1 tablespoon extra-virgin olive oil

1/4 teaspoon sea salt

1/8 teaspoon ground black pepper

Choices/Exchanges 0

Calories 15
Calories from Fat 10
Total Fat 1.0 g
Saturated Fat 0.2 g
Trans Fat 0.0 g

Cholesterol 0 mg
Sodium 45 mg
Potassium 65 mg
Total Carbohydrate 1 g
Dietary Fiber 0 g

Sugars 1 g
Added Sugars 0 g
Protein 0 g
Phosphorus 5 mg

TOTAL TIME 10 minutes
PREP TIME 10 minutes
COOK TIME 0 minutes

SERVES 8
SERVING SIZE 1 tablespoon

1/2 cup creamy peanut butter

1 tablespoon reduced-sodium soy sauce

1/2 teaspoon ground ginger

1/4 teaspoon red pepper flakes

Juice of 1 lime (about 1 tablespoon)

1/2 teaspoon stevia brown sugar blend (such as Truvia)

6 tablespoons water

PEANUT SAUCE

Peanut butter is on the healthy food list but should be enjoyed in moderation. The majority of peanut butter is heart-healthy unsaturated fat, which means it also comes with a good amount of calories. One tablespoon of crunchy or smooth peanut butter has about 90-100 calories, 4 grams of protein, and 10 grams of fat. Opt for regular peanut butter as opposed to reduced-fat varieties, which replace part of the fat with added sugar.

—————————————

1 Add the peanut butter, soy sauce, ginger, red pepper flakes, lime juice, and brown sugar blend to a blender or food processor. Blend until smooth. Add the water as necessary to achieve your desired thickness.

 Want to add an Asian twist? Blend this peanut sauce with 2 tablespoons of light coconut milk.

Choices/Exchanges 1 High-Fat Protein

Calories 100	**Cholesterol** 0 mg	**Sugars** 2 g
Calories from Fat 70	**Sodium** 140 mg	**Added Sugars** 0 g
Total Fat 8.0 g	**Potassium** 110 mg	**Protein** 4 g
Saturated Fat 1.7 g	**Total Carbohydrate** 4 g	**Phosphorus** 60 mg
Trans Fat 0.0 g	**Dietary Fiber** 1 g	

PESTO SAUCE

Pesto sauce is known to be high in calories, but in this delicious version, some of the oil is replaced with nonfat plain Greek yogurt, adding a touch of calcium and protein.

_____

1 Add the basil, olive or canola oil, and garlic to a blender; pulse until a rough paste forms.

2 Add the Greek yogurt, red wine vinegar, and salt and purée until smooth.

TOTAL TIME 10 minutes
PREP TIME 10 minutes
COOK TIME 0 minutes

SERVES 4
SERVING SIZE 2 tablespoons

2 cups fresh basil leaves

3 tablespoons olive or canola oil

1 clove garlic, minced

1/4 cup nonfat plain Greek yogurt

1 tablespoon red wine vinegar

1/8 teaspoon salt

 When purchasing fresh basil, look for bright green leaves without yellow or brown spots. Place the cut stems into a container of water and keep the basil on the windowsill for up to 1 week, changing the water every other day. You can also store basil in the refrigerator wrapped in a damp paper towel for up to 4 days.

Choices/Exchanges 2 Fat

Calories 110
Calories from Fat 90
Total Fat 10.0 g
Saturated Fat 1.4 g
Trans Fat 0.0 g

Cholesterol 0 mg
Sodium 80 mg
Potassium 125 mg
Total Carbohydrate 2 g
Dietary Fiber 1 g

Sugars 1 g
Added Sugars 0 g
Protein 2 g
Phosphorus 35 mg

CHIMICHURRI SAUCE

Simple sauces made from flavorful ingredients that are low in calories and saturated fat—like this Chimichurri Sauce—are the trick to healthy and tasty eating. You can make this sauce in just 5 minutes.

———————————

1 Add all the ingredients to a blender and blend until smooth.

 Serve with Roasted Salmon (page 158) or try it with Boiled Shrimp (page 159).

TOTAL TIME 5 minutes
PREP TIME 5 minutes
COOK TIME 0 minutes

SERVES 4
SERVING SIZE 2 tablespoons

1/4 cup water

2 tablespoons olive oil

2 tablespoons white wine vinegar

3/4 cup fresh parsley, roughly chopped

2 cloves garlic, minced

2 teaspoons dried oregano

1/4 teaspoon salt

1/8 teaspoon red pepper flakes

Choices/Exchanges 1 1/2 Fat

Calories 70
Calories from Fat 60
Total Fat 7.0 g
Saturated Fat 1.0 g
Trans Fat 0.0 g

Cholesterol 0 mg
Sodium 150 mg
Potassium 80 mg
Total Carbohydrate 2 g
Dietary Fiber 1 g

Sugars 0 g
Added Sugars 0 g
Protein 0 g
Phosphorus 10 mg

GREEN GODDESS SAUCE

TOTAL TIME 5 minutes
PREP TIME 5 minutes
COOK TIME 0 minutes

SERVES 4
SERVING SIZE 2 tablespoons

1/4 cup light mayonnaise

1/4 cup fresh basil

1/4 cup nonfat plain Greek yogurt

Juice of 1 lemon (2 tablespoons)

1 scallion (green and white parts), sliced

1 clove garlic, minced

1/2 teaspoon drained capers

This clean-tasting sauce is made with fresh herbs, garlic, lemon juice, and a combination of light mayonnaise and nonfat plain Greek yogurt to give it a creamy consistency. Use over fish, chicken, or beef. It also is a perfect dip to serve at a party with a crudité.

_____

1 Add all the ingredients to a blender and blend until smooth.

When selecting lemons, look for those that are bright in color without any spots or discoloration. To select the juiciest ones, give them a gentle squeeze. The juicier lemons are softer, with less pith and more juice.

Choices/Exchanges 1 Fat

Calories 50
Calories from Fat 30
Total Fat 3.5 g
Saturated Fat 0.3 g
Trans Fat 0.0 g

Cholesterol 5 mg
Sodium 130 mg
Potassium 65 mg
Total Carbohydrate 3 g
Dietary Fiber 0 g

Sugars 1 g
Added Sugars 0 g
Protein 2 g
Phosphorus 25 mg

LITE BALSAMIC VINAIGRETTE

One of the most popular vinaigrettes is balsamic vinaigrette, as it goes with many salads and can be used as a marinade or sauce for chicken, fish, and vegetables. This lighter version uses more vinegar and less oil than traditional vinaigrettes, but it is still bursting with flavor.

1 In a medium bowl, whisk together the balsamic vinegar, water, garlic, Dijon mustard, onion powder, brown sugar blend, and salt. While continuously whisking, slowly drizzle in the olive oil until incorporated.

2 Store the dressing in a resealable container in the refrigerator for up to 1 week.

TOTAL TIME 5 minutes
PREP TIME 5 minutes
COOK TIME 0 minutes

SERVES 7
SERVING SIZE 2 tablespoons

1/2 cup balsamic vinegar

2 tablespoons water

1 clove garlic, minced

2 teaspoons Dijon mustard

1 teaspoon onion powder

1/2 teaspoon stevia brown sugar blend (such as Truvia)

1/8 teaspoon salt

1/4 cup extra-virgin olive oil

 Extra-virgin olive oil works well for dressings and drizzling onto vegetables when no cooking is involved.

Choices/Exchanges 2 Fat

Calories 90	**Cholesterol** 0 mg	**Sugars** 3 g
Calories from Fat 70	**Sodium** 80 mg	**Added Sugars** 0 g
Total Fat 8.0 g	**Potassium** 25 mg	**Protein** 0 g
Saturated Fat 1.1 g	**Total Carbohydrate** 4 g	**Phosphorus** 5 mg
Trans Fat 0.0 g	**Dietary Fiber** 0 g	

TOTAL TIME 10 minutes
PREP TIME 10 minutes
COOK TIME 0 minutes

SERVES 8
SERVING SIZE 2 tablespoons

2 plum tomatoes, sliced
  (7 ounces)

2 tablespoons canola oil

1 tablespoon red wine vinegar

1 tablespoon freshly squeezed
  lemon juice

2 teaspoons Dijon mustard

1/4 teaspoon garlic powder

1/4 teaspoon dried parsley
  flakes

1/4 teaspoon salt

1/8 teaspoon stevia brown
  sugar blend (such as Truvia)

LIGHTER ITALIAN DRESSING

Italian dressing is made from traditional Italian ingredients such as tomatoes, garlic, and parsley. Making an Italian dressing is actually pretty simple—you take all your ingredients and toss them into a blender. After a few tries, you may skip the store-bought kind and choose to whip up a batch on your own.

———————————

1 Add all of the ingredients to a blender and blend until smooth.

2 Store the dressing in a resealable container in the refrigerator for up to 1 week.

 To properly store your tomatoes, keep them on the countertop or in another cool, dry place. Do not refrigerate them as the cold temperatures will make your delicious tomatoes mealy.

Choices/Exchanges 1 Fat

Calories 40	**Cholesterol** 0 mg	**Sugars** 1 g
Calories from Fat 30	**Sodium** 105 mg	**Added Sugars** 0 g
Total Fat 3.5 g	**Potassium** 60 mg	**Protein** 0 g
Saturated Fat 0.3 g	**Total Carbohydrate** 1 g	**Phosphorus** 10 mg
Trans Fat 0.0 g	**Dietary Fiber** 0 g	

POMEGRANATE VINAIGRETTE

Vinaigrettes are traditionally made using one part vinegar and three parts oil. With 120 calories per tablespoon of oil, the calories can add up–even if you're using a heart-healthy oil like olive oil. This vinaigrette replaces some of the oil with 100% fruit juice, which has fewer calories and a sweet flavor that beautifully balances out the vinegar.

1 Add the pomegranate juice, red wine vinegar, shallot, Dijon mustard, brown sugar blend, salt, and black pepper to a blender and blend until smooth. With the blender running, slowly drizzle in the olive oil and blend until combined.

2 Store the dressing in a resealable container in the refrigerator for up to 1 week.

TOTAL TIME 5 minutes
PREP TIME 5 minutes
COOK TIME 0 minutes

SERVES 6
SERVING SIZE 2 tablespoons

5 tablespoons 100% pomegranate juice

3 tablespoons red wine vinegar

1 shallot, finely chopped

2 teaspoons Dijon mustard

1 teaspoon stevia brown sugar blend (such as Truvia)

1/8 teaspoon salt

1/8 teaspoon ground black pepper

3 tablespoons extra-virgin olive oil

 You can substitute apple cider vinegar for the red wine vinegar in this recipe, if desired.

Choices/Exchanges 1 1/2 Fat

Calories 70
Calories from Fat 60
Total Fat 7.0 g
Saturated Fat 0.9 g
Trans Fat 0.0 g

Cholesterol 0 mg
Sodium 90 mg
Potassium 45 mg
Total Carbohydrate 3 g
Dietary Fiber 0 g

Sugars 2 g
Added Sugars 0 g
Protein 0 g
Phosphorus 5 mg

TOTAL TIME 10 minutes
PREP TIME 10 minutes
COOK TIME 0 minutes

SERVES 8
SERVING SIZE 1 tablespoon

1/2 cup parsley, roughly
   chopped

Juice and zest of 1 lemon
   (2 tablespoons juice and
   1 tablespoon zest)

2 tablespoons water

1/2 teaspoon stevia brown
   sugar blend (such as Truvia)

1/4 teaspoon garlic powder

1/4 teaspoon salt

1/4 teaspoon ground black
   pepper

1/4 cup extra-virgin olive oil

LEMON-PARSLEY VINAIGRETTE

Lemon and parsley are basic flavors that go with many salads and cooked vegetables. This vinaigrette can also be used as a sauce for grilled or baked chicken, fish, or tofu.

1 Add the parsley, lemon juice and zest, water, brown sugar blend, garlic powder, salt, and black pepper to a blender and blend until smooth. With the blender running, slowly drizzle in the olive oil until combined.

2 Store the dressing in a resealable container in the refrigerator for up to 5 days.

 When shopping, look for fresh parsley with bright green leaves and avoid parsely with wilted or yellow leaves. To store, wash the parsley and shake off the excess water, wrap in a paper towel, and then place in a plastic bag in the refrigerator for up to 7 days.

Choices/Exchanges 1 1/2 Fat

Calories 60
Calories from Fat 60
Total Fat 7.0 g
Saturated Fat 0.9 g
Trans Fat 0.0 g

Cholesterol 0 mg
Sodium 75 mg
Potassium 30 mg
Total Carbohydrate 1 g
Dietary Fiber 0 g

Sugars 0 g
Added Sugars 0 g
Protein 0 g
Phosphorus 5 mg

RED WINE VINAIGRETTE

Like other vinegars, red wine vinegar is very low in calories and is free of fat. It's a nice way to add a burst of flavor to dressings, sauces, or marinades without adding tons of fat, sugar, or calories.

_____

1 In a medium bowl, whisk together the red wine vinegar, Dijon mustard, oregano, garlic powder, brown sugar blend, and salt. While continuously whisking, slowly drizzle in the olive oil until incorporated.

2 Store the dressing in a resealable container in the refrigerator for up to 1 week.

Use this vinaigrette to marinate chicken or fish (for at least 30 minutes before cooking), or to flavor vegetables for the grill (marinate for at least 15–20 minutes before grilling).

TOTAL TIME 5 minutes
PREP TIME 5 minutes
COOK TIME 0 minutes

SERVES 12
SERVING SIZE 1 tablespoon

1/4 cup red wine vinegar

1 tablespoon Dijon mustard

1 teaspoon dried oregano

1/2 teaspoon garlic powder

1/4 teaspoon stevia brown
    sugar blend (such as Truvia)

1/4 teaspoon salt

1/2 cup extra-virgin olive oil

Choices/Exchanges 2 Fat

Calories 80
Calories from Fat 80
Total Fat 9.0 g
Saturated Fat 1.2 g
Trans Fat 0.0 g

Cholesterol 0 mg
Sodium 80 mg
Potassium 5 mg
Total Carbohydrate 0 g
Dietary Fiber 0 g

Sugars 0 g
Added Sugars 0 g
Protein 0 g
Phosphorus 0 mg

Index

Date Nut Bars, p. 87

About the Author

TOBY AMIDOR, MS, RD, CDN, FAND, is a veteran in the food and nutrition industry with close to 20 years of experience. She is an award-winning dietitian and recipe developer who believes that healthy and wholesome food can also be appetizing and delicious.

Toby is the founder of Toby Amidor Nutrition, where she provides nutrition and food safety consulting services for individuals, restaurants, and food brands. For 11 years, she has been the nutrition expert for FoodNetwork.com and a founding contributor to its *Healthy Eats* blog. She is a regular contributor to *U.S. News & World Report's Eat + Run* blog, *Muscle & Fitness* online, Shape.com, SparkPeople.com, and EatThisNotThat.com and she has her own "Ask the Expert" column in *Today's Dietitian* magazine. She has been quoted in publications like FoxNews.com, Self.com, *Oxygen Magazine*, *Dr. Oz The Good Life*, Mic.com, *Reader's Digest*, Shape.com, *Women's Health*, *Redbook*, *Men's Journal*, *Huffington Post*, *Everyday Health*, and more. Toby has also appeared on television programs including *The Dr. Oz Show*, *Coffee with America*, Fox 5 New York's *Good Day Street Talk*, and *San Antonio Live*. For the past 10 years, she has also been an adjunct professor at Teachers College, Columbia University. Previously, she was a consultant on Bobby Deen's cooking show, *Not My Mama's Meals*. In 2018, Toby was honored with the Media Excellence Award awarded by the Academy of Nutrition and Dietetics.

Toby is a *Wall Street Journal* best-selling cookbook author of *The Greek Yogurt Kitchen: More Than 130 Delicious, Healthy Recipes for Every Meal of the Day* (Grand Central Publishing, 2014), *The Healthy Meal Prep Cookbook: Easy and Wholesome Meals to Cook, Prep, Grab, and Go* (Rockridge Press, 2017), *The Easy 5-Ingredient Healthy Cookbook: Simple Recipes to Make Healthy Eating Delicious* (Rockridge Press, 2018), *Smart Meal Prep for Beginners: Recipes and Weekly Plans for Healthy, Ready-to-Go Meals* (Rockridge Press, 2018), and her latest book, *The Best Rotisserie Chicken Cookbook: Over 100 Tasty Recipes Using a Store-Bought Bird*, was released in early 2020 (Robert Rose, 2020). Toby trained as a clinical dietitian at New York University. Through ongoing consulting and faculty positions, she has established herself as one of the top experts in culinary nutrition, food safety, and nutrition communication.